14

1176

CHARLES HARRIS WHITAKER

THE STORY

OF

ARCHITECTURE

FROM RAMESES
TO ROCKEFELLER

HALCYON HOUSE · NEW YORK

NA
200
. W5
1936

HALCYON HOUSE *editions are published and distributed by Blue Ribbon Books, Inc., 386 Fourth Avenue, New York City*

THIRD PRINTING

PRINTED IN THE UNITED STATES OF AMERICA
BY THE CORNWALL PRESS, INC., CORNWALL, N. Y.

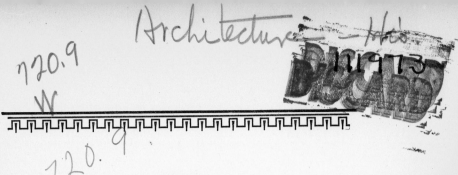

CONTENTS

[v]

ILLUSTRATIONS

REPRODUCTIONS IN AQUATONE

[viii]

TECHNICAL DRAWINGS

WOOD-CUT ILLUSTRATIONS

REPRODUCTIONS OF WOOD ENGRAVINGS BY J. J. LANKES

[x]

TO LOUIS HENRI SULLIVAN

1856—1924

Here I sit, Louis, thinking what I am to say about you and your ideas. Neither of us foresaw such a moment. We used to talk, whenever we had a chance, and we wrote a lot of letters. Now I am trying to tell the story of architecture, but that cannot be done without trying to tell the part you played.

I never think of you as an architect. When I got to know you, your days of building were over, but even so, nothing you ever did in buildings could change the memory of you, the man. I remember how timid you were when first I suggested that you write a story about your life. You could not believe that anyone would be interested. America had jumped forward into a hectic stride. Skyscrapers were rising like weeds. Who longer cared about Louis Sullivan?

So I had to plead and find some way to make you believe you still had something to say. Kindergarten Chats had been forgotten by all but a few of those who read them when they were printed. Now was the time to speak again, I said, for we both foresaw something coming, although it

[xi]

was nearer than we thought. What use? said you. Who cares? A lot of young men, now as in your day, I said. They face their future none too hopefully. The architect's position is far from secure. Big buildings are luring all sorts of people into the game. Small work doesn't pay. The future looks none too gay, in this year of 1922. You've lived through the period of the great dance. It's coming to an end. Then what?

At last you consented. What should be the title? Fortunately, the right one came to you. Following the theory you stated so well that all the world stopped to listen, the form of the title followed the function of the tale. You were to step outside yourself and look at your life. The story was to be about the Idea that made you want to be an architect. So it was The Autobiography of an Idea *that I published in the* Journal *of the American Institute of Architects, of which I was the editor. No doubt there are those alive today who will dislike seeing your name in this history, just as they protested at seeing your story in the* Journal. *Some of them were so vexed they besought the Board of Directors to put a stop to the publication of the* Autobiography, *but its members had more sense than that, even though some of them were a little fearful.*

As it happened, you never saw the book until you lay in your last bed, but after the story had been told in the Journal, *you came to spend some days at my home in the New Jersey hills. It was during those days that I felt the story of your life as your buildings could never have made me feel it. I saw you then, and see you now, sitting at the round table in our big room, reading the Psalms aloud by lamplight. I've never heard anything quite like that. My father could read, and declaim, and was a rare master of English, but the Psalms came from your lips as though the living David, with*

the flashing voice of a fervent young god, were pouring them
out in an ecstasy. The light fell on your worn and tired face,
but after a bit, there was no thought in any listener's mind
save the music of your voice.

I thought of Hans Sachs as he sat and sang, of the majesty
of the last movement in the Pathetique, and of the end of
"Don Juan" and the "Heldenleben." Yes, they were what I
thought of, for with all the music you made, I could still feel
your tragedy. Your country had passed you by. That was
what had happened, and I knew, as you read, what the passing had meant and how you had been hurt. It was plain then
that you had been crucified and lacerated, because you challenged the humbug of the art you loved. In every word you
read, I could feel the weight of the tragedy. But, like the
voice of the captain rising above the wreck, I could also feel
the exaltation within you that no tragedy could crush. You
had seen! You had beheld! You had known the rightness
that has forever belonged to craftsmen. You had heard and
accepted the everlasting challenge! Ah, that was a wonderful
evening, Louis, and I never told you how I felt about it. I
guessed that you guessed that I knew. You must have known.

What new day may be coming for architecture, no one
knows. It has been used to lure and deceive men into mad-
nesses that now claim their due. You and I foresaw and
deplored, but knew that we were helpless. The madness had
to take its course. Now you are gone. I cannot ask you to
write another story, nor can I ask you what you would say,
if you could speak. But I have taken down a copy of Kindergarten Chats to see if I could find a passage that you would
have me quote. I opened the pages at random and these are
the very words that my eye fell on:

"If we would know why certain things are as they are,

in our architecture, we must look to the people; for our buildings as a whole are an image of our people as a whole, although specifically they are the individual images of those to whom, as a class, the public has delegated and entrusted its power to build.

"Therefore, by this light, the critical study of architecture becomes, not the study of an art—for that is but a minor phase of the great phenomenon—but, in reality, a study of a new type of civilization. By this light the study of architecture becomes, naturally and logically, a branch of social science, and we must bend our faculties to this bow if we would hit the mark.

"Every building tells its own story, and tells it plainly. With what startling clearness it speaks to the attentive ear, how palpable its visage is to the open eye, may take you some time to perceive. But it is all there, waiting for you, just as every great truth has waited and waited, through the centuries for the man with eyes to see. . . .

"For no people can create except in its own subjective image. Hence what people are within, the buildings express without, and, inversely, what the buildings are objectively is a sure index of what the people are subjectively. In the light of this dictum, the unhappy, irrational, heedless, pessimistic, unlovely, distracted and decadent structures which make up our contemporaneous architecture, point with infallible accuracy the qualities in the heart, mind and soul of the American people that are unhappy, irrational, heedless, pessimistic, unlovely, distracted and decadent.

"The three chief borers of this young tree of Democracy are, first, inordinate greed, with all its attendant and ramifying evils productive of widespread unhappiness; second, the inherited feudal element in our education, with its at-

[xiv]

tendant poisoning of the faculties to such an extent as to render the attainment of happiness well-nigh impossible; and third, the inability or the unwillingness of the American individual to grasp the great and luminous truth that the foundation of Democracy lies in the individual, in his actual personal sense of responsibility and accountability, and his distinct willingness to accept them."

These words are fifty years old. In the meantime, the form of American civilization has followed its function; not the one that so many believed it was following, but the function that brought anguish and distress to millions, as the inevitable form took shape. You could not have saved it, nor anyone else. It had to be. But when the anguish and misery are gone, all in good time, the truth of what you said will be the same truth and there will never be any other. "Form follows function." Almost everyone thought, and still thinks, that you meant those three words to apply to buildings. Few were they who knew, as you knew, that the truth applied to everything. That nations take their form from their function, and from nothing else. It is impossible for the form of a civilization to grow out of the functioning of an imperial struggle based upon economic anarchy.

I might have opened Kindergarten Chats at a hundred other places. I might have looked carefully to pick out something I was sure you would choose. I took what came as I looked on the page, just as you would have taken whatever Psalm you opened to. Your words and the Psalms are part of the same rhythm. Your words, like the Psalmist's, have passed to the ends of the earth, and there are young men, walking the streets in anguish of mind, this very day, who will read them with the same thrill that came to the draughtsmen as they sat in those offices where designing was

[xv]

done out of books, fifty years ago, when Kindergarten Chats *was published. Their blood will tingle. The everlasting challenge is not dead. The sense of rightness is still within a million young hearts. All sages and prophets and craftsmen have helped to put it there, and you were sage, prophet and craftsman.*

But I shall always think of you as sitting at that big round table, in the lamplight, reading the Psalms of David.

C. H. W.

RAMESES TO ROCKEFELLER

I

HOW DID BUILDING

BEGIN?

AMONG the dates lost beyond hope of recovery is the far-away day when a man first began to build. That first fumbling effort to prop a bough, fix a post, or make one stone stay atop another, might have been a momentous one, as life is usually reckoned. So it was, and yet, after a score of thousand years, so is building still a momentous question. The first builder was probably less muddled and tangled, as to what to build and where to build it, than are those who conduct, arrange and finance the building of today. All about them, and rather mockingly staring them in the face, are the baffling problems of slum and skyscraper, congested city and dying farm.

[3]

Explorers in far places ever turn up the earth in delicate and careful delving; ever they find traces of man the incorrigible builder. The tale of the excavator is as endless as it is at present useless. The primitive builder had no past to trouble him. He could begin by facing his present squarely. As people try to do this today, when they also have great need to look daringly at the future, the past is more of a handicap than is suspected. It is often a tempting emotional refuge for the tired and faint-hearted, as it is a pleasant playground for those who hope to get a living without the trouble of facing either present or future.

Somewhere in that past of a thousand centuries, more or less, there was a first builder. What he tried to build, or how, we shall never know. Was it with wood he fumbled? Or with stone? Or with neither? For scores of centuries, wood and stone were his chief materials, but what of reeds and mud? With them, men in the Nile valley began to make rude screens against the sun. We cannot say they were the first builders, but Egyptian carpenters began with reeds. Wood was very scarce, stone for long impossible. Reeds were plentiful. Wise men took what they found. For tools they needed no more than their fingers.

As the carpenter began with long stems from the river's edge, so is it certain that the masons began with mud. It was even more abundant than reeds. Plastered onto the reed screens, it soon dried hard and added strength to wattle and more protection. Was it by mud-daubing that man learned to make bricks? Or had he noticed how the sun baked earth until its surface cracked into cakes that could be piled on top of each other? With fresh wet mud between, they made a wall. However knowledge came, slowly, out of water, sun and clay, brickmaker and bricklayer appeared. So began

[4]

the art of building in Egypt. Out of what previous knowledge it may have grown, who can say? In fact, none was needed to guide these first workers as they used materials at hand. First steps were fairly easy, but skill in making walls that would stand firm, and roofs that would not fall down, came only after long years of trial and test.

Man wanted shelter. Each step, as he played with his mud-daubed reed screens, led him onward. Did needs grow out of the delight of each fresh comfort and protection won, or was the longing for ease and comfort within man? A good guess might be that he took easily and naturally to comfort.

Through centuries to come, there was to flow away from these early beginnings by the Nile and elsewhere, traditions of knowledge, skill and craftsmanship. Now and then, a tradition would take timid root and wherever men drew themselves together for defense, or some common purpose of ease and delight, would gain a foothold and begin to grow. Tools multiplied and got better and better; craftsmen grew ever more daring as they grew in competence; cities rose, empires swelled to menacing size and grandeur and then burst into fragments. Over and over again was the work of the builders demolished and the ruins abandoned to Nature and her friendly and leisurely burial.

Yet the lure of craftsmanship survived. Under some new empire-seeker, the builders began again, perhaps with no traditions to help, or perhaps by gathering knowledge as they listened to the legends or looked about at such fragments as they could see. Once again they set valiantly to the work of writing the next chapter in stone. Nothing, it seems, not even the fear and folly of the game called "empire" could destroy the will to build, or conquer man's instinctive love of playing with a craft. In tantalizing mockery, the bit

[5]

of wood, the lump of clay, the rough block of stone, seemed first to taunt and defy, and then, suddenly, to yield in very rapture to the master hand whose cunning was guided by patience and the will to play the game.

Patience to achieve what? Buildings? Yes, but something more. Ever luring the craftsman on was that haunting vision of something he could not name. It sang and danced with him, wept with him, thought with him, looked with him, and loved with him. He was to find that the craftsman's life was a game to which there is no end. Perfection was always to be just a step ahead and yet never to be caught. That was the game.

The play at first was rude. The players were awkward, clumsy, dull. Neither mind nor eye nor hand had come to respond to one another save gropingly. All knowledge and skill had to be gained. There were, mercifully, no schools. Education was the reality of facing life. It was not long to remain so, for king and priest were just around the corner, but for brief moments now and then through the centuries, the craftsman had some liberty. The game developed. Players developed skill and cleverness. Yet no matter how happily they went to bed, after the triumph of the day's bout, there came, with morning, another challenge. No mistress ever so fertile as she whose beauty, floating airily into the senses of her wooers, kept herself forever just beyond their reach. In the moments of his greatest achievements, when all men said the work was a perfect thing, the craftsman knew in his heart there were further perfections still ahead. The game was never ended.

This enchanting playfulness, in itself a perfect recompense for being alive, was a thing of images and fancies. These were made up of lines, shapes, forms, patterns,

[6]

masses, colors. The game was to arrange them. That was all, except that things made for use had to be usable. That came first. Things that had not use, in a material sense, as their reason for being made, had their origin in fancy alone. Little did the workers suspect that their very skill in imagery was the means by which they were to be used unfairly and often dishonestly, in another game, as full of ruse and stratagem as the craft game was full of delight.

The first craftsmen players knew nothing of that. Mind, eye and hand slowly got acquainted. Mind imagined, eye saw dimly, hand felt the embryo thought or image and tried to record it. There came to the craftsman a sense of difference in the look of lines, shapes, outlines. Harmonies and pro- portions, as shadowy dreams, came swimming vaguely into the senses of the worker. At moments, his thoughts would run away with him, as hand and tool seemed to merge with wood, clay or stone, and become a living creative force. It was a grand game in those early days.

So, with reeds and mud, the Egyptians learned to build, shape materials, transform them, change appearances, alter the face of the earth as they pleased. Building craftsmen became possessed of knowledge that was to exalt races, as they rose to dizzy heights, and then were dashed into one hell after another. We are accustomed, as are people who still fear the truth, to mark only the dizzy and brilliant heights. The hells, less easy to look at because they are more truthful, we pass by, even though they are still all about us. Height and hell were never further apart than palace and hovel, although always it was hovel that triumphed as empires passed to oblivion.

The streams of building crafts and lore that flowed away from the Nile valley under succeeding groups of builders

[7]

were not the only streams, but they dominated the rise of what is called architecture in the Western world. There were other streams that rose, no man knows exactly where, so mixed and yet seemingly so plainly related are the traces that come to light in places as far removed as Egypt is from Central America. Whether man will ever connect the links that now defy him seems to depend on whether the oceans will be kind enough to raise their floors and let us look at what they now hide. For Earth, too, it seems, has a game, in which man cannot play. It is her own game for her own ends.

Eastward from Egypt rose another great craftsman tradition with the patterns and forms of which the West has almost nothing in common. If the craftsmen were a little less subject to the disasters of empire, so they may have been even more profoundly influenced by a priesthood more gifted in the arts (or the truth) of mysticism. This does not mean that the cultural or human content of life was either more or less. It was different, perhaps less volatile, and more soundly anchored to its feeling that life was a moment of transit, and under such ways and faiths, craftsmen developed a skill no less marvelous than the others. Its patterns and forms speak clearly and fully to Western minds only after years of intimacy, yet the tale of craftsmanship often seems far to surpass, in patient dexterity, anything the West has to offer. Then, one suddenly stumbles into the presence of those craftsmen of far-away centuries in Egypt, Crete or Mycenæ, and one is again reduced to utter humility. Surely, one says, no craftsmen ever exceeded these ancient workers in gold and carvers of stone. But at last, some kindly zephyr whisks away, if only for a moment, the emotional wrappings that have been put upon us deliberately, or that we have acquired

[8]

because they were so easy to slip on and so little trouble to wear, and we then come to see that there is nothing superlative and nothing surpassing. There is only the game—and the players.

II

THE ELEMENTS OF

BUILDING

ALL building begins with walls, but the noun "building" usually describes only those forms used for shelter, no matter what activity of man they house. Thus, even as building began with a wall, so it ends with a roof. Since the day when man first began, the basic problem has not changed. There is as yet no way to make a room save with walls, and no way to keep out the weather save with a roof.

But to get into the room there had to be an opening. At first, no more than a rude hole, it was the third vital factor in all building. Over tens of centuries, the holes grew into doorways with hinged doors that opened and closed, windows that let light in through thin slabs of stone or fabric, and finally through glass. The history of building methods and what are called "styles" is the story of wall, holes and roof. Each was in turn affected by advancing skill and the rising variety of uses and purposes that grew out of the actions and behavior of men.

We might assume that the first wall was a round tent-shaped enclosure, made of reeds, stalks, boughs, or what not. Or, that it was a square enclosing protection of thatch and mud, held up by stakes driven in the ground. In either case, there came the need for stability and tightness. It's a fair guess, from what we now know, that the first building to bear even a faint likeness to what we now call a house was round, for the natural step from the tent form would be a round-walled building. Such buildings were long used, and still are, in many places. Likewise, man could find nothing in the forms of growing Nature, whose materials he used, that suggested squares and right angles for a building form, although if any landscape ever did suggest flats and uprights, it was that of the Nile valley with its long level line of river and bordering plain, and the upright heights of stone that sentinelled the valley.

Whatever the reasons, however, the four-walled, square-angled building was not long in taking shape. With four bundles of bound reeds one got four stout corner uprights that gave stability. By joining the tops of these rude posts with flat bundles of reeds, stability was increased and there was made a resting-place for the lighter matting of reeds that made the flat roof. This could be inclined the better to shed water, as the builders in rainy lands one day learned, by having one set of posts higher than the other. This gave a slope to the rafters, and if they were extended a bit at the lower side, the water ran off all the better. One who has

[11]

BY FIXING REEDS, MAIZE-STALKS, PALM-RIBS IN THE
GROUND AND IN A CIRCLE, BENDING THEIR TOPS TOGETHER
AND TYING THEM FAST, ONE GOT THE RUDE SEMBLANCE
OF A DOMED ROOF.

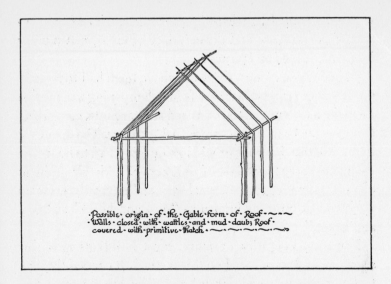

·Possible· origin· of· the· Gable· form· of· Roof·~~~
·Walls· closed· with· wattles· and· mud ·daub; Roof·
covered· with· primitive· thatch·~~·~·~·~·~·~

never built, or who has never dealt with the realities of rain falling on a roof, can have little idea of the problems that were to be set for builders before they learned how to prevent rain from undoing their work, and from making life wet and nasty for those who lived under any roof that could not defy the heavens at their worst.

By fixing reeds, maize-stalks, palm-ribs in the ground and in a circle, bending their tops together and tying them fast, one got the rude semblance of a domed roof. One could do the same thing with rows of bendable material set opposite each other in the ground and then bent towards the center of the wall space and fastened together in a long line. One then got the semblance of a gabled roof. Thus were probably evolved the three types of roof with which we still build: flat, gabled and curved. In their primitive form, scarcely unchanged after at least a hundred centuries, buildings as rude as these simple beginnings still serve in the arid lands

[13]

where the nomads, perhaps forever mistrustful of the illusion of permanence and the certainty of taxes, still wander in search of food and pasture.

In making openings, the walls above them had to be held up. If a door reached to the roof-line, the opening was simple. To make a lower opening, one used shorter posts, connecting them just as corner posts were tied together. The spanning lintel, whether for door or window opening, had to be strong enough to carry the weight of wall above. With this problem of wall, hole and roof, there slowly and naturally grew up a method of building known as "post and beam" or "post and lintel."

For forty centuries or more, most buildings men saw above ground were based on this method. It carried through to the Parthenon and far beyond. The bundle of rushes changed to wooden posts, which later grew into the massive stone columns of Karnak, and then into the robust glory of the Doric column in Sicily and Italy. In the later Parthenon, Doric column and order are said to have reached perfection. The primitive honest vigor of Paestum and Segesta gave way to delicate refinements that are said to be the last word— and so they are—in the fruition of a form for a purpose, but no more.

As walls grew stronger, posts were not needed. Door or window lintel could be fixed in the wall itself. This was a great advance for builders, but openings could be no wider than lintel was strong. No serious matter in such a climate as that of Egypt, where wall openings were a minor factor. It was serious, however, when it came to the beams that held up the roof. They set the size and shape of the house. Free

[14]

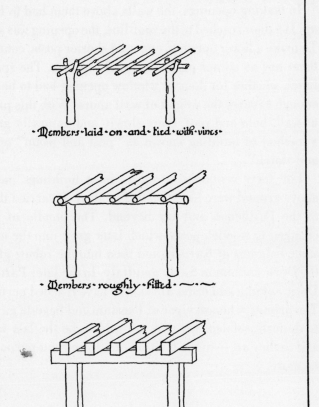

·Members·laid·on·and·tied·with·vines·

·Members·roughly·fitted·⌁·⌁

·Members·squared·and·fitted·⌁·⌁

DEVELOPMENT᛫OF᛫POST᛫&᛫LINTEL᛫FRAMING᛫⌁᛫

space in a room could be no greater than the strength of the roof beams would allow. To get a larger room than that, the space had to be cluttered with columns as roof-supports.

But the house could be expanded by the simple trick of putting two rooms side by side! Five walls were then needed, but the fifth wall that separated the two rooms made it possible to double the size of the house. And so it went, and has gone. These are the simple elements of buildings, no matter for what purpose or in what manner built. Walls and roof, wall openings and rooms. All buildings have them and it is their arrangement and treatment, not as ornament, but as straightforward building parts, that tell one how to distinguish the good, the honest and the useful, from the sham and the imitative.

Little by little, patient, groping craftsmen learned to make walls that defied all forces that Nature pitted against their wit and courage. First, a battered wall, the base wider than the top, and easier to build than one with exact vertical sides. The posts found a new use in the free standing column. It helped to make great monumental rooms, covered walks and peristyles. As such useful spaces are hardly to be classed as ornament, the column can hardly be said, through its use for these purposes, to have passed into the merely decorative class. Arcades and peristyles add a useful note to which we are now so accustomed, at least in a Grecian temple, that we sometimes forget that when use is plainly not the object, the column is both useless and a too costly decoration.

Just as the stout walls of masonry made the post useless, so had the roof form of the tent put yet another idea in the mind of some builder. The rough dome-shaped roof plastered with mud had suggested to someone that a mud-daubed dome could be set on brick walls. Not exactly a dome, for

[16]

the problem of fitting a round dome to a square wall enclosure was not so simple, as we shall presently see. But
what of the half-dome, half-gable, where the wattle had been
bent over two parallel roof-joists? Very likely the idea came
into some builder's head just from seeing what happened as
the wattle one day fell away and left the hard clay daub as an
unsupported roof.

How it happened, we can only surmise, but out of these
rude trials in which the delights of the game were never-
ending, there came the brick arched roof, more or less in
the shape of a half barrel. This was anywhere from thirty
to fifty centuries before Christ. For reasons we may suspect
but about which it is well not to be too dogmatic, the builders
were trying to build stronger tombs. Had wood proved too
short-lived—or too easy to break through? At all events,
wooden tomb walls were giving way to brick and then to
stone. Wooden roof-joists were giving way to great stone
girders, and not long after, we assume the builders had
learned how to set a brick arched roof on the tomb walls.
For centuries the effort to provide an assured security for
the departed was to become the chief activity of Egyptian
builders.

Over these endless years of heroic quarrying, transporting and raising, the story of the simple house as shelter has
to be picked out of records so scanty as to be practically
non-existent. The climate of Egypt was so wonderful that
shelter was no great matter. It is a fair guess that house walls
grew in strength, size and height, but for long were devoid
of more than the most meagre openings. The brilliant sunshine gave as much light in the rooms, through the entrance
holes, as anybody wanted. As walls passed through succeeding stages of trial and test, they also clung to the patterns

of the woven reed or stalk walls and the forms that grew out of their joining to the horizontal roof supports. Patterns became so familiar that builders felt the need of clinging to them as parts of knowledge gained, even though the reason for them had gone. Thus walls became not merely elements in the body of the building, but things that had grown into a sort of pattern. This was not the only motive that led to wall decoration, but from the feeling for patterns, however, many forms were certainly derived and carried over into buildings for centuries after the patterns or forms had anything to do with the bones of the building. Even in the Parthenon, with all its refinements and harmonies, there are forms that have no relation to the principles of stone posts and lintels. It is a fair guess that the pattern of metope and triglyph grew out of the appearance of the joining of wall to roof in the earliest reed or wood buildings.

Decoration, it also seems, grew out of the craft game that workers were playing. As they slowly got better tools and more mastery over materials, they grew keener on the trail of decorative pattern, the meaning of which related to some remembered event, some shape that had caught the fancy, or something connected with life, death, people, animals, the heavens, or any of the myriad experiences of a race that faced a world of unknown moods and powers.

The art of writing was on its way. Symbols told simple stories and set down the thoughts of potter, weaver, builder. The great outside expanses of building walls were tempting sheets on which to scribble. Papyrus and tablet were playthings, compared with these wide surfaces. As time went on, the blank spaces of columns and walls, on even the most stupendous of buildings, were completely covered with a host of symbols. Everything—every part, every shape—be-

[18]

came symbolic. Not only was the temple itself contrived to fix an idea of mystery and power, but all was made more impressive by adding a bewildering array of symbol that made for obedience and submission. The tricks of symbology were never to cease. Truth was to become, under their sway and guidance, whatever those in control of the forces that gave shape and effect to government could make people accept as truth.

At the long story of these early builders and their heroic persistence, we can take but a passing look, not forgetting that it is but one of many beginnings. It happens to be nearest to the Western world, in direct line of descent, but there were other builders no less skillful, no less persistent, of whom only faint traces are blown to us like an air from some mystical garden. How many times the builders tried, or were commanded, to entrench, ennoble and build a durable civilization, we can but guess. What we know is that, so far, they have never been able to find a foundation on which to put a social order that would endure. But that, I, for one, would assert, was not the fault of the craftsmen who made the buildings.

III

FORM BEGINS IN

EGYPT

T HE building forms that began to take shape in Egypt some thousands of years ago were the forerunners of what the Western world calls its architectural heritage. The legacy is not clearly traceable. There are missing links in the chain of sequence sought by those who wish to trace all building knowledge to single or related sources. The procession of forms remains, however, and that is quite enough. From mud-daubed screens the craftsmen slowly advanced to corner post and roof beam, to a house of reeds and mud, to walls of sun-baked cakes of earth, to walls of brick, shaped to use and fancy, and finally to such mastery of stone as men are not like to see again.

[20]

The form and shape of buildings changed very slowly, but the game grew ever more interesting and the players more skillful. If one likes the sort of play in which imagination and invention are permitted to flow freely, it is not too difficult to believe that the early craftsmen had a pretty good time. One of the pleasantest idealisms is that of the workman singing at his work. Whether those early Egyptian screen-weavers and mud-daubers sang over their labor, we do not know, but the history of music goes so far back as to let us at least guess that it was not long before the craftsmen had a tune. There were no shops, no factories, no necessity for speed, no loans for piling up the menace and threat of debt with interest, and the two clocks that governed all things were the sun and the Nile.

With the river down, all work went to the garden. With the Nile in flood, there was building to be done. Population increased and thought had to be given to general arrangement of buildings. Planning had a simple and natural approach. It dealt not alone with the single building but with the relation of each to all the others, and with the relation of all to the mode and manner of life. There were for long no problems of private rights. As the Nile alone gave food, so did it point the way to the communal plan. Houses needed to be beyond reach of the flood, yet as close as possible to the land the river uncovered once a year, in order that men might live. For the long period between harvest and planting, food had to be stored, and the location of the storehouses for the use and convenience of the hungry determined the size and location of the groups that made the communities. The source of life was close, simple, direct. Away from the Nile stretched only the sandy wastes and the stony arid hills.

A natural economy evolved. Based on food supply, it

gave the builders a clear need to satisfy, a basis for what to build and where to build it. The idea of making a civilization has never departed a hair's breadth from that simple basis: what to build and where to build it. Simple primitive races manage to arrange their building with a straightforward directness. The more learned always make a mess of it. Could it be possible that architecture is the evidence of an endless series of far more truthful records than we like to admit?

Before any great monumental building could be done, there had to be not only tools of precision, but tools for quarrying, lifting, rolling, raising. Through the ensuing centuries it was a slow onward march, a pageant in which time counted for nothing. If one could have asked the marchers where they were going or towards what goal they were headed, the answer might have been quite as intelligent and socially far-seeing as one would get by asking the same question today. Would that be true of the building craftsmen? Weren't they interested beyond the day's work? What led them on? There was no clink of coin, and for many centuries the only driving master was hunger. How far forward did the builders look, as they got the better tool or learned the new trick or manner of doing things? Did they see an ultimate better and easier life growing out of their labor? Did they see their children in better houses, with a good house for everybody? Or was it just the day's work and the day's bread?

However these things may have been, those who were to pretend to look into the future after death, and use their assumed knowledge for their own ends, were slowly ap-

[22]

proaching. They may have been present when man first began to build, but whether or no, it was not long before they saw the builder as one who could be used to further their schemes. Whether king or priest came first does not matter. Nor does it matter whether they sought power or whether it was thrust upon them. Both began to use the builder to proclaim certain things to all men, and in no unimpressive terms.

There came at last the day of the stone mason. There came the day when as dauntless a race of builders as ever lived were to turn away from rotting wood and crumbling brick. There were the hills, always at the back of the Nile-watered plain. They lifted themselves high and stood as fixed forever. Builders, thinking of things that would stand fast and long, must have looked at them, approached them, examined them, felt of them, and dreamed of how to outwit the firmness and fastness of them. One might think of the slow calling and the slow wooing of the stony hills as a gesture of Nature, as though she were saying to the builders: "Time to cease playing with reeds and mud, and the wood so scarce and fragile. Time to look away from the plain and see that the most durable material I have to offer is the stuff out of which I have made the hills."

Nothing, she might have been saying and they might have been hearing, would stand fixed forever or endure always. One could see that, if one had the vision to see beyond the crest and the outline of things as they appeared. Slowly cutting their way through those very hills, in order to find the sea, had come the snows of which the builders had no knowledge, falling on mountains they had never seen. Had they these visions or were the Nile and the seasons no more than things going by? And the hills the changeless forms that

[23]

suggested only changelessness and thus gave a beginning to the thought that if buildings could be in stone they would last long and leave the builders free to go on and on, rather than stop and patch, repair and rebuild.

At last the wooing came to an end, it is plain, for stone tombs began to appear. Concern with life after death was what the builders were asked to give their hands and skill to; or did they give it of their own accord? Whatever the reason, more and more were they set to the service of king and priest on tombs of stone that would make safe and sure the agreeable life to come, and on minor temples as part of the ritual by which the departed were laid away. Not for a moment was it in the minds of king or priest that the builders should be set to the task of making life steadily easier and more agreeable for the multitude that lived and toiled day by day on earth.

Tomb and temple were to be used for thousands of years to turn men's minds away from the pleasant task of building a secure and stable way of life on earth. Builders were to labor for some other purpose than their own gain and benefit, as they steadily sacrificed themselves to the life to come. The long centuries of Egyptian craftsmanship may well be reckoned as a titanic effort to deny the physical evidence of death and, by ever more colossal and impregnable tombs, to rob life of that strange terror that came when eyes no longer looked and voice no longer spoke.

Life must go on! So, over long periods, the multitudes of empires spent their lives, to the point of complete sacrifice and eventual destitution, in building for the king such a tomb as would guard him inviolate until his never-dying self should in some manner resume his being. As for his subjects —well, they could afford to take chances. They were not

[24]

burdened with the tempting possessions that also had to be made safe and sure for the king and that probably had more to do with the impregnable tombs than was generally admitted.

Whether derived from tomb building, or from the instinct for rightness, or from both, the early Egyptian had an opinion. Of that, no doubt whatever. He believed in solidity, precision, rightness. His word for monument meant "firm thing." As to what he may have meant symbolically by the pyramid tomb, if anything, there has been offered no proof that satisfies all minds. Some think the form related to occult and cosmic ideas, understood only by the "initiate." Perhaps this is a question that ought to concern us deeply. If the pyramid tomb, or any other building, contains knowledge that will tell man how to behave in order to establish a decent relationship with the cosmos—which surely includes his fellows—we ought to find these things out.

My own guess is that temple and tomb were part of the fear tradition and the system of power and tribute that grew out of it; that as time went on, the king, aided and abetted by the priest, knew very well how to make the most of it. In time, others also discovered that there were ways of escaping one's share of common labor, and that if one used one's wit and took advantage of the credulous natures of those who liked to work and who got a pleasure and even a joy out of it, one could be well fed and clothed and have a better house to live in.

What has all this to do with building? Everything—for tomb, temple and palace were to dominate the work of the builders. Skill and knowledge were used to obscure rather

[25]

than to liberate the mind of man. Instead of a common movement towards an ever-growing ease, stability and security, life was to be dominated by the ideas of king and priest, and these ideas were to be fixed by the builders in stone, and set before men as truth. War and religion were to become the chief activities in all attempts at national life, and buildings were to be used to glorify these activities.

This need not lessen our admiration for the builders. Their works and marvels were not a bit the less, as they went on glorifying an unknown heaven and making preparations for a secure hereafter on the one hand, and shouting the glories of victory and the triumphs of empire on the other.

In Egypt, twenty to forty centuries had flown since the reed-weavers and mud-daubers. King and priest were well in the saddle. Khufru reigned at Memphis. Great tombs had been followed by greater ones. The mounds of earth above the early simple graves had grown to colossal pyramids. Temples of ever-growing grandeur were on the way. The record, to this point, covers not years, but centuries. The Nile valley, for hundreds of miles, bore witness to a pageant of prodigious human labor and skill. If the result, expressed in terms of devotion, is one of the wonders of time, so also was the result as told in terms of building.

Builders had now reached a mastery of limestone, sandstone, granite and the flinty diorite, such as has never been surpassed. If they began with such boulders as could easily be detached from their beds and rolled to some tomb site, and of which the number was limited, we can do no more than gasp at what they did when quarrying had to be learned.

To make the Great Pyramid of Khufru (Cheops), there were cut from the hills across the river, some forty miles away, no fewer than 2,300,000 blocks of stone, each weigh-

[26]

ing two and one-half tons. In the king's chamber, high in the heart of the pyramid, for the whole was a tomb for the royal family, there are nine stone beams that weigh from sixty to seventy tons. What courage and what labor! How did these builders long-cut, cross-cut, and then undercut these great blocks? The legend is that it took ten years to get ready to begin the actual building—ten years to make the causeways over which the blocks could be moved from quarry to river and from river to the site of the tomb. Ten years more were used in piling the stones and in adding the casing. For, after the great blocks had been piled step-like in a rough pyramidal form, the whole was entirely covered with smooth-dressed limestone, of which it is reckoned from the few fragments that have survived desecration and pillage that there must have been something like 115,000 slabs. Again we marvel! So great was the skill of these builders in fitting the casing slabs, that a skilled mason of today would be puzzled to know how those Egyptian craftsmen ever used cement on the edges. The joints were so perfect they must have looked like lines ruled off in faint, yet perfect precision on the vast smooth expanse that reflected the sun as in a flame. The pyramid, to the Egyptian, was the ever-burning light of life continuous—at least for the king!

Where, in certain places, limestone was not thought either worthy or strong enough for the tomb that was to make safe and sure the royal hereafter, the builders journeyed some five hundred miles up the Nile to Syene (now Assouan). To quarry the blocks of granite sought they drilled holes into which were driven wooden wedges. These were soaked with water until the swelling wood burst the granite from its bed. Then the blocks were rafted down the river to the pyramid causeway. Time did not count. There was no money. Life was only for raising food and building tombs.

The base of the Great Pyramid is roughly 755 feet square. The apex was 482 feet above the base. Variations in measurements are exact to a 10-1000th of the whole. The pyramid faces north with a precision that could not be bettered by the most modern astronomer with the most delicate instruments. A half dozen cathedrals could be set on the area covered by this heroic effort to get a king to—wherever he is.

A hundred thousand men, says Herodotus, worked on the Great Pyramid of Khufru, over three-month periods. No one seems to doubt this as a credible statement. The periods would apply to the times of year when the Nile was in flood, and when there could be no work in the fields. As to the legends of slaves driven by brutal masters, few longer believe the great pyramids to have been carried on quite so heartlessly. Rather do we guess their builders to have been more light-hearted than their monumental tombs suggest. They lived in abundant sunshine, seemed not to have lacked food, while clothing and shelter were small matters. Nor could such heroic buildings have been possible to other than a well and devotedly organized army of workers whose animating force, one guesses, could hardly have been a man with a whip. No such craftsmanship could come from chain and manacle, whip and goad. Great skill has to be won in some other way.

The method by which the blocks of stone and the great stone girders in the king's chamber were raised in place is no more than a guess. Probably it was by a combination of two of the simple elements of mechanics, for these at least must have been known to the builders: the inclined plane and the lever. To quarry and raise those 2,300,000 blocks

[28]

of stone, there were needed not only a hundred thousand men, highly skilled and wisely directed, but tools! For cutting the great blocks in the quarries, there were copper saws, each point shod with some abrasive such as a jewel or a piece of corundum. For dressing the stubborn surfaces, there were rasps, scrapers, hammers without handles, mallets with handles, a variation explained, apparently, by heavy usage of the first and light usage of the last. There were bow-drills, bits, wedges, cradles, rollers, adzes, the square, the plumb-line and bob, the lathe, but, curiously enough, no crowbars. A great amount of copper must have been needed. Whence it came, there have been many guesses. There was none in the Egypt of that day, although there were deposits in the Sinai peninsula.

How had the tools evolved? Whence came the craftsmanship? It is as impossible to say as it is unimportant to know. There are no direct and infallible links in the history of building. Never is there a positive proof that this or that race was the first to use this or that tool or to build in this or that way. There is the pageant—and the game. During the centuries since the reed and mud beginnings by the Nile, many kings and peoples had passed in long procession. To judge by the meagre records, there must have been a continuing mixture of men with aquiline noses, pointed noses, snub noses, and then the straight-bridged noses of the latter historic dynasties. After all, there were men who knew how to make tools and weapons at least a thousand centuries before Egyptian builders built a tomb.

Over later centuries, unto this very day, migrants and wanderers carried knowledge about until there was a great admixture of craft methods, but never anything resembling a universal way of building. It is certain that different peoples, at the same or different times, got to build in the same manner with no borrowing whatever, because neither people knew anything about the other. Nothing is of less moment, in the history of building, than fixed dates and infallible links that prove authorship of anything.

One thing is certain, the pyramid of Khefre, who followed Khufru, was smaller, and so on for succeeding monarchs until at last there were no more. It is not difficult to imagine, at this particular moment in Egyptian history, that, as Breasted says, "Menkure (who later followed Khefre) was not able to extort more from an exhausted nation." The consecration of the whole state to a series of kings' tombs that would endure forever had consumed and at last exhausted all resources.

Centuries rolled by between the fall of Memphis and the rise of Thebes. The pyramid age was one of great power and achievement, of massive undertakings, heroic effort and fine workmanship. And then a low sinking, and a silence. One might say that in a nationally concerted act of pious endeavor, based upon earthly life as a transitory flash and the hereafter as a permanently arranged state of something better, the builders had spent their skill in magnificent attempts to defeat death. They, and their fellows, we might thus assume, were not interested in preparing the way for an agreeable life on earth. But such an assumption has to face the fact that only the king was provided with a death-defeating guarantee.

No proof exists, or ever will, of what was in the minds of the people of that day. No record can ever tell that about any people. One may assume and deduce, but one will never

[30]

know the thoughts that lay behind the long efforts of the tomb makers or any other builders. One may look at succeeding eras and compare similar great achievements with similar ends. One is then likely to conclude that the builders have many times risen to great heights of creative power and technical skill, only to leave their works as an exotic flowering that soon withered, even as the root and bole that bore it sank ever to a slow but sure decline. Many and many a time did some great human flood sweep over the builders and their buildings, as over all else, and then—silence and a slowly rising new splendor that went the same way.

After the great days of Memphis and the pyramids, there were centuries that left little trace. The era of temple building that began in the XIIth dynasty, some thousand years after Khufru, came to an end. The earlier temples, as adjuncts of pyramid tomb and burial precinct, had likewise ceased to be built. The whole land was impoverished by the sacrifices exacted, and apparently there were some who decided that the needs and pleasures of life on earth took precedence over the hereafter, for the tombs were rifled of all the treasures stored against the need of the one-time kings in the life to come. No tomb was sacred. Even the colossal pyramid of Khufru, with all its massive safeguards, did not escape the general pillage. So thorough was the rifling that rarely have modern seekers found a tomb where other riflers had not been there before them.

It was then that the builders turned to the rock-cut tomb. In this hewn vault they once again attempted to insure a safe journey to the hereafter. After burial, deep in the rock-bound sanctuary, the tomb was sealed, and the excavation piled with sand and buried from sight. Kings returned, in principle, to the very grave that had given rise to the

[31]

pyramid. The temple form slowly revived but, no longer an adjunct to the tomb, served as a simple element in the primitive ritual of worshipping ancestors who waited in the hereafter. As a separate structure, it did the royal honors but had nothing to do with the burial precinct. That, it had been discovered, was best not advertised to the public. The centuries of rock-tomb and temple rolled by and suddenly there was Thebes. And then there was Karnak!

This colossal temple did not rise magically or quickly, nor did it indicate a rebirth of more than what so many historians have called "megalomania." Thebes began its story at the moment when dates become fairly authentic and creditable, some fifteen or sixteen centuries, B.C. Karnak was already some hundreds of years old. Like all temples, it had more and more been taken over by the priesthood, as the domain of a cult that could be developed profitably by a privileged class deriving income from ever-increasing possessions. The great god, Amun, for example, who held title to the property, and to whom, and to whose wife and son, Karnak was largely sacred, had greater wealth and income than the king. He owned more than eighty thousand slaves and vassals, endless herds and gardens, together with ships, towns and cities.

From the time that Amasis came to power in Thebes, the temple became the mystical abode of an impressive religious dominance, the power and wealth of which was masked by a title vested in a god. As flattery for such kingly vanity as priests found useful in extending their sway and income, the temple also took on an overpowering majesty of size, something so big and bewildering as completely to silence

[32]

PLATE I. THE PYRAMIDS. PLATE II. THE STATUES OF MEMNON IN THE PLAIN OF THEBES. (After the ithograph by Louis Haghe, from the painting by David Roberts.)

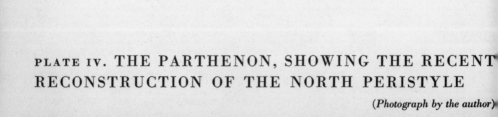

PLATE IV. THE PARTHENON, SHOWING THE RECENT
RECONSTRUCTION OF THE NORTH PERISTYLE

(*Photograph by the author*)

PLATE VI. THE TEMPLE OF NIKE APTEROS

(Photograph by the author)

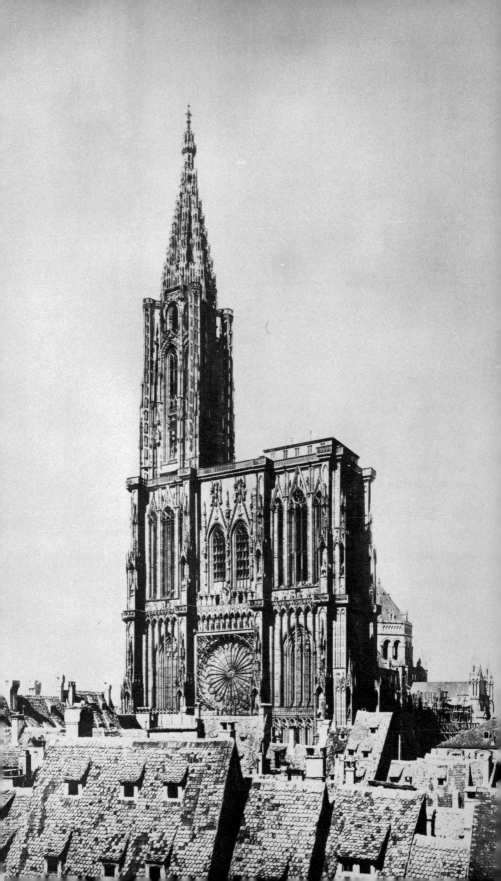

(

PLATE XV. ST. PETER'S, ROME

(After the engraving by Piranesi)

any questioning and to win subservience from all subjects and vassals.

Karnak was probably the first great central religious edifice ever raised by builders. Its extensions and accretions continued for more than ten centuries. It grew to an area of 338 by 1120 feet and covered more than sixty acres. In the use of post and lintel the masons of Thebes dared to bridge spaces in a manner that must have been more fearsome then than today, when the audacious risks on which the builders staked their skill and prowess still fill the beholder with a sense of awe. What save fearsome thoughts could have filled men's minds in Karnak's day, as they looked up at those gigantic blocks of stone laid across other equally gigantic columns? Well indeed were their minds prepared for humility and subservience as they approached the temple by an avenue lined with rows of sphinxes and terminating at the enormous pylons, larger than the façade of any subsequent cathedral. Behind lay the precincts of the god and the mysteries, the assumed knowledge of which was reserved for those who profited handsomely by the assumption thereof. One wandered literally amongst a forest of columns. In the great Hypostyle Hall, one hundred and seventy by three hundred and forty feet in area (about the same as that of Notre Dame at Paris), the massive roof was held up by one hundred and thirty-four columns in sixteen rows. The two central rows towered above the others as columns sixty feet high and twelve feet in diameter. They thus formed a kind of clerestory through which light, falling like a benediction from Ra himself, found its way into the great Hall.

There was also the great columnar hall of Thothmes, there were courtyards of columns, aisles of columns, separated from each other by towering pylons, while over the surfaces of all, walls, pylons and columns, was written the tale of the kings of Thebes, each of whom had sought to surpass and outdo his predecessor. Fergusson, one of the first of the modern historians of buildings, marvelled at Karnak in these words: "No language can convey an idea of its beauty, and no artist has yet been able to reproduce its form so as to convey to those who have not seen it an idea of its grandeur. The mass of its central piers, illumined by a flood of light from the clerestory, and the smaller pillars of the wings, gradually falling into obscurity, are so arranged and lighted as to convey an idea of infinite space; at the same time the beauty and massiveness of the forms, and the brilliancy of their colored decorations, all combine to stamp this as the greatest of man's architectural works, but such a one as it would be impossible to reproduce, except in such a climate and in that individual style in which, and for which, it was created."

From Karnak, temple and tomb builders roamed the Nile valley. Under Rameses they built with a vigor that slowly and surely devoured the wealth of both production and tribute. With the most lavish and prodigal use of craftsman and slave, of materials as costly as they were precious, Rameses built new temples, restored, rebuilt or enlarged many old ones, and left as his most striking monument in buildings the great rock-hewn temple of Abou Simbel. Then, little by little, the Egypt of Thebes went the way of the Egypt of Memphis. Not even the wealth gained in war and pillage —and it was in no mean amounts that the plunder rolled in —could endure the cost of such profligate waste. Again the land was impoverished. There followed the Exodus and a great loss of man-power. Once more all but the most skillfully concealed tombs were rifled. Once more a silence. Once again the centuries rolled by, until some three hundred years before the Christian era, the Ptolemaic dynasty arose. Once again Egypt became powerful, rich, and there was another straggling era of temple building, continuing into the Roman dominion. And then—a long silence. The most prodigious efforts that builders ever attempted over forty centuries, and in which they quarried, moved and piled stone in endless millions of tons, became no more than a tragic record of ruins and decay.

In this building period of forty centuries or more, what had the builders finally learned? Very little. The craftsmanship at Karnak was far below the high level of that at Memphis. This may have been due to the prevalent use of the stream of slaves brought back in the Theban wars of conquest and capture. In planning also, the Theban builders never attained the marvellous exactitudes and simplicities of the Great Pyramid. That had been set on a site that would bear its weight. Karnak, on the contrary, had been set on ground through which the great weight forced upward a continual seepage of water carrying salts, and these ate away at whatever stone they touched. They left a problem to those who would preserve the ruins that has involved no end of study and money.

In the crafts, the Egyptian builders clung to their forms with a stolid persistence. Nothing would induce them to seek an easier and simpler way. All effort, in the ruins with which we are familiar, went into the ponderous and the grandiose, as expressed by massive walls, pylons, posts and lintels. Even in the rock-hewn tombs and temples, where all loads were borne by the natural rock itself, these four elements persist, as outward form, as stubbornly as when the

[35]

builders went through the herculean labor of quarrying, transporting and putting in place the colossal blocks and beams with which they built.

One may say that this tenacious clinging to form was because of unwillingness to experiment. This in itself is a denial of the very basis of craftsmanship, and inclines one the more to believe that religious dominance held the craftsmen well and steadily in leash, never letting their fancy flow very far. Once or twice, as in the rock-hewn temple to Queen Hatshepsut, or the tomb of Beni-Hassan, in Theban days, is there evidence that some builder was dreaming of daintier things and forms. In either or both of these, one might easily conclude, was the beginning of the Doric order, although there is no proof for or against the theory and never can be, unless an army of dead builders shall one day arise and tell their own tale.

Spencer has observed that "primitive man deviates into novelty only through unintentional modifications." The story of how those simple columns found their way into the temple of Queen Hatshepsut may be no more than such a deviation. Or we might accept these columns as the first faint trace, in a building, of the concept of social justice that was here trying to make an appeal, as some moralists so confidently assume, and as the reign of Ikhnaton may serve to give an inkling. Whatever the truth, and whatever place assigned to that long heroic labor, one finds it impossible to accept it as evidence of how to make buildings for a civilization based on the common good. The builders' effort was colossal. The ruins are grand to the point of sublimity. If any of them tell the tale of first gropings for a social form based on justice, security and stability to all, we shall have

[36]

to conclude that the process was as painfully slow then as now.

Through forty centuries in Egypt, dwellings for the privileged classes grew ampler and were made pleasant with pool and garden. Chiefs' houses were of planks, twelve to fourteen inches wide and six or seven feet high. Set upright, overlapped, lashed at the edges, they could be moved close to the fields when the Nile receded, and back to high ground, in a day, when the water rose. Peasant houses were often no more than a screen, or with a sort of portico room at the back. Then came steps to the roof, and a second story, with an attic for grain on top of that. Brick arches and palm columns, of many different forms, were used. When the earthen floor was damp, it was overlaid with baked clay.[1]

There were planned streets, giving access to mansions of forty to sixty rooms, with roof spaces and sun chambers, courts and stairways, granaries and outbuildings. The climate was so dry and kindly that hardship in the matter of shelter was probably so little that "housing reform" was never discussed. Any idea that buildings were the prime factors in any plan for social balance was to lie fallow for many long centuries.

In sculpture, however, by and for itself and as an integral part of building, Egyptian craftsmen touched the topmost heights. Here was straightforwardness—the very essence of integrity. Never were kings so exalted in stone as were those monarchs of Egypt. Never was sculpture so scorned as ornament and so securely built into buildings as to be in and of their very bones, sinews and fibres. Here, in a rhythmic flow of the inorganic, buildings radiated a simple organic whole that has never been excelled. With sculpture and carving,

[1] *Social Life in Ancient Egypt.* By W. M. Flinders Petrie.

temples came to be as wondrous as storied documents as they were glorious examples of sheer building prowess.

After Karnak, a profusion of temples. If they were a part of the dawn of conscience, so were they also a part of that unceasing mirage that has lured man, whenever raised to power, to deny all semblance of conscience. As time went on, the ruling class learned, ever more artfully and more skillfully, to use buildings for the purpose of acclaiming the social justice to which mankind might look forward—but never enjoy.

IV

FORM IS REFINED IN

GREECE

THE traveller, if he approach Athens by day, whether by land or sea, cannot well escape a distant view of the Acropolis and the outline of the ruined Parthenon. The effect of the sight of this rocky eminence, on Western peoples, differs, one supposes, in the degree of awareness of the kinship that is theirs. If one feels the blood-stream running deeply, then the air of Athens is charged with a vibrant thrill, as though one had come Home at last, and into the presence of a great throng, of which each invisible member was as eager to speak as to listen, yet unable to utter a sound.

The wise traveller will know better than to be other than very gentle with such a host of personages. Nor will he be

[39]

in any hurry to break the spell. Rather will he seek to modulate his manners to the murmuring silence and slowly prepare his spirit for the climb to the top of the rock. At last, on some sunny morning when the shadows are playing in the Propylea, he will stand and watch their frolic. The sounds of Athens, far below, will be no more in his ears. Then and there the many voiceless questions will suddenly become so many faintly audible whisperings, as though in clear yet mystical communion. The craftsmen of that day will speak at last, and listen with delighted ears, and one may have speech with them according to one's capacity for such talk.

The number and variety of questions will be infinite. Many, like myself, will ask to know nothing farther back in history than the day that Isadora Duncan danced in the long peristyle. They would like to know, as would I, whether any flight or gesture of a goddess could match that upward fling of hers in the Brahms Waltz, as she soared to we know not what Olympus. We, who remember as though it were yesterday, would no doubt be thinking of dancing rather than of architecture. But the pedants and the lovers of documented dates and tight-fitting historical sequences would ask more proper things. They would very likely wish to know how the Doric order came to Athens. No importance will attach to the answer, even though it could be found. It does not matter in the least, for when all is said and done, the Doric order rests squarely on the use of post and lintel. The pedants refer to it as "trabeated building," the word "trabs" being a good equivalent for the beam or lintel. As to its appearance in Greece, some suggest that a wandering Greek got to Egypt and saw the temple of Queen Hatshepsut, or the tomb of Beni-Hassan, or both, and came back with a memory of how the columns looked. Others think that some Egyptian wandered away from home and invited attention to a new style of column in his country. The first is more likely than the second, for the Greeks were no mean travellers in their day, while the Egyptians were not much at roaming.

What more natural, others ask, than that the trabeated idea came down from the north when forest-dwellers came southward? Wooden post and lintel came long before stone, and were used as late as the last days of Knossos, somewhere about 1500 B.C. There were wooden columns throughout a great part of the Ægean civilization of Crete, Tiryns, Argos, Mycenæ, and although nothing appears in the ruins to suggest that the Ægean builders were much concerned with the perfections or refinements of post and lintel, it might well be that the Doric order rose in Greece and was suggested by no outsider. It is certain that the temple of Hera at Olympia, built about 700 B.C., had Doric columns of wood.

There were centuries in the history of the stony area known as Greece about which nothing is known. No buildings have survived, which may mean that they were of wood, or that none was built. After Tiryns, and Mycenæ, a great gap. And there at the same time, and long before, was Crete, a great and flourishing civilization, in many ways far advanced over Egypt. Apparently its builders preferred to use their labor in generally advancing the comforts of living—in devising bath-rooms and toilets that were flushed with running water, rather than in squandering their time and the substance of the people on awe-inspiring temples. Crete was a great maritime power, yet the traces of her sailors and their wanderings and tale-bearings are lost in an obscurity as deep and dark as that which surrounds the Achæans of Homer's day, the Pelasgians, the Dorians, and all the migrant tribes that came south from the cold land of the great woods.

Just as in Egypt, so are there here no clear sequences. Over all lies the patina of many vanished races. One of these, we assume, came south with a knowledge of how to forge and weld iron, and so to conquer and subdue the men who knew only bronze. Soldier and builder, shepherd and villager, make a pattern of rude outlines only. In that pattern, somewhere, and yet at no point that man can fix, lies the secret of how the Doric order came to be.

There is also the intriguing possibility of the lost island of Atlantis, and the contribution it may have made. Rumors of it reached Plato, who mentions it and who seemed to be going to write more later, and who may have died before he could record all he had heard. The legend of that vanished island still persists, to this day, and there really is no reason why an island should not have sunk into the Atlantic and have carried down a great civilization along with it. The sea has swallowed down and vomited up many an odd bit of land, in its day. A vanished island would, if the sea should some day uncover it, help to settle many questions, utterly unimportant though they be.

On the Acropolis, such things seem trivial. Standing in the Propylea and looking through the inner columns at the two temples ahead, it suddenly occurs to one that history is inevitable and changeless only up to the drawing of the breath; that the present lasts no longer than that breath; that the future is the one thing with which man can have any concern. All the rest is beyond his reach. But the future begins with each filling of the lungs. Nothing but what is ahead is of the slightest moment, and the pattern of what is to come is now, as it has always been, in the hands of the living. What other hope has man than in that pattern and its weaving?

It may be with such meditations as these that the traveller walks away from Athens, over which the past hangs so grandly and yet so tragically. So may he be thinking as he climbs the last flight of steps and sees through the columns the glorious temple to the Virgin Goddess—again to remember that belief in parthenogenesis is far older than the Christ legend. The noble austerity and majesty of the mass are accented by the position of the temple on the highest point of the Acropolis. From the moment one leaves Athens until one at last sets foot on the floor of the portico, one climbs and looks upward.

The Parthenon is so many things that one is for the moment quite overcome. Some time will pass before one begins to see the temple not only as the work of ten or more years of building, but also as the fruit of a hundred years of patient trying and testing, during which four generations of craftsmen, working in Asia Minor, Sicily, Italy and Greece, sought to bring the Doric order to a form that entirely pleased them; at least we must assume as much as that if we accept the usual historic version of the Parthenon as the greatest of all Greek buildings. It is so easy, in thus accepting, to give credit for it to the men whose names have come down to us by the historical method—Pericles, Callicrates, Ictinus, and Phidias, whom Plato called "a wise stone-cutter"—and so easy to forget, by the same very defective historical method, the long procession of building craftsmen who, year by year, played with their changing ideas of form and proportion as succeeding variations passed the ultimate test by which like and dislike were determined.

Had it not been for this great unsung host of stone-carvers and stone-hewers, there could have been no Parthenon. It did not spring from any single mind. It was not born of any single concept. Rather was it the fruit of a slowly ripening experience over a century of trial and error. Year after year the builders studied the result of their labor, looked at it, lived with it, and noted what pleased them and what did not.

In gradually refining the form of the column and all the parts of the temple, from the huge solid base to the acroteria on the peak of the pediment, the Athenian builders had an advantage over the tomb and temple builders of Egypt. Almost at the edge of Athens lay Mount Pentelicon, stored with abundant marble of good strength and fine texture. It could be cut, dressed, shaped and carved in delicacies and precisions that were impossible in the stone used by the Egyptian craftsman. All the more glory for the marvels they wrought, one is tempted to exclaim.

Whether the Egyptians would have departed from their tradition, had they known Pentelic marble, is no more than an interesting speculation, but the Athenian builders were certainly not interested in the fearful and the awesome, the ponderous and the colossal. They had a different way of looking at their gods and goddesses. The temples they built for them were meant to be noble and gracious works in which neither skill nor material should be spared. In this respect they differed from the builders of Memphis, who had an equally fine concept of craftsmanship, only in the quality of appearance they sought. Though no more than mythical and momentary, the Greek temple, as abode, had to be a fitting place for immortals. They were very much alive and wanted no tombs in which to await a hereafter.

There was likewise no host of priests, as at Karnak, set apart as a privileged class drawing revenue of all sorts. The Greek temple was not a place of daily or even weekly ritual and ceremony, but a place apart, to which men might

[44]

go when it came time to celebrate. Then the happenings were as festal as they were religious, and while the temple was meant to advertise certain ideas that would inspire respect and make people pay and go to war without too much murmuring, the element of fear, in its form, was small indeed, compared with the grandiose awesomeness of Karnak.

Standing today by the ruins of the south peristyle of the Parthenon, where the fragments of columns and wall lie as they fell under the Venetian bombardment, one may come to feel, if one is sensitive to presences, the spiritual attendance of a great army of craftsmen. The thought of them is a part of the pleasant comfort and serenity that flow from ruins. In these, where sun, wind and rain have long bathed and cleansed, those fixed ideas the building was meant to impress upon the beholder are gone. The message, once set forth in symbols that were even clearer in their meaning than are our words of today, has disappeared. The very stones have regained their purity.

One is no longer asked to believe in the virgin birth, or to be afraid of the wrath of the gods, even though these ideas were no more than an excuse for proclaiming the glory of Athens—and Pericles. One is set free. No abstract notions and emotionally acquired reverences or idolatries intervene to confuse one's natural feeling about a work of craftsmanship, and thus to make one timid about either knowing or saying whether one likes or dislikes it. Only so can one come to intimate and honest terms with the beauty that flows simply from line, form and color, from harmony and proportion, from the relation of part to part and of all parts to the whole. Only so can one really know how one feels about a piece of architecture as a work of building.

It is at such moments, as though by a revelation, that one

[45]

hears the faint clink of hammer and chisel, the hum of pleasant talk and the friendly sounds that come from workmen who are seeking the utmost, who are matching all their wit and skill against a rude material, and who mean to get from it all that can be had in strength, grace and harmony. One feels instinctively that not only were there many happy craftsmen at work on the Parthenon, less free, perhaps, than their Egyptian forbears, for they were more trained and restrained by rules, but that from this building there stretches away an uncountable train of craftsman workers, backward into the centuries, and then forward, for more centuries, building, building, building—playing with tool and material, until, now and then, they found the form that suited the purpose to perfection.

Thus the historical method of giving the credit for a building to some particular person seems ungenerous. No building ever had a single author. One cannot point to a single feature of building, anywhere, and say that it first appeared in this building, or that. The whole historical method, in so far as it applies to credit and authorship, rests only on the concept of society as a struggle for individual glory and reward. It completely denies the endless sequence—when it deals with buildings—the endless procession of workers and thinkers, each making his humble contribution.

These things remain true, no matter how keenly we reflect upon the toiling slaves that quarried the blocks on Pentelicon and helped the oxen to drag them to Athens and up the steep of the Acropolis, or upon the silver that helped to pay both workman and slave, mined at Laurion under conditions so revolting and inhuman that one shudders at thought of them. That the philosophy of the craftsmen builders was overwhelmed by that of the money changers does not alter the nature of the craftsman and his attitude towards his work. Craftsmanship still remains one of the great satisfying pleasures of men. As a method of teaching wisdom, honor, justice and patience, has the world yet found anything so good as the pitting of hand and brain against tool and material?

Why did the Greeks build temples? As earthly homes for their gods and goddesses, we have answered; yet the Greek temples sprang also from the same concepts of power to rule and take tribute that had fastened themselves on Egypt under a form of rule that was hereditary rather than elective, as at that moment in Athens.

The result differed but little, for, although the Parthenon lacks the sternly masterful note of Karnak, we shall have to accept the fact, however melancholy the truth or however it may shock our emotional cravings, that the temple at Athens was a kind of propaganda. The temple builders there worked exactly as had their forerunners at Memphis and Thebes. The requirement, no matter how far it was refined and beautified and made noble in proportion and radiant with sculpture, was a building that would advertise ideas and lead to such submissions as would minimize the discontent of the slaves, lead free citizens to pay taxes cheerfully, and, with a conscious pride of glory, go forth obediently to war. One remembers very well what happened to Socrates, for example.

The Greek temple, however, was very simple in form, sometimes with but one room and seldom with more than two. An easy way to understand the Parthenon, is to think of a great stone box two hundred feet long, seventy feet wide,

was a great building that would advertise powerful ideas and

and forty feet high. Around the box stood a row of columns, each thirty-four feet high, eight showing on each end, and seventeen showing on the sides, a total of forty-six. At the ends of the buildings were porticoes, or recesses, to give shelter at the entrance, for Athens, unlike Egypt, had plenty of rain. The roof of these porticoes was a projection of the roof that covered the temple, and, to help support it, there was an inner row of six columns in the portico. (The total length of the Parthenon was two hundred and twenty-eight feet, the width one hundred and two feet, and the height, from base to peak, fifty-nine feet.)

A single roof thus covered the rooms, the porticoes and the peristyles formed by the spaces between the rows of columns and the outside walls of the two rooms. It was supported by the outer rows of columns, the walls and by columns in the rooms. The roof was almost certainly of wood framing and covered with thin slabs of marble, and although there has been endless guessing as to whether the Parthenon in some manner got light through the roof and how it might have been let in, the best guess seems to be that light came only through the open doors.

As the Parthenon, like the temples of Egypt, was a post and lintel building, all wall openings, or distances between columns, were limited in width by the strength of the beam or lintel that spanned them. It is also plain that any roofed building, under these conditions, is bound to be long and narrow. It may well be that the Grecian craftsmen preferred such a form. Its harmonies and proportions were no doubt as satisfying to them as they are to us. Still, we shall never know what form they might have used, had they chosen to use a dome for a roof, or known how to make a truss support one without rows of columns inside the building.

[48]

We might dare to imagine, for example, that they would have liked a wider Parthenon, and thus a wider room in which to set the great statue of Pallas Athene. But as they could not make a wide room free from columns, it seems fair to guess that the Parthenon was made as wide as could be with two rows of interior columns as roof supports. These rows divided the larger room (Naos) roughly into three aisles, of which the center one was used for the statue. The rows were formed of two slender columns, one set atop the other. The builders felt, we may imagine, that in the room of Pallas Athene, only Doric columns would answer. But if one large Doric column with the correct diameter for its height were used, it would take more floor space than could be spared. Hence the smaller columns, of perfect proportions, placed one atop the other. So was floor space saved and the honor of the Doric order preserved from indignity. In the smaller room behind the Naos, used only by mortals, single Ionic columns were used. They are slenderer than Doric and floor space was here of no importance. This theory may be knocked into a cocked hat if it is true that the small room was originally designed to be known as the Parthenon (virgin birth) and sacred to Pallas Athene, but even so, it is as pleasant a theory as any, and the answer is no longer of any moment.

Besides the walls, columns and roof of the Parthenon, there are a great number of parts, each of which has its place as an integral part of the Doric order. These have been so carefully measured, and their size relation to each other so studied, that those with a mathematical mind assert that one can take any minute part of the Parthenon and by the simple process of multiplication according to the deduced formula for the Doric order, arrive at the finished work. Larger or

[49]

smaller buildings could thus be designed by making the size of the initial part larger or smaller. (The same theory is applied to the pyramids, as well as to certain at least of the Gothic cathedrals.)

The theory may very well be true. It is not difficult to believe that all forms, and even sound and color, are reducible to mathematical rules. Whether pleasant forms can be attained by a conscious mathematical arrangement, or whether anyone can derive pleasure from such a method of work, is quite another question.

Above the two long outside rows of columns in the Parthenon runs an upper structure, known as the entablature, roughly divided into two horizontal belts. (Architecturally, it is divided into architrave, frieze and cornice.) The lower belt, just above the columns, runs in a continuous stretch around the building. The upper belt is composed of alternate spaces known as metopes and triglyphs, the first plain and the second marked by three vertical divisions of the space, hence their name. What a chance for sculpture! What the subject? Why not the great Panathenaic festival that commemorated the union of certain Greek states under the leadership of Athens? And so it was.

The sculptured story began at the eastern end, over the portico through which the procession entered the Parthenon, with the maidens bearing the sacred peplos, or robe, to replace the one that Pallas Athene had been wearing since the last procession, four years before. Thence the figures continued around the building in truly processional array—priests and sacrificial animals, young men bearing olive

[50]

branches, utensils, offerings and making music; then the chariots and their drivers, horses and warriors.

As a piece of decorative sculpture it must have been completely satisfying. The scale and spirit of the figures were enhanced by their faultless execution and by the subtle manner in which the relief established a living relationship with the beholder below. The whole was an incomparable ornament to the noblest building the workers ever raised in Greece.

The metopes in the belt above were used to tell a single story rather than a continuous one, although the result was more or less a running tale of the Athenian legend, battles of gods and giants, Greeks and Amazons, and so on. But the two horizontal bands, one continuous and the other a series of alternate sculpture and triglyph, were so superbly balanced that not a line nor a figure was allowed to dominate or interfere with the harmony of the whole composition.

Another belt of sculpture ran inside the peristyle, while the gables, or tympanums, in the pediments over the porticoes, were reserved for the Immortals. Here the figures were greater than life-size, as befitting the space and the glory of a temple to Pallas Athene and her Olympian kin. For the goddess herself, there was the great statue in the Naos, carved by Phidias, and covered with gold. Poor Phidias! Accused of having cheated in the amount of gold he charged for, as covering, he proved his innocence by taking all the gold off and having it weighed in the presence of his accusers, but that did not save him against the final plotting of his enemies, and he died in exile.

How much color was used on the Parthenon? The question is still an open one, and is likely so to remain. There is a pretty general agreement that the smaller projecting parts

[51]

were highly colored, mostly deep blue and red. The flat background of the sculpture is also generally thought to have been painted. Color was also applied to the garments worn in the procession, while a further gorgeous note was added by the use of bronze wreaths, weapons, reins, bridles, shields and sandals. These were fastened to the figures, and where this was not possible or desirable, a similar effect was perhaps gained by using gilt or gold leaf.

Very probably the whole surface of the building, where color was not used, was given an ivory tint over a priming coat of wax. Such a conclusion seems to be supported not only by minute test and examination but by the very probable dislike of the Athenian builders for the brilliant glaring whiteness of freshly quarried Pentelic marble.

In the Parthenon is no major straight line, either vertical or horizontal. The great base is curved. On the long sides, it is four inches higher in the middle than at the ends. On the shorter sides, the center is higher by three inches. The end walls recede and are thus curved away from the beholder as he faces them. The side walls slant, the columns are inclined at different degrees, their base diameters vary, and by the peculiar curve known as the "entasis," they grow slenderer as they rise.

Why all these refinements, as they are called? We shall never know for sure. Some affirm they were merely to correct optical illusions, and thus to make major horizontal and vertical lines appear to be truly so, as they would not appear were they correctly built. Everyone knows, for example, that two straight parallel lines, such as rails on a track, appear to meet as they recede. The Greeks also found that the long straight base line of a building appeared to sink in the middle when seen at a distance. The refinements

[52]

corrected these false appearances. Others prefer to believe that the builders did these things because of their sheer love of looking through and beyond the material in which they worked, looking, as it were, inside of Nature herself, and thus seeing her forms and her truths, really hidden from the eye by the appearances she chose to give them. Thus the Athenian craftsman could not be satisfied with mere rectangular precision. That was not Nature's way.

Somewhere within or near these conjectures lies the truth. Undeniable evidence, one hopes, will never be discovered, any more than we shall ever discover, let us also hope, the source of many other raptures and refinements. As we are without knowledge of their source, so can we the more marvel at their beauty, those timid beauties that would flee with a blush, once we violated their retreat, and laid bear their inmost secrets!

Sitting on the north steps of the Parthenon, in a flood of sunshine with wisps and fleeces of cloud playing under the canopy of deepest blue, the Erechtheion assumes a most friendly aspect. Even though all but the soul of the craftsman has fled the Parthenon, it still keeps one at a respectful distance. It invites no intimacies and certainly no familiarities. But the little Erechtheion, just a stone's throw away, has a touch of coquetry. One might imagine that having been so overshadowed, in history, by its august consort above, its four porticoes were now coyly disporting their charms in a manner to attract attention, at least. There may be even something plaintive in the look of the east portico, for the sixth of the columns that composed its front was taken away to London, and the mutilation is neither pretty nor creditable.

Suddenly it occurs to one that after the rigors of the Parthenon were over and the long task finished, the craftsmen may have laid down their tools, heaved a sigh, taken a long breath, a good swig of resinated wine, and then said to themselves and to each other: "Now, let's build something just for fun." So, in a burst of freedom and relaxation, they built the Erechtheion, choosing the more playful Ionic order rather than the Doric. Somebody, many years before, had built a little Ionic temple on the sandy plain below, by the banks of the Ilissos, but the experiment had not succeeded in dethroning the Doric as the correct godly shelter in Athens. But when the long devotion to the Parthenon was over and Doric had at last reached its final perfections, there may have come a natural wish to have done with it, if only for a holiday. One can grow as weary of perfection striving as of all else, and the Ionic bases, capitals, columns, architraves and cornices offered a tempting variation from the classic austerity of the Doric.

Whence came the Ionic order? No one knows. In embryo it flits in and out of history like a will-o'-the-wisp. There are suggestions of it in Egyptian scarab and lotus-leaf capital, in goldsmithing from Mycenæ, in carving from Babylonia. A drawing of a peasant's house in Lycia, made by Sir Charles Fellows about a hundred years ago, is so suggestive of the temple of Nike Apteros as to startle one with the likeness. A good guess as to how the Ionic got its foothold in Greece, however, might be that it expressed the slow evolution from bulkiness of massive strength to the graces and charms of delicacy. The Doric column is the very essence of uprightness and dependability. It radiates a feeling of security, while the Ionic suggests something more dainty and even slenderly flirtatious. Then too, while the Ionic gave freer play to the fancy of both builder and stone-carver, in the greater variety of treatment the order permitted, from moulded and ornamented base, as in the Erechtheion, to intricate spirals of the volute in the capital, it likewise required less marble and lighter weights to handle.

Evidently, we might guess, there was a spirit of play abroad. Fifty years after the Ionic temple by the Ilissos, there was built another little temple known as Nike Apteros. They put it on a great bastion, high on the Acropolis. There, after having been demolished in warfare and then picked up and put together again, it still stands. Like a radiant young queen, it looks down over the plain that leads to the sea where lie Phaleron and the Piraeus, and afar to Salamis, Eleusis and Corinth. Not only the Ionic order but the whole spirit and site of the building indicate that something was going on in the builders' heads.

Ionic columns were also used, soon after in the Propylea interior, but the Erechtheion gave Athenian builders the most fun with that order. To the three porticoes, of which the north one is as perfect as anything ever built, they added the portico of the maidens, plainly as a bit of sculptural dexterity and with no thought of feminine humiliation. The grace, serenity and tranquil poise of these six figures (one is a replica, of which the original is in the British Museum) carry no suggestion of undignified burden-bearing. Rather do the figures suggest devotional contemplation of great wonder and beauty. True, the experiment was seldom repeated, so that the builders may have got themselves talked about in Athenian houses whence womankind seldom issued

[55]

but where there was no doubt some interchange of views, even though it was a man's world. There may have come a powerful protest from somewhere, but it is more likely that the builders had the sense to know that it was not wise to dare an experiment too many times. One success was enough!

For a hundred years after the Erechtheion, there were random Ionic temples, from the ruins of which it is said that many were in the best tradition, but the decline of the art of building, both in imagination and in craftmanship, was as swift as it was inevitable. The Ionic was followed by the Corinthian (which was never a truly Greek order of building), in which the slightly modified column was crowned with a larger capital, ornamented with a design based on acanthus leaves. Their ends curled outward at the points, as if to remind one of the Ionic volute, while a memory of this also appeared in the scrolls that connect capital with abacus, the square block that sits between column and beam. The oldest example of this order in Greece is the Choragic monument (also known as the Lysicrates monument) in Athens. Slender Corinthian columns are used to hide the jointings of the circular marble slabs that form the round body of the monument, where a very human note lingers in this inscription: "Lysicrates, son of Lysithedes of Cycina, was the choragos (leader). The youth of the Achmantide tribe won the prize. Theon played the flute. Lysiades, an Athenian, was the poet; Evenetes was the archon (elected ruler)." Yes, there was evidently some fun to be had, in Athens, in the year 336, B. C.

The temple of Zeus, largest ever built in Greece (also known as the Olympeion) was placed on the plain, south of the Acropolis and near the Ilissos. A few of the huge Corinthian columns still stand, to remind us, perhaps, that

[56]

the "bigger and better" idea eventually set in, in Greece, as elsewhere. This vast hundred-columned temple was intended to proclaim once more—although the message was this time a Roman one—what Pericles had attempted to proclaim from the Acropolis.

The one secular building still standing in Athens, in which one senses an effort to be simple, human and pleasantly useful, is the Tower of the Winds. Simple and friendly, useful and lovely, this little building was a part of everyday life at the beginning of the first century, B. C. It stood at the edge of the Agora, where all Athens came to shop and to gossip. On top, holding a wand, was a bronze Triton that turned with the wind and pointed the direction. Sun-dials told the time to passers-by. On sunless days, one looked inside at the clepsydra (water-clock), said to have been contrived by Andronikos, the builder, (how it worked we do not know) and which gave the building the name of Horologion.

Andronikos is said to have learned about time measurement from the Syrians, the most advanced astronomers of his day, and to have studied in Alexandria. In any event, it is pleasant to believe these meagre gleanings from his life, and to think of him as a serene observer of the heavens who had the skill to combine his wisdom with stone, and so to make a most agreeable building for the use and delight of men.

If he marked a moment on the fateful path that led from Syrian priest, who first measured time by water dripping from a hole near the base of an earthen pot, to the day when Seth Thomas of Connecticut put an end to craftsman clock-makers everywhere, one finds it hard to grudge him his craftsman delight. He could not foresee that the tick

[57]

of the clock would act powerfully to divert man from that contemplative observation of the cosmos, whence alone he might learn how to deal with the evolutionary phenomena of tool and machine, and wedge him ever tighter in a regimented procession of time-clockers and turnstilers, in a march that verged ever nearer and nearer to the tragic grotesque.

Nothing is left of the houses where dwelt the Athenian builders, workers, slaves, and the populace generally. This is perhaps a valid excuse for treating the history of that great day in building, as is generally done with other periods, as one entirely concerned with temples, theaters and a few odds and ends of monuments. Yet the Athenians had no such climate as Egypt. They needed much better protection against weather, and this, it is assumed, they got mostly with houses of sun-dried bricks. The more privileged, as in Egypt, had plenty of space, generally depending about a central courtyard. As for the multitude, they probably got what they could as best they could, as is usual with multitudes.

The vast sums spent by Pericles, on a public works program that would give work to the idle and the result of which would proclaim the glory of the Athenian republic in a manner to command respect, merely consumed all the wealth there was. The little derived from production and trade would not have gone far. As in the time of Rameses, it had to be supplemented by booty and tribute, but even that came to an end. When the citizens of Athens at one time murmured a bit at the high cost of Pericles' public works program, he told them that if they were unwilling to keep on paying the bills, he would defray the balance out of his own pocket. But, said he, if I do this, all the glory must be mine! None shall go to Athens! Would the Athenians like such an arrangement? No, they wouldn't, and they'd go on paying, as they did, although we may be sure that there were plenty of wise Athenians who knew what the end would be.

It came, and soon. The downfall of Athens was sad, tragic, lamentable. One of the moments of promise, for all mankind, was rudely blotted out. A philosophy had begun. It dealt with people, their life, their communities. The builders had learned something about making plans, for colonized towns had been sponsored by Greece in other parts of the Mediterranean. The art of building seemed, for a moment, to be coming into its own and to be on the eve, perhaps, of using the skill of its craftsmen for making, not single buildings such as cost more than any state could bear, but towns in which to live with comfort and convenience. There were sinister interests to reckon with, then as now, but there was also a rising flood of intelligence. Suddenly, all was over. The moment had gone.

What had the builders learned? Very little, in one way, and quite a good deal in another. As in Egypt, the bulk of their effort had gone into a few works. There had been no attempt to distribute the builders' knowledge in a planned effort towards a better city all round. The labor on the Acropolis was not required as a means of defense, but was used to satisfy the wish for glory and vanity, when all is said and done. Whatever verdict we render on the triumphs of sculptor and craftsmen, there was here no social effort towards a juster sharing of the wealth that derived from common effort.

On the other hand, the Greek builders had refined the

post and lintel building, and while it would be unfair to say that this was because the Pentelic marble was easy to tool, dress and carve, that factor played a part, none the less. The Athenian builders, following after the temple of Hera at Olympia, Athena at Corinth, Concord and Juno at Agrigentum, Poseidon at Pæstum, Athene at Segesta, Thesus at Athens, produced the Parthenon, and then the temples of Poseidon at Sunion—one of the divine spots of this earth —and of Apollo at Bassæ, where the glory and beauty of solitude are lifted to the heights of ecstasy. From the usual historic standpoint, one stops at the Parthenon, after which there seems little more to be said (which does not mean that one should forget Delphi, Epidauros, and many another spot where the buildings lie low in ruins, but where the soul of the craftsmen still lingers on).

Yet if one is thoroughly happy at Pæstum or Segesta, even more so than on the Acropolis and should dare to ask why, there is no need to be frightened at one's boldness. The earlier Greek temples have qualities that sing the fine and careless rapture of craftsmanship. They have vigor, robustness, solidity and a lack of that complexity that arrives when the worker begins to embroider too much, as though one were weaving into a good old form some shade of meaning that will later pervert or destroy the simple directness of the form itself. There will then be confusion where once was straightforwardness.

It is, in these matters, as though one built a simple building where justice might be sought and had. Over the door, a symbol or the one word Justice. Everyone would understand, but as justice became more artful and less easy to get, and as the building where one sought it grew more monumental, and filled with the mysteries of law and the

[60]

wiles of lawyers, the plain word would no longer do. We should get the words "Equal Justice under the Law," as they appear in the new building of the Supreme Court at Washington, while an even lengthier attempt to explain something that once had no need to be explained appears on the County Court House at Cincinnati, in these words: "Equal and Exact Justice for All Men of Whatever State or Persuasion, Religious or Political."

It is ever thus, it seems, as the simple is twisted into the complex, which is why one plainly has the right to be as happy as one can with the simpler primitive forms of many a well-known building, even though the grander one is catalogued as the finest of its kind. There is no "finest building." The greatest charm and most satisfying architecture are found, for many a lover, not in costly monuments, but in minor simplicities, where purpose is combined with grace and form, and where one is asked to believe in nothing but a clean and quiet lodging for the night, some pleasant talk over food and drink and some happy memories to carry away.

The Parthenon, in 435 A. D., ceased to be sacred to Pallas Athene. By imperial decree from Constantinople, then the seat of the orthodox church, it became a Christian shrine. Pallas Athene was baptized and named St. Sophia. Some time in the eleventh century, thanks were given in the Parthenon to the Blessed Virgin, to whom the temple had then become sacred, for a victory over the Bulgars or somebody. In 1205, it became the Catholic Church of St. Mary. In 1458, a Turkish ruler dwelt hard by in the Propylea, and although for a moment he restored the Parthenon to the

Greeks for their own house of worship, it soon became a Mohammedan mosque and a minaret was added to the west front. In 1687, the Venetians, besieging the Turks who still held Athens, dropped a shell in the Parthenon, then used as a powder magazine. The explosion blew the interior pretty well to pieces, leaving the two ends and parts of the sides standing. The north peristyle has now been rebuilt from the fragments, with the addition of a few concrete parts.

In 1799, Lord Elgin came to Athens. In 1816, much of the Parthenon sculpture was in the British Museum at London. Poor Pallas Athene! Her patience is long-suffering and she is slow to wrath!

On the Acropolis, the shadows lengthen. The roofs of Athens slip behind the same soft veil that now steals about Hymettos. The clear-cut Grecian profiles lose the sharp brilliance of their edges. The hills that rise beyond Phaleron and Salamis are outlined masses in a dying golden radiance. Above the Propylea hangs a cloud of burnished golden splendor, as though Zeus had sent a blessing for the end of the day. Amidst the silence and the deepening shadows, one seems to stand where the waves of man's long groping break softly on the white Athenian strand. Endlessly they follow, from east and west, like lingering lappings of a long unrest, like the ceaseless rhythmic surge of host upon host of craftsmen builders, in search of a civilization for which they might build a fitting home!

V

FORM IN ROME

IF A single word would serve to make a good general picture of the work of the Roman builders, it would be "official." There was no nonsense or straying emotions about planning and doing, in the minds of those who were out to build the world's biggest empire. Other empires there had been, but now was to be only Rome. The single-minded purpose wrapped up in that word also governed what to build and where to build it. The same thing might have been said of the Egyptians, as they worked for the tomb in which the dead might await the life to come. It might be said, to a much less extent, of the Greeks, as they sought power with the subtlety and refinements of their temples. But the Romans had something else. They had the swift vigor, the pounce and the punch that lead true empire seekers to those moments of triumph as alluring as they are deluding. When triumphs are mounting and the tribute is pouring in, it's an exciting game and one not easily outlawed. Ideas of national empires and of big and little private and personal empires are still abroad.

As for the Roman builders of buildings, where lies our concern, the thread of their tale may be picked up somewhere in the fourth century, B. C. The welding to Rome of the nearby lands and peoples was well under way. The Etruscans had long been building, in what is now Italy, and their masonry laid the rude groundwork for what was ahead, although no builder of that day could have dreamed of the kind and size of the buildings that would be needed to carry out the idea. Never before or since has empire genius used builders so cleverly, first to sow the idea of sway by mastery and an army of soldiers, and second, to plant the cheaper idea of mastery by law and an army of bailiffs. Never before or since, although countless undertakings, big and little, national, religious, commercial, professional, have used buildings to gain power or to hang on to what power they had, has there been such a show of official building propaganda as that which helped to weld the Roman Empire.

Besides the Etruscan groundwork, there were the Greek temples in the South of the peninsula and on the island of Sicily. No mean buildings, these, but whatever the Romans thought of them, or whether or no they took them much into account, following events seem plainly to show that they had their own clear ideas as to what was best in buildings. Their practical minds (using the word "practical" in its common meaning of opportune profit rather than any idea of far-seeingness) knew, by unerring instinct or by genius, as one wills, what was good for the empire business and

[64]

what wasn't. Their main idea of forging and welding never got lost in details. The empire was lost, of course, by neglect of human details, but that is a part of the delusion of what is called practical, and one can scarcely see where the Romans differed greatly, in this respect, from any other "practical men," such as always take to empire making, even those who are still at it, this very day. The process is hard on the multitude, as so many know now, and as the Romans soon learned. The builders, in each succeeding effort, never get a chance to do more than build for the beneficiaries of whatever empire is being put on the map.

In the course of the next two or three centuries, the rude knowledge gained from the Etruscans was fused with the more delicate refinements of the Greek builders, although the result was anything but delicate. Post and lintel gave way to the arch, but in the process, the Greek builders, many of whom are said to have been carried off to Rome and other places, were never again to repeat the glories of the day that had been theirs alone. Rather were they to be used to decorate and embroider the huge constructions of Roman engineers —theaters, arenas, baths, arches—things for amusing and impressing the populace, from which Rome meant to derive all possible tribute with as little fuss as possible. Pericles and the Acropolis may have been an example, in the art of glorification, on which the Romans cast an eye, now and then, but it was not the sort of thing that could tempt them to forget that tribute was what they were after. Glory—yes, but profitable glory, first, last, and always, for that, no one will deny, is what tempts men to play the empire game.

This did not mean that a little booty would be overlooked, or that the bosses were unaware of the value of culture or of giving a push to "art appreciation." Greece was rifled of her treasures of sculpture, bronze and pottery. The Greeks, their day of tribute-taking over, had no way of protesting. But the Greeks, as builders and sculptors, may have felt even more bitter over the cultural despoilment they had to endure. That indignity is evident, if one but takes a casual look, in the Roman use of the creative and imaginative simplicities into which the Greek craftsmen had put such deliberate thought. As these details passed from their logical place in the "trabeate" to become decorations for the "arcuate" method of building, they were only stupidly useless pretensions.

The Etruscans had long used the arch. For many centuries, they were thought to have invented it. They had built other things, as well, but it was the arch that took the Roman's eye. From the earliest moment, apparently, these empire builders were not slow at seeing far more in the arch than any other race had yet seen. First, it could be built of small stones. No need for the colossal lintels of Karnak, Mycenæ and Athens. No need for either giant monoliths, or sectional drum columns. Both involved great labor in quarrying, moving, dressing and raising into place. The Romans had plenty of labor, but none to waste on slow perfections. The Greeks, using no cement, revolved their sectional column drums, one atop the other, with fine sand between, before putting them in place. The bed surfaces were ground to a razor-like precision. They fitted so perfectly that the two stones were as one. The joints, hardly visible, were the joints that a craftsman loves, for to him there are neither good nor bad ones. Either a joint is one or it isn't.

Nothing like that for the Romans. They were in a hurry. An empire cannot stop for fine jointings in stone. There can be no pauses, and craftsmen cannot consider and deliberate.

[66]

The empire doctrine has to have constant pushing. The propaganda and publicity must be unceasing. The salesmen must be always on the jump, and as buildings were one of the chief goods used in "selling" the empire idea, the problem for the bosses at Rome was to keep up speed. In this, the arch was a great help, not only when built of masonry, but even more so when the builders learned to make it of concrete. The smallest stones could then be used. All the refuse of the quarry could be dumped into the concrete. Faster and faster, bigger and better, north, east, south, west, the course of empire took its way.

The arch had another quality, quite apart from its ability to span a space, bear a load, and the ease with which it could be made. It had a note of triumph in it. Whatever may be the reason, there can be a triumphal arch, but there cannot be a triumphal equivalent in a square opening. From post and lintel one may get many kinds of thrills, but they are not triumphant notes of conquest. It takes the roadway arch for that, which may be wholly because of what the Romans said so loudly to the whole world, then and afterwards, with their arches. The slender spire will exalt, the four-square upright tower will dignify and even be boastful, but it is the arch through which troops can march that shouts the note of empire, victory, conquest, power.

Only one other building form carries this same note, though differently, but the dome is the very essence of the arch principle and carries the kudos of the royal crown as well. With arch and dome, it might be truly said, Rome built and proclaimed her empire. Had her builders their poetic moments? Did they now and then get free of officialdom and let their fancies go a-roaming? Or was it that they now and then, by some straightforwardness that sought no end

[67]

but safe simplicity, attained to greatness? One can hardly sit by the river Gard, near Nîmes, on a summer evening, without feeling a superb note of poetry in the glorious group of arches. Here, at least, one feels the note of triumph to have been quietly subdued. One is in the presence of the simplest possible bridge that could be used to span a river at such a height that the water supply for the city of Nîmes was carried in an open trough at the very top of the structure, to flow by gravity from source to destination, twenty miles away.

There may be something in the arch over water that is truly infinite, or it may be that man is no more than a creature of emotional whims and fancies. An arched bridge, however, still strikes a note, in most people, such as neither cantilever nor suspension can yet awaken. Is this merely an emotional tradition, and will men some day wonder, as they glory in their cables, trusses and cantilevers, at the poetic nonsense of those who went completely daft over the sweep of an arch over water, who got a great joy out of such bridges as Ceret, Ronda, Pont Neuf and Waterloo, or out of the littler ones such as Echternach, Collegeville, or in the valley of the Musconetcong, or the tinier ones that carry one across a thousand rivers in both the old world and the new? In another century they will all be gone, for speed on the highway will no longer tolerate them. Yet the question still persists: Is there something infinitely more precious than speed, in that round frame of water and sky, with the swish of water and the dance of sunlight? Could the Romans have thought, by that very token, that the arch might come to mean an infinite empire?

Fergusson, in his history of architecture, remarks that as the object of Rome was empire, conquest and wealth,

[68]

she thus reached "a pinnacle of greatness that no nation had reached before or since," but that "her arts have all the impress of this greatness, and are characterized by the same vulgar grandeur, which marks everything she did." Ruskin, in much the same vein, complains that the Romans "went in for a cheap and easy way of doing that whose difficulty was its chief honor," a characteristic Ruskinian economic looseness by which, however, one can guess that he was really thinking of the fact that when the instinct to create dries up because the chance to create has been taken away, there is no compensation that will undo the wrong.

As to "cheap and easy," he probably had no better idea of what the words meant than has anyone now. Modern empire builders are just as befogged, in that matter, as were those of Ruskin's own land and time, or those of today in any land or institution whose object is empire. "Cheap" and "easy" are a pair of as artful young pickpockets as ever were let loose. What labor should be saved, how it should be saved, and what to do with the gains (?) that result from the saving, who can tell us? There seems to be no reason for chiding Rome on that score.

As a matter of fact, the Roman use of concrete probably gave work quickly to far more people than masonry would have done. It takes time to learn to be a mason. It is no small trick to pick a stone, dress it, fit it and slowly build a wall that will stand straight and endure. My guess is that it would be better to take that long time, not only because it teaches the learner what can never be had from books, but because it now turns out to have been very unwise to turn half the world idle in order to make things cheap and easy. But for empire builders such things are never taken into account. Roman slaves could learn to mix concrete in a short time, just as today a man can learn, in a day or two, to operate a machine that makes bolts by the million. But just as no one stops to think of what becomes of the bolt-machine operator, so the Romans never stopped to think what became of the concrete mixers. They could turn out a vast amount of work without costing the state what it costs to teach a trade. It is likewise highly probable that the Romans were greatly concerned to keep both subject and slave so busy that they had no time in which to think of the high cost of empire. It is only when idleness begins that empires begin to totter.

As the new Rome on the seven hills gathered itself together and made itself master of all within easy reach, and then set out on a conquest, the extent of which few could then have dreamed, there was an abundance of building materials. Quarries of tufa and peperino, both volcanic and long used by the Etruscans lay in the hills. Marble aplenty and the lovely limestone known as travertine lay waiting in the hills of Tivoli. Of lava no end, in the South, where the wonderous "pozzolano," spewed and ground by volcanic action, made a perfect sandy conglomerate for concrete. There was clay for brick, but that was hardly empire material, and was used, together with slabs of stone, as time went on and straight masonry abated, for facing only. Great quantities of alabaster, porphyry and rare marbles, quarried by armies of slaves, were brought from far lands and also used to hide the uninspiring concrete. Whatever may have been the dream, and whatever the plan of propaganda in the minds of the bosses at Rome, concrete was to be the backbone of Roman official building.

Yet the builders were never finicky, or perplexed when

[70]

they couldn't get the things to which they were accustomed. If the materials they found on the spot, in whatever part of the empire they worked, were usable, they used them. In Egypt, Greece and Asia Minor, they worked in the style of masonry they found there. The tale of their labor is beyond the telling. From Egypt to the West of England, from Timgad to Echternach and Trier, they roamed, building and teaching to build. Walls, walls, walls, and roads, and then buildings. A record of their wanderings is likely to turn up wherever men dig much in the lands where once they hustled and settled. Some of their great works are without a rival in the sheer impressiveness of the imperialistic trappings that shouted the glory of Rome. No idea was too big, no plan too vast. If their courage in walls was brilliant, their daring in vaulting was dazzling.

Egyptian, Assyrian, Greek, Etruscan had known the arch and how to make a rudely vaulted roof. But they knew how to make it only in brick or stone, laying it up over a form that could be taken down when the last stone was in place. An arch, or vault, so laid, exerts a lateral thrust. The weight of the stones tends to push them out of the circle. The remedy for this is walls at the sides. By them the arch can be made to carry a very great weight, but to span great distances or vault great areas, the weight of the arch stones requires the solidest side walls and foundations.

The Romans learned to pour their arches and vaults in concrete, all in one piece. There was then no side thrust. The dome vault was like a pottery bowl, the arch vault like a pottery half-barrel. Inverted, they sat on the walls which then had only the weight of their concrete to support. It was the first great labor-saving jump for the builders since the discovery of post and lintel, although the Egyptians might

[71]

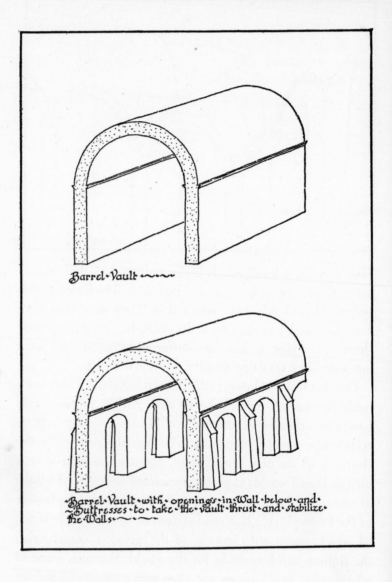

Barrel·Vault

Barrel·Vault·with·openings·in·Wall·below·and·
Buttresses·to·take·the·vault·thrust·and·stabilize·
the·Walls

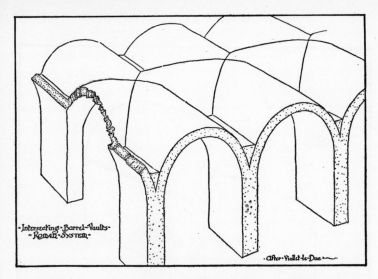

Intersecting·Barrel·Vaults·
·Roman·System·

·After·Viollet-le-Duc·

have done it, a hundred centuries before, had their minds
not been so bent on their idea of rightness. The Greek builders would probably have spurned it. They may even have
done so, which wouldn't be at all unlikely, for, during their
short shrift, they had a very different program and were
interested in a very tiny empire, as such things go.

On went Rome! On swept the Roman builders! Their work
could be counted in millions of tons. Arches to emperors;
basilicas as halls of justice and trade exchanges, their
rectangular apsidal plan soon to become the pattern for the
churches of the new Christianity, about to be offered to a
torn and tired world; superbly appointed baths, of which the
great ones of Caracella were to make a pattern for the façade
of the Pennsylvania Railroad station in New York; bridges,
of which many still remain as the greatest contribution
the Roman builders made for the world; theaters, some of
whose walls, as at Orange, are filled with a power and a glory

[73]

that transcend all words; aqueducts that carried copious water for miles to great cities; leagues of roads such as have never been excelled in durability and over which the people of rank and wealth could roll, in their luxurious carrucas, in such ease as travellers had never before known; some temples, many of which were torn down by the Christians in order to make churches; the mighty Pantheon, many arenas, and a colosseum much given to bestial brutality and where, towards the end of the great experiment, a hundred thousand people could sit and forget their own misery in watching the torturing deaths of other victims; the Circus Maximus, begun in the time of the Tarquins, restored by Claudius, and by Trajan given such a garb of splendor with white marbles, gorgeous mosaics and statuary as to make it what many historians have called the most magnificent building in the world, into which there could pour and find seats no fewer than 485,000 spectators. Let us end the record with the Golden House of Nero, one of the most insolent gestures of lavishness ever flung in the face of an emperor's subjects, said to have covered an area as great as that of the Vatican and its gardens, with St. Peter's thrown in. Vespasian tore part of it down to build the Colosseum; Titus demolished another bit to make some baths, and to make more baths Trajan finally finished it off so well that scarcely a trace of it now remains.

Looking at the record, one has to admit the genius of somebody. The Roman empire went to pieces, of course, but its traditions go marching on! For a long time they have had, and still have, a great effect on buildings. For a longer time, their speech has clung; why? Is it not because the people who took it over were also bent on empire? By sheer audacity (there is no other way to make an empire) the Roman bosses

[74]

created the legend of power through sumptuous magnificence, insolent ostentation, imitative vulgarity, and the pretense of legality. Against that dazzling legend the truth of the shameful record has made scant progress. Empire, it seems, is as alluring as ever, in spite of the record, for the idea is not confined to foreign conquest. It has permeated all trades, callings, vocations and professions, and overflowed into forces that play havoc with all buildings and all builders. Are there any building workmen left who do not dream of an empire in which their rights and wages shall be as they say, no matter what happens to all other workers and all buildings?

Through the centuries, what had the Roman builders learned? Much more than the Greeks, one might say, for they learned to make stout walls with less labor, build tight fireproof roofs, use stucco, concrete, mosaic, and a fourth mongrel order of post and lintel called composite, a combination of parts of Ionic and Corinthian. If they had been given a chance to plan and build a civilization rather than an empire, one feels they might have done some fine things —things that ought to have lived. Had they been used rather than misused, as craftsmen have ever been, one feels that they might have become great craftsmen, with a feeling for grace and rhythm and a sense of decoration that would have turned them away from the tawdry and the vulgar. That feeling may be founded on nothing more than one's own abiding faith in craftsmen, when they are left free to follow the challenge of tool, material and purpose, for there is always the everlasting challenge, never ceasing to call for rightness.

In houses, the Roman builders got to building pretty,

showy and sumptuous places—for the rich. They learned to heat and drain, supply water from faucets and even to contrive an elevator. Pompeii tells this tale very well. As for the multitude, its members lived as best they could. After fifty centuries, that habit had not changed. When the end came, and even long before and during the whole imperial effort, the plight of the real builders of empire was too sad to talk about. Many historians have told the tale of bread and circuses. With tribute wrung from all lands, and wasted in profligacy on official building, Rome had tried for an empire. In it, the work of the builders was to roar so loud that no protesting or complaining voice could be heard. Any lamenting by the oppressed, impoverished, dispossessed, or the victims of the Roman holidays, was to be drowned in the blare of architecture.

VI

FORM IN BYZANTIUM

THE scene shifts. It is the beginning of the fourth century in what is known as the Christian era. Constantine is founding the Eastern Empire at Byzantium. The fast-growing organized worship and ritual, slowly complicating the simple teachings of Jesus Christ, must have looked to him like chance conferred by the gods. Why not use the new religion to bolster up the empire idea, then a little ragged, and also to support the fiction of justice through legal institutions? Both fictions had been workable, and the end of the Western Empire was even then almost two centuries in the future. Still, this new Christian idea was making headway. Why not kill two birds with one stone? First, cheer on the new worship. Let it act as a brake on complaint over the pluckings that Constantine had in mind. If the meek were to inherit the earth, let them be content with meekness. Second,

[77]

abet the people in razing the temples and in building new churches. That would keep them busy and less inclined to murmur as the weight of empire settled down heavily on their backs.

The new capital had to be created, however. To be the seat of empire there must be population and riotous embellishment. So the builders were again set to work. Many were brought from the old empire, and at last, one might have said, they were to make something that would really add to the pleasure of being alive. There was a shortage of houses, and timber was the only material handy. It was cut, wholesale, in the forests of Belgrad near by. Used long before it had time to season, however, the result was a shoddy jerry-built community such as one might see, on a comparable scale, in either Brooklyn or Chicago today.

For churches, there had to be a new model. Temples, associated with pagan gods, were not to be considered. The long devotion of the Greek builders on the Acropolis, where they sought a perfect form in the building that housed their goddess, was of no use. Christians could have none of it. What to take as a pattern? The business-like Roman basilica, naturally, since in form it was well suited to the purpose. The curved end where the judges had presided became the apse for priest and ceremony. The hall and side aisles, where trade and commerce had been carried on, were right as they were. Add a portico, and call it a church.

The builders of Byzantium, however, had no such luck as at Rome. The land about the new capital was generally poor in good building materials. Constantine, however, in all his lavish propaganda for the new style of empire that was to be called Christian—and he and his successors were no mean squanderers—had the advantage of the best that had gone before in other lands. The world was his, so to speak. He could rifle and plunder almost at will and in those very lands where it was most worth while. From tomb, temple and monument, many of them stored or adorned with the richest treasures of craftsmanship, the loot poured in by land and by sea. The swashbuckling Golden House of Nero at Rome was to be outdone by the Great Palace, begun by Constantine and added to by his successors. It was a veritable small city in itself with its own quay on the Marmora. Within its confines, according to Young, were one hundred and fifty-three private baths—no mean number for that day, small as the count seems beside the boast of the modern hotel. There were fourteen separate palaces and four thousand, three hundred and eighty-eight family mansions; the entrances were guarded by no fewer than fifty-two porticoes; there were two theaters and a university, while four law-courts looked after justice.

Of all these buildings, nothing remains. What became of the new theory of autocracy by divine right and defense, resting also on justice by due process of law, is a question apart. How successful Constantine was in fixing these ideas as part of the Roman legend that was long to serve as a recipe for empire builders—in spite of the ruin that overtook him, and all that had gone before—is also quite another matter. Of the churches built by his builders, one only now stands as perhaps belonging to his era. St. Irene marks, however, the first probable use of those features that slowly changed the Roman basilica into the Byzantine church. Likewise does it echo the days of damnation and heresy, of believer and unbeliever. Before its altar, bishop and prelate besought God's aid against the imperial edicts that ordered the church to give its blessings and shelter to such heretics as Constantine found useful in empire making.

So fierce were the early disputes over dogma and ritual that the builders had not only to build a church but almost to fortify it. Old forms were set aside, but there was no change in taxation and tribute. The adoption of the Christian church was, in many ways, an even more torturing form of persecution than the material privations the multitude had so long borne. Henceforth it was to be more and more obliged to do at least lip service to ideas that had to do with conscience, that curious mixture of mental freedom and slavery that was to go on tying ideas of right and wrong, even up to this day, in harder and harder knots. Not only had the multitude to pay the cost of the churches, but also the wages of the army of functionaries who claimed to be their spiritual betters and masters. It took a thousand people to run St. Sophia, some time later, and eleven thousand shops are said to have paid rental to the church as support for them and for the hundred singing eunuchs, two hundred choir boys, one hundred choir women, three hundred musicians, ten bishops and eight hundred priests. Each of these activities had its effect upon the changing plan and design of the church, which also became a treasure house. Byzantine building, fused with ideas from Rome, Greece and Persia, is the tale of endless sums wrung from subject and slave wherever they could be taken. "The edifices of Justinian," says Gibbon, "were cemented with the blood and treasure of his people."

The bronze horses of Lysippus, now adorning Venice, first stood in the great marble-benched Hippodrome at Byzantium, some four hundred and fifty by twelve hundred feet in area. Here also stood the gilded Milion column, marking the empire's center, from which all highway milestones were measured. This huge arena was another populace-amusing burst of building swagger under Theodosius, he who officially banished paganism, naming the Orthodox Church as the one and only. Into it, early in the next century, the Parthenon, well on its way to its thousandth birthday, was formally inducted. Under the same emperor, razing went on apace. Old pagan buildings yielded much-needed building materials. Never were builders busier. Little by little they changed their ways to keep pace with new church forms and ritual. By skill in using the dome, they were getting ready to build one of the outstanding buildings of the Western world.

When Justinian came to power, early in the sixth century, there had already been a church where St. Sophia now stands. Three of them, in fact, (perhaps more) for Constantine had built a basilica. It had been rebuilt, but the dome they tried to put on it fell down, and the next church was burned. Here then was a good chance to back up the idea of empire by divine right under God, and Justinian, calling his builders together, put them under Anthemius the mathematician. By his genius and daring in the use of the dome, he carried the builders on one of the most triumphal journeys they ever made. Under the hands and skill of the craftsmen, many of whom were probably Greeks and had also worked at Rome, the domed vault their ancestors in Athens had refused to play with achieved here a splendor such as the Roman builders never reached.

The great central dome of St. Sophia is one hundred and seven feet in diameter. This is some thirty-five feet less than that of the Pantheon at Rome, but on the eastern and western sides of it are two half-domes that cover semi-circular apses, while each of these has three smaller recesses covered with semi-domes. By such a use of the principle that so intrigued the Romans, the builders of St. Sophia contrived to get a nave one hundred and seven by two hundred and sixty-five feet in area, free and clear, or more than twice the area under the Pantheon dome. Weight and thrust of the main dome is taken by four enormous piers, while the supporting semi-domes, springing partly from these same piers also act to buttress them and strengthen the whole. The domes and semi-domes are knit together, as it were, to give not only rigidity but to create the appearance of an immense vaulted space into which pours the light that has sent many a worshipper a-dreaming and many a chronicler into rhapsody and ecstasy. This light enters through forty arched windows set in the lower part of the main dome and through others that likewise pierce the semi-domes. Above these streaming shafts of light rises the great central dome, its peak one hundred and eighty feet above the floor.

To adorn this structure, Justinian searched the empire far and wide. Nothing but the most precious materials would do, the finest marbles "white with rosy streaks, green, black, blue, with veins of white." There had to be also porphyry and polished granite, and temple after temple in Greece and the Eastern empire was ravished and stripped. Monster monoliths and great slabs were brought from Egypt, Baalbec and Greece. There were portals covered with gold-leaf; there were jewels; there were pearls, of which some five hundred thousand were woven into the curtains of the rood screen. The choir was enriched with carved cedar, with amber and with ivory, all of which was, some centuries later, to be snatched and scattered by the soldiers of the true cross. The

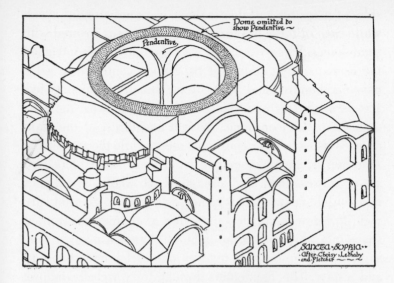

Dome omitted to show Pendentive

Pendentive

Sancta ·Sophia··
·After·Choisy ,Lethaby
·and·Fletcher

gorgeous mosaics, hidden from the faithful by coats of plaster, were overlooked in that sacking, as they were when the next band of "Crusaders," under Mahomet, were intent upon destroying whatever related to the true cross. (In December 1933, it was announced that after two years of painstaking labor, these mosaics had been cleared of the paint and plaster by which they had been hidden from Moslem eyes.)

With ten thousand workmen, it is said, Anthemius labored for some six years. He had then managed to spend a sum that would likely be somewhere between fifty and one hundred millions of the dollar of today. The golden treasury of one of the richest of empires was dried up to a point where the people were starving, and there was no longer any oil with which to light the church. To Memphis, Thebes, Athens, Rome, there was added Byzantium. These are not the five empires that alone used the builders as agents and

[83]

salesmen for the empire idea, but they are the five around which the tale of the Western world revolves. There were still, at the end of Byzantium, no other means for propaganda than buildings, and a first principle of empire builders is to take over whatever methods there may be, at the time, for publishing what they wish and suppressing what they do not wish to be known. One has thus to consider the work of the builders not as an actual labor of service and skill in the work sense, in an art they were slowly mastering, but the use of that art for ends that were entirely at variance with any idea, in the minds of those who bossed the show, of building a pleasant world in which people might live in peace and justice. The one idea, when all is said and done, was to collect as much as possible, for the few and from the many, and then to throw a beneficent halo over the groans of the payers. To do this, the riotous luxury of buildings was used to advertise the glory of king and priest and the idea that one had better watch out and be respectful and uncomplaining.

One looks at St. Sophia with many a mingled feeling. Its splendors have been but barely touched upon in the brief description of its structural wonders. It has suffered many indignities, yet remains a triumph. "It rises to the heavens," wrote Procopius, "and towers above the neighboring buildings as a ship rides the waves. The dome floats as though it were hung from heaven with chains of gold." Sir John Mandeville remembered it as "the fairest church in all the world," while to Byron it was "not a patch on St. Paul's." Frederic Harrison esteemed it as "the most harmonious, most completed, and least faulty of all the great domed and round-arched temples. It unites sublimity of construction with grace of detail, splendour of decoration with inde-

[84]

structible material. It avoids the conspicuous faults of the great temples of Rome, or the Pantheon of Paris. Its glorious vestures of marble, mosaic, carving and cast metal is unsurpassed by the richest of Gothic cathedrals, and is far more enduring. Though twice as old as Westminster Abbey, it has suffered less dilapidation and will long outlast it." Young calls it "disappointing," but Fletcher says it is the "masterpiece of Byzantine architecture," an opinion shared also by Waterhouse.

Moslem in outward form, the Christian legend still clings to it. Young says that "on the eve of the great Christian festivals of Christmas and Easter, both Turks and Christians avoid the church. For then those destined to die within the year will see ghostly lights burning on the altar, pale gleamings of the ancient glories of gold and jewels and a dim congregation of long-dead worshippers. They will hear faint echoes of solemn chanting until the four angels in the dome beat their wings and the vision vanishes." [1] He also adds that when the Russian emperor sent envoys to Constantinople to inquire about the new religion and report as to its worth for the Czars, the verdict was that "in this church one is more than elsewhere in the presence of God, for the rituals of all other countries are there entirely eclipsed by a grandeur which we ourselves will never forget." So, in all probability, Young finally comments, was Russia saved from Mohammedanism. So, also, does one get, in this hunt amongst the struggles of churches to survive and confer power, a good idea of the part they played and the purposes for which they were used.

What had the Byzantine builders added to the craft of building? A very great deal. They had united arch and col-

1 *Constantinople.* By George Young.

umn in forms of such delicacy and grace as the Roman
builders were incapable of imagining. Surpassing this
achievement, however, they had gained a triumph in the
use of the dome that puts them in the very front rank of
creative builders. Others had put a dome on a round building, as in the Pantheon at Rome. No one had put a dome on
a square building, although many a builder had no doubt
scratched his head over that problem, ever since the baked
clay dome had taken shape in Egypt.

In St. Sophia the problem was solved. The dome rests on
a combination of piers and arches. Together they furnish a
series of buttressed reinforcements of the greatest ingenu-
ity. No such daring leap had ever before been taken by
builders. The colossal lintels at Karnak were a risk, based
upon long years of experimenting with the strength of stone.
The system of piers, arches and domes in St. Sophia was
based upon principles that had never before been tested.

It was plain, to any builder of sense, that when a circle
was superposed on a square of like diameter, four corners
were not covered by the circle. There lay the problem of
putting a round dome on a square-walled opening. It was
solved by the Byzantine builders, very likely because of the
arithmetical skill of Anthemius, by building four great
piers, twenty-five feet square. These were connected by four
arches, on the tops of which the dome was set. By them its
weight is distributed to the piers, which in their turn are
heavily buttressed on two sides, while the other two sides
are reinforced by the semi-domes. There remained but the
problem of filling the spaces between the inner faces of the
arches and the dome. This was done by building a vaulted
ceiling, in shape like a triangle bent to conform to the surface
of a globe, and called a "pendentive." The trick was done.

There was a completely enclosed space in which a circular dome had been united with a square-walled room! It was a triumph indeed!

It was the followers of Islam (and to a certain extent those of the Greek and Russian orthodox church) who carried away the general ideas of the Byzantine builders. They became not the pattern for the Christian churches that were soon to arise in great numbers all over Europe, but for the mosques of later Egypt and Arabia, and, by a circuitous journey, were to arrive at Cordova, the Alhambra, the Alcazar and the Giralda, though much varied by their travels.

Indeed, this roundabout wandering of the Byzantine is often cited to prove that had it not been for the bulwarked empire city by the Bosphorus, Islamism rather than Christianity would have spread westward and taken root all over Europe. Deprived of this route, it was by way of the Moorish empire that the Byzantine got to Spain. Whether this is a reason for exalting the skilled and hard-working wall builders of Constantinople is not here to be decided. One can admire their skill and devotion as one pleases, and marvel at the great Wall with its ninety-six two-floored towers, its moats, battlements, terraces and posterns, without being forced to decide whether "they protected the culture centre of civilization from tidal waves of barbarism for ten centuries." If one were asked to agree, one would be likely to suggest that any answer would depend upon what is meant by "civilization" and by "barbarism." Neither word appears any too honest, and neither could be used clearly and truly to describe any period of history. One could build up a mass of evidence, for both words, in all so-called civilizations and excepting none. Even in the twentieth century, one finds it difficult to use either word, in the generally accepted

[87]

sense, as a valid description of any group of humans still on earth.

Whether the builders of Constantinople or its walls concerned themselves with such things, no one knows. One assumes that they built the walls because they were bidden to. They may have believed them necessary, just as they may have believed in St. Sophia or the Great Palace, as parts of some scheme of life that would work itself out. One guesses, however, that they mostly built as told, and so, once again, as in the building history of preceding empires, no one can tell us what might have happened to either barbarism or civilization, if the builders had been allowed, or had even been commanded, to put their skill and knowledge to such use as would make a fine city for everyone.

So long as all nations are still a depressing mixture of palace and hovel, now as for five thousand years, it would perhaps be safer not to be too insistent on the word civilization, except in the original sense of people living together in something larger than a hamlet. Building, let it not be forgotten, has been as potent in sowing the seeds of decay as in nourishing the plant of growth. Since the Egyptians began throwing up mud-screens in the Nile valley, there has been no change, in that respect. One can build either way, for growth or for decay. A thousand cities, since Memphis, barricaded themselves behind great walls, but none was strong enough to stall off the rot that lay behind them. No city rose, or has yet risen, where the builders were asked to do what they have so long known how to do—make a fine city for all who dwell therein.

In 476, Romulus Augustulus concluded that the Roman game was up and sent a message to Constantinople, where the Eastern Empire had still a hundred years to run, to say

[88]

that there was no longer an emperor at Rome. The signs had been plain for many a year. The rot was everywhere and over all. Good land deserted and run to waste, fleeing people who had to escape the tax-gatherers, the breakdown of trade, the dole, public works programs, and the last insolent luxuries of the bosses made it only too plain that the old malady was back again, as ever before in all empires.

Gone were the youth that made soldiers, but gone also were the tillers of the land, and that was indeed the end. Tribute, out of which the poor had managed to get a crust now and then, had also dried up. The same profligacy had pauperized the tribute-payers all over the empire. When any part of it had competed with Rome, or any great Roman owner, orchards and vineyards had been cut down. The joint stock companies at Rome, by which the powerful cheated the state in its empire speculations, had led to corruption in the highest places. The culmination of trickery and treachery was at hand. "Only a state composed of bandits and liars could have devised the law of prescription and the statute of limitations," cried Heine, "and then have sanctified them in the devil's bible—the code of Roman Civil Law."

In setting about the building of a civilization worthy of the name, the Byzantine builders were no farther advanced than the men of the pyramids. They had more knowledge, a wider range of materials, and more varieties of skill, but they were as helpless to use either in the common interest as the Roman peasants were helpless to do more than slay their children, as the end of the empire pageant hove in sight, because they had no food for them. Of the gorgeous spectacle that was meant to dazzle people into believing in and paying for the empire idea, nothing useful remained save roads and bridges. Useful indeed, they were, to the next race of builders, but their price was infamous. As for that day and purpose, one leaves them with no sense of regret. The price of the Byzantine method of building arch and dome together was equally infamous.

Within the limits of the present city of Istanbul lie buried the dreams, ruins and relics of the Eastern Empire of Constantine and Justinian. Here and there, in wall and battlement, or in St. Irene or St. Sophia, a memory remains. Other churches have risen, for upon the ruins of Byzantium was founded the empire of Mahomet. Neither its history nor its building shall concern us here, but if one is sensitive to things of the spirit, again as on the Acropolis, there will here be awakened within one a reverence, not for empires and their makers but for the things of the spirit that nourish and sustain the craftsman. Here one is again in the presence of a departed host of builders who wrought grandly and well, in stone pier and towering dome, in delicate carving and mosaic. They won their victories over materials, they fulfilled desires, and carried the art of walling and roofing space to new heights of skill and glory. As had served their ancestors, ever since Memphis, however, so served they also. So far as bettering the march of the multitude was concerned, they had added nothing. The Byzantine multitudes had died on battlefields and in slum and hovel, as had long been the custom for the disinherited. Thereafter, they were to be more dispossessed, but, as a reward, be blessed for their meekness.

VII

ROMANESQUE AND

GOTHIC

T HEY used to call the period between the fall of Rome and the rise of Charlemagne the Dark Ages. How dark a time was it? One can guess that little groups, here and there, began to take heart. All about were lands in ruin, lands gone to waste, and the ruined building of emperors. Life was no easy matter, but for a blessed moment there was a breath-ing-space. Emperors and priests were out of the picture. Not for long, of course, for new ones were on the way, as ever. More land empires were soon under way, while a newer form of empire was being dreamed, for a new church was slowly to come to power. Its agents worked in a sick and disillusioned world, for even though the pagan gods

[91]

were gone, it was no easy task to persuade men to put their faith in a new one.

Perhaps the ages were called dark because there was so little evidence out of which to write their history. Perhaps there was so little evidence because people were too tired to build. Perhaps they found solace in going about their life in a natural way, raising food and wine, sowing and reaping crops, clipping wool and making clothes, building plain houses, and generally doing what people would do if they were free from tax-levying and war-making overlords. Perhaps also, the new church, still unsoiled by the smear of empire, was spreading the simple gospel of peace on earth to men of good will. Perhaps those dark ages were, at least in comparison with those that had gone before, a fairly happy period, when the builders were not being used to propagandize for empire, for surely no one can say that the people of empires ever found great happiness in their buildings! The craftsmen? Yes, no doubt they were often happily busy, as is the habit of craftsmen, but for the multitude there was never happiness just because vast sums were spent on buildings, rather than for them. The vast sums had to be taken from them, always, whether they liked it or not, and it is fairly easy to imagine they would have preferred to put the money into better food, more wine, clothes, shoes and houses that the sun might shine into, just as slum-dwellers today would prefer a decent house to a seventy-story office building or a five-million-dollar church. These things are so simple that no one would dispute them, were it not that the empire makers and worshippers have been able to throw the halo around art instead of around life!

From the crumbling of the Roman Empire (it never came to other than a geographical end, but like the soul of John

[92]

Brown's body, went ever marching on, changing leaders now and then) organized religion was to play a heavy rôle in telling the builders what to do. Another new empire of the mind was well under way, although its founders had no such idea in their heads. Once again, using buildings as propaganda, all thought of man as creature was to be diverted from the realities of a body on earth and the search for a decent way of life amongst men, and encouraged to wander freely in the complicated paths of an unknown heaven in the hereafter. That wasn't by any means the main idea of the Sermon on the Mount, but that, alas, was too simple. No empire could be erected on such plain language as that.

So the Sermon on the Mount became the basis for a propaganda that slowly shut its eyes to what went on, as men ploughed and reaped, bought and sold and struggled to possess the riches of earth. The effort to adjust and adapt it to the business of exchanging goods, and the horrors of usury, led to fights and compromises that have never ended. Kings and bishops, powers temporal and spiritual, worked hand in hand when it suited their purpose, quarrelled and punished each other when either got the upper hand. Together, they devised ways of extending their empires, spending enormous sums in crusades that had trade and profit as their real objective, setting up the Inquisition when there was danger that much tribute was likely to forsake the empire treasury, hunting heresy for the same reason, excommunicating when they could not commit murder, splitting nations and peoples in order the better to subdue them, pitting nation against nation in the name of God and asking Him to give victory to each, on the battlefields where millions died like swine in a carnage of butchery.

Amidst this record of the ceaseless struggle for power and tribute, one senses the quiet life flittings of good men and true, simple-hearted workers, givers of kindness and bearers of those lamps of patience and tolerance by which alone there was kept alive some spirit of comradeship and even of gaiety. In all of this, craft after craft was added to that of mason and carpenter. The procession became a gay one indeed. Again and again the builders were called in to try for something better than the last time. There was rivalry in the priesthood. Churches were becoming the centres for the collection of much revenue. Farther and farther afield they were being pushed, as the crushed lands of empire slowly picked themselves out of the ruins and began to live again. The work of the builders was nothing short of wondrous. The ten centuries of church building make a pageant the like of which is not to be found, as an example of what craftsmen can do when they are set to a task. (Yes, one remembers the seven thousand churches that the Mexicans built under the Spanish domination.) The ruins of empire lay all about. There was everywhere a litter of temples and monuments. Those that could be used without tainting the new religion were turned into churches, while the Christians ravished and pillaged the old temples, in order to make new ones, apparently with no qualms. Anything could be violated if it had pagan associations. The ruins of Rome formed a vast quarry whence stone might be taken, with only the labor of carrying it off. Masonry came into its own again. Not the marvellous cutting of Memphis and Athens, but after a time and by slow recapture, the good solid substantial stone-walled building, where the stone was laid up in a copious bed of lime mortar.

The resources of earth were still abundant. Land was still

[94]

fertile, if one but treated it as a friend. Trade became freer and wider, roads grew better, travel easier and ships began to voyage, though timidly and not far, to bring back news of other craftsmen who made fine things for their own use. The wider use of money gave a growing spread to the exchange of goods, as it steadily built the system of usury that quietly ate away all the social blessings that freer trade and increasing skill should have contributed to raise the ease and scope of life for all workers everywhere. Things went a little faster than in the days of Memphis, Athens, Rome, but in other respects, the world had not changed its ideas very much. The new church grew to be reconciled to poverty and slavery and was even induced to suggest, after a while, that it was a very good thing to remain in the station of life into which one had had the privilege of being allowed to arrive, by arrangement with God, and be thankful for the chance. No! Things had changed but little. There were the kings still wanting their palaces, and the priests who had merely changed their frocks were still wanting to rule and be paid for it. All of them? No, indeed. There were saints among them, men who gave and gave and never took, who wanted nothing but to live quietly on the simple basis of the Sermon on the Mount, to make the earthly journey of humans a peaceful business of work with plenty of play. They had wisdom, the infinite wisdom that knows why people cannot be happy unless they can make play out of their work, and be free from the need of getting a profit from their neighbor, or, and far worse, taking advantage of his needs and preying on his misfortunes.

Over the surface and in the bones of the early Christian building, from the sixth century on, there is written this simple philosophy. The builders were happy, once again.

There was no joy in pouring Roman concrete. There was some, perhaps, but for a few only, in facing it with marble. But a building, to express the happiness of that "first fine careless rapture," must have happiness poured into it. The Roman method of building, based on bravado and humbug, may have left the builders exultant or proud or vain—the few of them who had any chance at plying their craft—but between the ruins of it and those of the early Christian churches, one senses the difference between vanity and piety.

The new church, like the old temple, was based on a legend. As the Greeks embroidered the life and the loves that went on at Olympus, so were the Christians to embroider the legend of a babe born of a virgin in a stable manger. To the Greeks, their gods were ever-present, though invisible. To the Christians, their God was also ever-present, but enveloped in a strange fog of fancy and fear. The Greeks, for a time, feared the wrath of Zeus, we may assume, and believed in the manifestations of that wrath. The Christians feared the wrath of their God, and likewise believed that much of life was a system of reward and punishment meted out from the throne of an angry God.

To the builders, however, there was the Christ legend, as a source upon which to draw for their forms and patterns. Most of this legend was not new. The idea of the virgin birth was far older than Christ. Easter was a festival long before He came on earth. Even the idea of one God was lost in the remote past where it had been born. In a new combination, these legends were now come alive again. Men were still too fearsome to believe in themselves. Life had still to have a support that lay outside the visible world; at least there must be some agency to which could be assigned those evils and misfortunes that appeared not to be man-made. For man was still afraid to examine himself and his life and behavior. He could not realize that things were in his own hands, and that the world would be what he made it. That each tick of the clock began a new future over which he alone presided. That the inevitable past was no more than a carry-over in which skill and wisdom were much mixed with fear and emotion.

Yet in spite of this mixture of timidity and tradition (Does it not still persist?), the evidence of which is written plainly on the churches of a thousand years in Europe, there is also written the tale of a happy craftsmanship. There never had been a like writing in stone, over so long a time. In places, late in the Middle Ages, and afterwards, crafts-men got free to build other minor buildings, and even some good houses to live in, and in these and those that gradually went to make the old towns and cities, a newer and more human writing came to view. But the outpouring of stone-cutting and stone-carving inspired by the Christian legend, in the early days when its simplicity had not been hopelessly obscured by the nimble theologians who had to find a way of reconciling the trickery of landlordism and usury with the Sermon on the Mount, is a grand tale.

One cannot look at it without feeling the truth of the in-junction that except as ye remain as little children, ye can-not enter. That, in a nutshell, is the truth of craftsmanship. Always, if it is to be fine, there must be contained within it the simplicity of childish wonder utterly free of fear. In the pattern that runs over the surface of the early churches as though they had been sprinkled with the breath of a great and fervent adoration, there is childish wonder, but not quite free of fear. The Christ legend began to be embroidered, very simply, with imagined scenes from the life of the holy family, the pilgrimage of Jesus, the death and resurrection, the ascent into heaven, and the life that there went on. Over the fronts of the churches and even in places where no eye could look, save by climbing to dizzy heights, there was cut and chiselled the childish wonder of men who dared not believe wholly in themselves.

Can one blame them? Far from it. They suffered from a tradition, as men still suffer, that weighed down and over-laid them with fear. Where the tradition had its beginning does not matter. It may have been born out of primitive man's inability to do other than shiver with fear at the awe-some whims and caprices of Nature as she darkened the heavens, or dazzled her skies, as she chose. It seems easy to think this to have been so, and thus to imagine that it was easy for king and priest to use such fears, and others connected with the wonder and sadness of death, to hold the multitude in material subjection and under tribute. At all events, they did, and the hand of fear still lay upon the men of the new Christian day, or was soon put upon them, as though a great weight had closed the door against any examination or any escape.

Yet there was one avenue of escape! With hammer and chisel one could in some strange and happy way come to terms with at least a part of the material world and find it responsive and even kindly. Here, if one had the will and the patience, one could become a Master, in his own right and by his own hand. A Master that drew no tribute and asked for no recompense save the just reward of his labor! This was the open door! There will never be another like it! Through it lies the broad road to fearlessness. Yet the craftsmen could never wholly escape. The constant message, star-

ing them in the face, was bidding them to submit and fear
and pay. Intent themselves on asking questions, for there
can be no craftsmanship without questioning, their whole
labor was poured into the making of buildings that were
meant to silence all questionings. It had been noticed, by
those who wanted power, that the easy way to dominion is
to keep people from asking questions.

Now and then, in a piece of carving here and there hidden
from all but the most curious searcher in triforium or tower,
comes the vision of a workman who was almost ready to
question and to dare to believe completely in himself. One
seems to see him daring the heavy hand of fear, daring to
make an image that was ironic or sarcastic, as though the
maker were confessing his doubt and was about ready to
utter a new faith that if the church's God created the world,
it was men that made it difficult to live in; that the first task
of man was to make a decent world and not to be bothered
about what was to happen afterwards. If anything was to
happen, the result could not be made any the worse by having striven to build a decent earthly world for all men.

Thus do gargoyles and monsters seem to be both symbols
of evil and yet almost playful symbols of men who were
timidly seeking an avenue of escape from the tradition of
fear. One can fancy the workman as he chiselled, and guess
what was going on in his mind as he furtively cut the grotesque figures of men and animals. They were images that
grew primarily out of the frightening ideas of the devil and
his purgatory; but do they not, over and over again, seem
to tell another story as well? Do they not express all
sorts of doubts and timid ridicule? The surfaces of a thousand churches and cathedrals are an open book, on which
all of these things, in a thousand variations, are written and

written, with great skill and great beauty. They are the multitudinous echoes of the days when the empire of the church was coming to the very power that was to enfeeble it.

The mason, during the thousand years after Romulus Augustulus, was to carry on the wall tradition in stone, and to a much lesser extent, in brick. After Rome, there were the several centuries, already referred to as the Dark Ages, when building was by no means a major occupation. No doubt the simple-hearted could get on without pauperizing themselves to build a church. The growth of the new institution, dependent for its buildings upon the gathering of wealth by the people at large, was not rapid. Behind the masons who slowly began to resume their craft, lay forty centuries of masonry, and yet it was to take them almost another ten centuries before they had recaptured the skill of the masons at the Great Pyramid.

The Roman method of building was a highly organized mechanism of smart engineers and cheap labor. It left a heritage, however, and it is not strange that for many a long day succeeding builders tried to work in the Roman manner. That is, roughly, to get a good-looking outside appearance on a wall. Away from Rome, stone was not easy to find, and it was hard to carry it from one place to another. Many a city perhaps grew up because it was near a stone quarry. Verona, for example, with its nearby red and orange marbles, or Fiesole and Florence, with their sandstone quarries that the Etruscans had worked.

Indeed, the story of masonry is almost the story of geology. With a map on which is traced the stone beds of earth, one may follow the mason on his course and well understand why he did many things. It was the great hills of limestone that chanted their refrain to the builders of Memphis, even as the Nubian sandstone deposits likewise intrigued the builders of Philæ, Abou-Simbel and the great avenue of sphinxes at Thebes. It was the limestone beds of Greece, fused as they had been by the heat of great pressures into fine marble, that gave the Greek masons a way of doing things differently, and more delicately. So also had the "poros" stone taught them the art of surfacing a wall with plaster, just as the Egyptians had surfaced their reed thatch with clay. Poros was perfect for giving a binding union with plaster, and although this form of wall might have been thought totally unworthy of a god or a goddess, there were such walls at Selinus, Ægina and Olympia. The Romans found the same stone for plaster in their "tufa," whose spongy lightness was one of the chief reasons for their skill in vaults and domes.

The Greek builders ignored the colored marbles hard by Athens, the red and gray ones and the green schist deposits, but the Romans used them greedily, even as they went to the islands of Paros, Naxos and Samos for other marbles, and finally ransacked their whole empire for all the brilliant or unusual stones to be found.

The Egyptians had known mortar, but it had no strength. It was the Roman builders who first found how to bind stones together in a wall that would be as strong as though it were one stone. In such a result, the Egyptians had not been interested. They wanted their stone work to look like one piece of rightness. This required the most perfect joints, as in the limestone covering slabs of the Great Pyramid, where the mortar, used in joints that were a fiftieth of an inch wide, was more to hide the marks of the joining than to cement the slabs together. For keeping a wall true, both Egyptian and Greek mason depended on weight. Now and then they clamped stones together with metal or, as in the columns of Greek temples, keyed the drums together with blocks of cypress. Their only enemy was the earthquake. Weight of stone alone sufficed, except when earth shook and rocked.

The Roman mortar mixture, strong as stone itself, served not only to bind but to distribute the weight of one stone on another. It was not then necessary to grind surfaces as in the drums of the Greek columns. Mortar made a rough cushion so that no one stone rested directly on the other. The stones touched at high points only, but all uneven roughnesses were bedded and padded in mortar which thus received and distributed the weight equally over the contacting surfaces. This speeded up the laying of stone walls, by saving labor, but it was a useless method when one wanted a wall that looked to be of one stone, a tradition that persevered pretty well all the way from Memphis to the beginning of Christian church building.

Before the Roman builders lay good examples of Etruscan masonry, where stones were laid in courses and the joints properly broken, as they should be. But the process was laborious, when compared with concrete, and any Roman concern with the rightness of craftsmanship was to show itself, at its best, in fine river spans for carrying roads or water. Concrete arches were perfectly in keeping with such purposes. At such times, one feels that these later builders were one in spirit and principle with their Egyptian and Greek forbears. At Memphis, when they came to make their "firm things," they sought rightness in the relation of material to purpose. The Greeks, in their golden day, had also to find the perfect form that fitted both material and purpose. The Roman search for rightness was based on empire, not upon delicate relationships. Preceding empires were far less plain-spoken, with their propaganda, than was Rome. Its gods were pagan, but its empire building was what would today be called business-like. Those who ran the show sought power and tribute openly and frankly. They used buildings to sell the idea in the open market and without much religious humbug. Their builders were taught so to build as to put fear of and respect for Rome in the hearts of all tax and tribute payers. Naturally, there should be shown an apparent good intent, in all public works, for that would silence any murmurings over the cost.

When that day had passed and another empire experiment had gone the usual route, and when a new religion had routed the pagans and their gods, it is not strange that the new builders still worked on in the same manner. They attempted nothing grandiose. The people who walked amidst ruins were too tired and too poor, for many a long day, to spend any great energy in glorifying anything or anybody. But when, some centuries later, the church was strong enough to begin calling for buildings, the Roman tradition of heavy walls and piers of concrete, with dressed facings, still clung. The results were often disastrous, for there was neither the skill nor the materials with which to make them properly.

Not until the builders came to know and get the feel of the great limestone deposit that stretches across Europe from the valley of the Meuse to the West of England, did the fine craft of masonry come to the perfections it had known at Memphis and Athens. Ever more skilled the masons grew, until at last they rose to the mastery of stone that gave the world its Christian legend of Gothic churches and cathedrals.

Even though cataloguers and classifiers have never ceased disputing as to what is Gothic and what is not, one need not mind. A good guess would be that it makes no difference whether they agree or not, and that if one likes the smell of roses, no name will add to the fragrance.

Romanesque, which cannot be closely confined to any time or area, was marked generally by heavy walls. The builders were passing from the inert mass of their Roman forbears, where concrete piers and domes knit themselves together in a bond of cement, to the live mass, where vaulted roofs and masonry walls had to depend on a proper calculation of weights and thrusts and a safe way of keeping these forces in balance and equilibrium. The early basilicas, with low roofs of wood, involved no very great problem, for there was no great weight to be borne by the walls.

Wooden roofs, however, could burn, and frequent fires led to serious disasters, for the new churches were often stored with precious things. What other answer than to build roofs of stone, vaulting them with the simple semi-circular forms the earlier builders had used? The art of concrete had been lost, one might conclude, for in spite of all the difficulties, stone-vaulted roofs began to appear. In these, it was quickly evident, weight of roof increased with width of church, and this increase had to be met with thicker walls. By resting the barrel vault on arches, its weight could be distributed at certain points in the wall, rather than through the whole wall. Vaulting could also be in the form of two barrel-vaults at right angles and seeming to intersect each other. This so distributed roof weight and thrust that they had to be offset only at those points in the wall from which

[104]

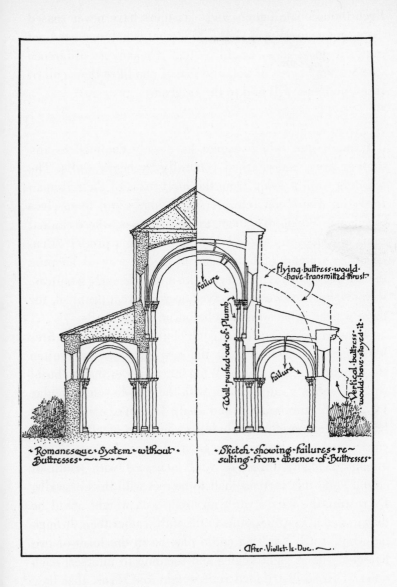

Flying buttress would
have transmitted thrust.

Failure

Wall pushed out of Plumb.

Failure

Vertical buttress
would have stayed it.

. Romanesque. System. without .
Buttresses . — . — . —

. Sketch . showing . failures . re~
sulting . from . absence . of . Buttresses .

. After . Viollet . le . Duc . — .

the arches, or vault sections, sprang. Hence came the buttress (a pier attached to the wall), and so, little by little, there finally developed ribbed vaulting in which the roof was broken into many sections, each supporting and reinforcing the other. The roof could thus be lightened, width of church increased, and the whole structure carried to heights that had not before been possible. Ribbed vaulting is, to many, the very essence of craftsmanship at its highest, and it must be ranked as one more great victory for the builders. This is not to assert that earlier builders had not known the principle, nor to ignore the marvellous stone-work of the craftsmen of Persia and the Orient. Origins are never to be cited with exactness, a point that can scarcely be over-emphasized in tracing any history.

If one is interested to trace the story of Romanesque building, one may find its early churches as fine a tale as the builders ever wrote. Here is a pleasant song of rugged simplicity, such as might have told the faith of people to whom a good king was not an owner but a kindly guide, and to whom the church was a place where justice and security were a matter of genuine concern, where human relations were thought a part of life, quite as interesting and even more needful than divine relations. One could easily come to feel that way in the tiny chapel at Vaucluse, for instance, near the spot where Petrarch wrote his sonnets, in Provence. The room is so little and so humble, yet so full of peace and security, that one well might wonder whether the loftiest nave in Christendom could bring one nearer to his God than here in this simple church of a thousand years ago.

If one began a serious quest of the Romanesque, however, one would go back to Italy, and to the churches of St. Apollinare at Ravenna, one without and one within the city.

[106]

Nave~

Aisle~

- Romanesque · Vaulted · Church ~~·~

- After · Viollet-le-Duc ·~·~·~

These are plainly related to Byzantium, for Ravenna was once an official outpost of that empire, but the moment of change in building technique is none the less plainly marked, albeit the note is here more sumptuously Byzantine than simple Romanesque. (Many esteem the mosaic in S. Apollinare Nuovo, where a procession of white angels walks against a background of gold, as one of the exquisite creations of the craftsmen of that day.) These churches mark the beginnings of a building era that was to take one form in Lombardy, as at S. Zeno in Verona, or S. Michele at Pavia; another form at Pisa, in the Cathedral; or in S. Michele at Lucca, or S. Miniato in Florence; in still another at Rome, where the basilicas long clung, while one more variation is marked in the cathedral of Monreale at Palermo, where the basilica exhibits the blending of many traditions.

S. Zeno at Verona is demurely gay with its plain, delicately moulded façade, flanked by a towering campanile, yet it is quite a different gaiety from that in the porch of St. Trophîme at Arles, where the whole note of joyous craftsmanship is framed in a vigorous doorway of great beauty. One might guess the difference to be due to the luscious red wine of Provence, but one might also guess there was always a greater gusto in those Provençal craftsmen, as in their Burgundian and Rhenish brothers farther north. To many they will appear to have had a feeling for that good lusty mass that the Italian builders never had. One may likewise feel their Romanesque buildings to be more heartily structural, more solid-walled, more vigorous bursts of stone masonry, and more expressive of a gay and robust life in a world where good things were in abundance, rather than telling the tale of a life of cloistered devoutness. To those who so feel, their churches will be brimming over with a

[108]

naïveté that is as delightful as it is rare in buildings. They would prefer to spend their days amidst the churches of Arles, Arles-sur-Teche, Aulnay-de-Saintonge, Beaulieu, Bellenaves, Chateauneuf-sur-Charente, Clermont-Ferrand, Fenioux, Montceaux-l'Etoile, Poitiers, Retaud, Rioux, Souillac, and Talmont-sur-Gironde, than in looking at all the rest of the churches in Christendom, and especially in not looking at the grander Romanesque churches and cathedrals at Caën, Mayence, Worms, Toulouse, or Cologne, although the Church of the Apostles in this Rhenish city has, however, a faint echo of the charm that hovers over the apse of the cathedral at Lucca.

These things are a matter of preference. One may easily escape from cataloguers and pigeon-holers, who are seriously convinced that one must proceed from a fixed point and follow a fixed route, simply by ignoring them. It is of course pleasant suddenly to come across a certain thing in Spain which convinces you that it is intimately related to something else in Burgundy, or to find that French or Italian workmen have apparently been wandering away from home with their tools and their fancies. But these discoveries are amusing rather than vital, unless one has to make money by talking about them.

The variety of forms and the manner in which French, Italian, German and Spanish builders came to play with round and pointed arches, and with vaulted roofs, from the eighth or ninth century on, forms one of the enchanting chapters in the pageant of the builders. There is, in the tale, no precise beginning, nor can the tragic end of it be marked on any calendar. It is, at its finest moments, a joyous tale of merging and blending, of fancy and great daring, of freedom and yet order, of hard-won experience that grew out of

[109]

taking the risks by which alone knowledge could be gained. The cathedral of Beauvais is often cited as the great piece of audacity in which the Gothic builders failed completely, but by the time Beauvais was being dared, the old craft spirit was also far gone, and for reasons to which we shall presently come.

It seems odd that the word "Gothic" was the most scornful name of which the jibers and jeerers of that day could think. They didn't like the new methods of builders who were setting out to use lighter walls and build higher churches. So they called the upstarts after the Goths, who were the bogey-man barbarians of the day, a kingless host of marauders without a country. They roamed from the Baltic to Trebizond, and their chiefs upset the dreams of many a would-be empire maker. As a host, they passed quite out of the scene, chuckling a little, one might guess, at having given their name to one of the greatest bursts of creative craftsmanship that men had ever known, and which was used to the glory of the new God of Hosts, in whose eyes there were to be no empires and no country for those who followed Him!

The gradual change of robust Romanesque into delicate Gothic is another clear and shining example of what the builders could do when they were set a task, and were not yet ready to ask whether it would be better to build good houses for everyone rather than palaces and churches. So building, it was for all craftsmen a golden day. The Christ legend was taken over by painters and sculptors, by weavers and glass-makers, by smiths who forged iron and hammered brass. From the Adriatic to Bristol Channel and North Sea, and from the Baltic to the Mediterranean, the pageant

[110]

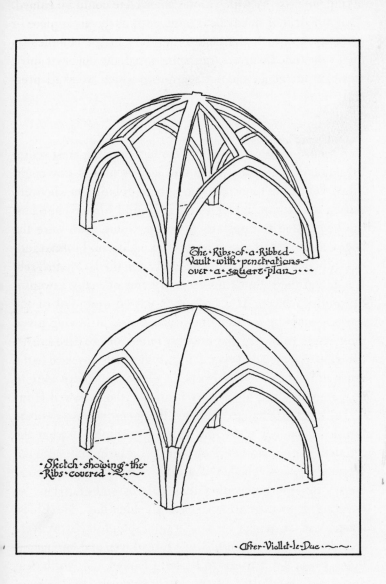

The · Ribs · of · a · Ribbed ·
Vault · with · penetrations ·
over · a · square · plan · · · ·

· Sketch · showing · the ·
· Ribs · covered · · ·

· After · Viollet-le-Duc · · ·

wended its unhurried way. It left behind a record in craftsmanship such as men are not likely to see again, unless all present empires be destroyed and succeeding civilizations, if any, be thrown back upon the search for such rightness as will tell them how to build something that will endure. That was the faith in which Romanesque and Gothic builders worked, although the very institutions they were helping to found were to betray them, at the critical moment.

Under the influence of growing congregations and changing ritual the church plan changed. The basilica was extended on the sides, by transepts at right angles to the nave, giving a cross-shape to the plan, and the name of crossing to the intersection. To the growing array of larger and larger windows in the nave, made possible by the rapidly advancing skill of the masons in heightening and lightening walls, great rose windows began to appear in the transepts. Indeed, it might be said that without the invention of painted glass, there would have been no such Gothic as we now know. Fergusson even remarked that it would have been truer to call it the "painted glass" style, since he contends that most of the builders' skill came to be spent in contriving the largest possible windows for the display of colored glass. At all events, windows grew larger, and became more and more decorative. To strengthen the great surfaces, and the many small pieces of glass, joined with lead, delicate stone muntins were added in a great variety of forms, the "tracery" of the middle period in Gothic known as the Decorative.

Thus, even as the Romanesque departed from the naïveté of its early days, so went the Gothic. It grew steadily more ornate, and even vulgarly efflorescent, as though it were concerned, finally, with a boastful display of virtuosity rather than with a sense of rightness. In its later days, it was even

[112]

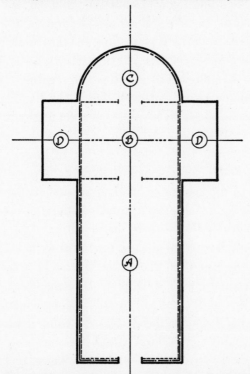

·Dotted·Lines· show· Greek·Temple·~·~·~
·Dot·and·dash·Lines· show· Roman·Basilica·~
·Solid·Lines·show·Christian·Church·~·Cruciform·Plan·~

·In·the·Greek·Temple:~ "A"·is·the·Sanctuary; B·is·the·
·Treasury·of·the·GOD·~·~·~· In·the·Roman·Basilica:~
·A~is·the·Public·space; B~is·the·space·for·the·Lawyers; "C"·is·
·the·space·for·the·Judges·~·~·~· In·the·Christian·Church:~
·A~is·the·Nave; B~is·the·Crossing; "C"·is·the·Sanctuary;
·"D"·"D"·are·the·Transepts·~·~·~·~

·~·Note·that·the·Greek·Temple·was·oriented·with·the·Entrance·to·the·East·~· In·the·Fifth·
·Century·A.D·the·Christian·Church·was·officially·Oriented·so·that·this·was·
·reversed·and·the·Entrance·was·and·has·been·since~·to·the·West·~·

known as "flamboyant," which means boastfully trying to show off, and nothing less, but for that the craftsmen were not to blame, as we shall see.

If one traces Gothic through its various manners in France, England, Italy, Germany, Spain and the Low Countries, one will note differences that rose out of different ways of looking at things and also out of different conditions. French cathedrals usually began as bishop's seats, and mostly in walled towns where space was at a premium and where the process of building generally began by demolishing much-needed houses, as was also true in the Low Countries and Germany. This tended towards a ground plan that was short and wide. The English cathedrals generally began in connection with abbeys. Land being plentiful they chose a long and narrow plan. Occasionally, as in Westminster at London, there is a compromise, in details, for while nave and transepts are purely English in feeling, the apse is quite as purely French. All sorts of mergings and blendings may be found, in almost any cathedral, and it is rare indeed that any one building may be pointed to as perfectly pure.

To get some inkling of what Gothic building meant, one must look at the whole record. The variations are as infinite as the craftsmanship is glorious, for it was above all a day of craft freedom. That is the first lesson the Gothic age has to teach. It was a day of even greater freedom than the day of the Parthenon, for in Athens there was a fixed and fairly rigid framework of rules within which a craftsman had to work. In Gothic days there was hardly a limit either to daring or fancy.

The Gothic that came to its final perfections in the thirteenth century, or even earlier, if one prefers the earlier, goes back to the day when the first men with the first tools

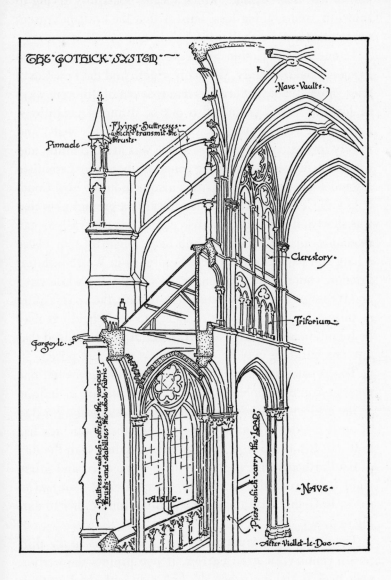

THE·GOTHICK·SYSTEM·~~

·Nave·Vaults·

·Flying·Buttresses·
·which·transmit·the·
thrusts·

Pinnacle·

·Clerestory·

·Triforium·

Gargoyle·

·Buttress··which··offsets··the·various·
·thrusts·and·stabilises·the·whole·fabric·

·Piers··which·carry·the·LOAD·

·AISLE·

·NAVE·

·After·Viollet-le-Duc·

sought rightness. There is no difference in spirit of crafts-manship in any age, no matter by what name one may call it. Craftsmanship is craftsmanship, the feeling for rightness, and depends on freedom of the individual to develop him-self to the utmost. What other freedom is there, one wonders, when all is said and done, for is not craftsmanship born of imagery and fancy, and is there any other pure freedom that man is ever likely to know?

A Gothic church or cathedral no more smells of draught-ing-boards and written rules than the Sermon on the Mount smells of pew-rents and church investments. All craftsmen had their ways and their training, yet there was never a halt to that individual fancy or skill that so enriches the whole pattern as to leave Gothic a living dynamic record, even though seven centuries have passed. Master minds kept an eye on the whole labor, and so knit the fabric together with-out too many errors at those points where craft met craft. That is why the great Gothic cathedrals are as fine a lesson as ever set before man, although one must be careful, as one cons it, to take account of the fact that in making use of the lesson it was church that failed, not craftsmen.

In the fabric of Amiens, as in many another, the basis and plan for a decent way of life are written as clearly as though they were a flame in the sky. Running over and through the stones, as the tree's unseen roots spread and mingle in that rhythmic strength by which bole and branch soar upward as the outward and visible sign, is the law of order, the prin-ciple of freedom, the necessity for equality. No clearer les-sons have ever been written. No philosophers ever probed deeper than did those craftsmen when they wrote their sim-ple lesson. Plainly, they said, the way to a civilization where men shall live in peace and justice is by and through the

[116]

craft spirit. It is the only path. There will never be another.

Is that what the builders had learned when the great day of Gothic was over? No, indeed; they wrote the lesson unconsciously, which is why they wrote it so truly and so beautifully. They were seeking for rightness as workers, not as talking preachers. They had, however, learned two marvellous things about buildings: how to use the ribbed vault and how to create masonry as alive and full of muscles, sinews and nerves as is the human body. From the simple primitive contented aliveness of the early Romanesque, they leaped to the restless aliveness of the athlete whose muscles could be seen playing beneath his skin and whose movements ravished one with the sheer grace of their rippling interplay as each fibre of the body danced and played its unerring part, no matter how delicate or how vigorous the movement. The loftiest pinnacle in a Gothic fabric is as clearly related to and sustained by the solid base and buttressed wall as sensation in the human body is carried from delicate finger-tip to registering brain. Everywhere is aliveness, litheness, suppleness and no pride of part over part. It is all order, freedom, equality.

The Parthenon is also a law of order, yet one can hardly feel it to be so brimming with freedom and equality as a true Gothic building. That embodies the purity of rightness, as well, but within its vibrant fabric lies an even more profound lesson. To the purity of the Greeks, the Gothic builders added the ecstasy of fancy. They loved the joyous play and were always ready for a frolic with any part of the work. They could try the same part in any number of ways and without feeling that any result was a perfect end. Rather was it a pleasant halting place where one sat down and had a bite from a loaf and a swig from a bottle, and then prepared to resume a journey that was to go on endlessly.

What happened? Sad to relate, the church, perhaps all unaware, had been drifting away from the path that leads to civilization and was seriously engaged in trying to forge and weld a religious empire! When the question of the new system of dealing with land had to be decided, the church chose for the empire method, in spite of its long record in favor of common rights. This is not to deny that the church may have imagined its choice to be only a temporary compromise, a momentary departure that could later be corrected. The evidence inclines one to believe differently.

Whatever it thought, it turned out, for the builders, that their conquest was not to end in the use of their skill to make better houses, towns and cities. Nor were they to be asked to put sunlit streets in place of dark alleys, or to let sun and air into the damp dungeons where the multitude was born and where it ate and slept until it died. Nor yet were they to build in the name of order, justice and security, and so bring men to the beginnings of a decent way of life for all. No, none of these things was to be asked of them. The Sermon on the Mount had fallen into the hands of theological hair-splitters, and the history of that golden day of craftsmanship was to prove hardly more than the effort to build a church empire.

One guesses there was anguish of spirit as good men and true wrestled with a question they knew was to change the destiny of men. No doubt there were prayers and that men besought their God to show His truth, to reveal Himself once again in that hour of mortal avarice. Land was His offering to man. Life could not go on without free access to it, even though that need had already been a source of persecution

[118]

by sinful overlords and empire seekers. Now the king would sign papers that gave outright ownership, not only to the land a man needed for his own house, garden and crops, but for the land that other men needed for the same uses! Great areas were henceforth to be owned by a landlord who could make other men pay rent for their use.

To the good men and true who believed in their Lord Jesus with all their heart and soul, such things could not be —must not be! There could be no ownership title unless it were given by their God directly. Not even the king had the right to give that, and many a pleading went up, one may be sure. The church, however, was at work setting up an institution dependent upon property and income therefrom. It thus came to the unhappy state of all institutions. This was a pity, for the craftsmen of a thousand years, as in the centuries from Memphis to Rome, were used almost entirely in building to the power and glory of institutions that were a denial of the spirit of craftsmanship as a basis for human relations.

One may look at the long and glorious record of the church builders with profound emotion, or with profound questioning. One may lose oneself in the delights of form, the solaces of shadows, the peace of cloisters, the soaring of spires, the exultant flings of buttresses, or the majesties of naves with their proud towering piers and heaven-piercing arches. Or one may decide that the only way to found a religious institution is to put it in the hearts of men and never give it a building. As soon as it gets one it will begin to lay up treasure on earth, and the rest of us, sinners though we be, will then know that the institution doesn't mean what it says. Then one has an institution and no faith.

Also one might speculate at great length as to why builders kept trying to build higher, wider and longer naves. Was it merely the joyous delight of daring? Was it a matter of growing congregations? Is there some profound relation in height above as one kneels in church? Is one more in the presence of his God in Amiens and Canterbury than in a simple whitewashed church in Holland, or in the little chapel at Vaucluse? Or is it that the will to empire always pushes the builders into a squandering of the common substance, an unconsidered waste of labor, materials and what is called wealth, all of which might be used to far better purpose? Such were the influences that slowly ate away the hard-won gains of the craftsmen, even as they were tempting the church to forget why it was there.

For whatever reason one may choose, human relationships were to shift the basis of a decent respect for the rights of others, as had been set forth in the Sermon on the Mount and which had gained some headway, and slowly to evolve into a struggle of the individual to get and keep what he could. It is quite a strong tendency, one may admit, in the relations of men, but now it was to move steadily forward under the sanction of the very church that had come into existence to establish not only the Fatherhood of God but the Brotherhood of Man. This brotherliness had been tolerably possible under the ancient system of land tenure, where ownership was vested in the commonalty. Under the growing system of legalizing individual ownership, it was quite a different story.

In meeting this profound change in the basis of society, the church was caught in its own toils. Bit by bit, and in ways that were sometimes devious, it had become a very large

[120]

owner of lands, and as landlord was deriving a good income from them. The principle at stake was plain, but the temptation was too great. Instead of using its influence to put an end to landlordism, the church compromised by pretending to curb the rapacity of landlords. As we now know, once the theory of landlordism got itself fairly rooted, it was difficult to break up. The delight of income from rent rather than from labor was too enticing. Men who had once been allowed the use of what land they needed, even though they paid in kind for the protection of a feudal lord, were now to be dispossessed and left to make the best terms they could with the landlords. The church lost a golden opportunity to save men from a pitiful mistake. It compromised, which really meant that it surrendered, in the end. For the sake of its revenue it gave in, and never again was it to be the power it might have been in the destinies of mankind.

To the craftsmen it was an unforgivable betrayal, although they were long in finding out how serious the matter was. They had given of their utmost in building the power and empire of the church, and when both were needed in their defense, the church forsook them. Its power at that moment was at the highest point, but to bishops, landlords and usurers, the physical institution of property and income had become far more engrossing than the idea on which the church had supposedly been founded. On its simple human base it had rested for several centuries, until, all unnoticed, it had been buried in property, theology and compromise. Even under the feudal system, where the use of land obliged a payment to a protecting overlord, dispossession was almost impossible. One might be punished for not paying, but there could be no landlessness. Everyone knew that man could not live without land. The change to landlordism, to many an historian and student, was one of the crucial partings of the ways for man. A vast control over life was to be had by land ownership, henceforth, and although no one may then have foreseen all that was to happen, the change was profoundly and vitally to affect all buildings, all builders, all empires, all efforts towards civilization, all relations of men to one another.

One finds it unpleasant to remember these things and to admit them as true, as one walks in the cloisters of Arles or Tarragona, or muses in the close of Salisbury or the tree-shadowed yard at Exeter, the apse of Amiens, in the enchanted light that pours through the windows of Chartres or York, or is held mute and breathless in the mystic shadows of the cathedral of Barcelona, or by the sheer nobility of Burgos. Beside the towering splendor of Durham, where Norman and Gothic builders entwined their crafts in one of the most majestic of cathedrals, as before all others in the long procession, one has to be resolute if one is not to become lost in the story of the builders. Tradition and training bid one forget all but the sight and the emotional intoxication. Reason and the will to know oblige one to remember and to question, not the skill, nor yet the content, but purpose and result. Where else is one to look but in the life of the ever-present day that is *now*, if one is to understand what the builders did, why they did it, and what the effect has been? For we have still to build, and who is to tell us what and where?

If the upset of the communal land system was to tempt the church from its plain path of rightness, the rise of usury, as money became a banker's game, was to force it into an even more sinister compromise. Usury was not only to raise further havoc with all builders and all buildings, but with

[122]

all ideals of justice and peace. Together with landlordism, it was to grow into a complete denial of an ultimate decent way of life. Money, it had been found, could be used not only to compel borrowing from those who controlled the supply, but could be used to cheat both the craftsman maker and the user of things, who was often a craftsman as well. As trade had long passed from the barter stage, men dealt less and less directly with one another, face to face, each with a knowledge of good work in his mind, but took money for their wares and services and then sought the tradesman for what they wanted or needed. He had variety from which to choose, which was all to the good, but it was not long before craftsmen found that tradesmen were getting the best of it. The new trading middlemen paid less and less, and charged more and more. When they got fairly to competing with each other, the craftsmen were caught in a money mesh indeed. It was the slow and sure rise of that petty trade that was eventually to develop under landlordism and usury, and break down completely the whole basis of rightness on which the crafts had rested. Ahead, under ever-tightening bonds, was the maelstrom of the competitive money-price system; but who saw to what it would lead?

At what precise moment the craft guilds rose, one cannot say. No one knows how far back runs the idea of joining together in order to defend a group or class from the attack of another. Each human offense has always brought forth a human defense, however long it may have taken to cohere and entrench. That may be the process by which "earth floods to justice, though it seems asleep." The craftsmen of the Middle Ages, however, began to see that under the spread of landlordism, usury and the money-price system set up by traders and now in use everywhere, and which was operated with no regard for the factors that had determined the worth of a craftsman's labor, there must be some control, or else competition by money-price only would undermine every craft and lead to the loss of all skill and quality. Men were getting to have no concern with these things as they bought and sold. For the craftsman, landlordism had begun to cut away his old independence. Trade was henceforth to rule, life to become impersonal, value a measurement in currency, and currency a will-o'-the wisp.

The fight to have price determined only by quality was a bitter one. Whatever the guilds had been, a real work now faced them, and thus there came the "fixed price" and the "just price." Both were attempts to check the havoc of price competition, and while no one would now pretend they were perfect devices for the purpose, they put up a good fight to keep the forces concerned only with money from destroying the one basis on which craftsmanship could rest. The story is confined to no limited period nor to any one country. It is traceable, through several centuries, from Rome to Edinburgh. It led many craftsmen into vigorous methods for maintaining the quality of their product and the price asked for it. It was probably the nearest to a just age of trade for money that men have ever come, or could come, with landlordism and usury sniping and sharpshooting from every possible vantage point.

The builders, by the time the Middle Ages were well advanced, had grown from the two trades of mason and carpenter into a goodly number of other skilled trades. Even the carpenters were divided, as between the rough labor of joists and rafters and the skilled work of joiner and cabinet-

[124]

maker. The tendency was to tighten the ranks of each craft. The apprentice served his time and, if judged competent, became a journeyman. Ahead was the master stage, generally not awarded until competence had been duly proven, although no doubt there was favoritism and a tendency of the masters not to fill the ranks so full as to put themselves out of a job. There were degrees of competence running through all the trades. Some masters were more skilled than others, more inventive, better organizers. There had always been such differences, and even in Egypt, Athens, Rome, Constantinople, there had been an organizer and director. It is the custom, at this point, to refer to these very early men as "architects," to which there can be no objection, so long as it is made plain that these men were generally skilled builders, which few architects are at the present time.

It is natural, certainly, that a profession should seek to justify its worth by pointing to an ancient line of ancestors. It doesn't prove anything, of course, for whether Imhotep was an Egyptian architect, or Ictinus was a Greek one, leads to nothing at all. The idea behind all this is the publicity that all callings seek to promote. No doubt, if the present architects could have their own way, no one would be allowed to build except by paying them. This is no more than just, if other callings are to have a similar monopoly, but again, it proves nothing. If all professions guaranteed their clients against harm from incompetent practitioners, there might be some reason in monopoly and in forcing the use of certain workers for certain work. It is well known that over various periods, the medieval guilds were responsible for the trade acts of their members. They put their seal on his work and stood ready to make good. It was the one moment when a whole class of paid workers, whether they be called crafts

[125]

or professions, has been on a fair and honest basis with society as a whole. The attempt to point to a long line of craft ancestors insures neither competence nor honesty. Carpenters and masons are the oldest crafts in the world, by thousands of years, but that doesn't mean that because a man calls himself carpenter or mason, he is one. Nor does calling oneself by any name, be it architect, engineer, doctor or lawyer, prove anything. Nor will any effort to tighten class lines and hunting-grounds prove anything, until every organized class is willing collectively to make good for the bungling of those incompetents who now pervade all trades, crafts and professions.

Into the building industry, generally at about the time the Renaissance began to spread its ideas of class and to take over the skill and knowledge developed by building craftsmen for use by a white-collar profession, there began to intrude all sorts of strange people who, having no craft knowledge of their own, wanted to tell skilled craftsmen how to build. Most of the celebrated buildings of the Renaissance were directed by men who served no apprenticeship as carpenter or mason, any more than the architect of today serves one. In the golden age of Gothic building the man who ran the job was a master builder. He had arrived by passing through the mill, was usually the most competent builder not otherwise engaged, and the terms of his contract were often as severe as they were amusing. He did not call himself architect, a word derived from two Greek words that mean master of craft; more precisely, a master carpenter, which is less important than the fact that the word came into current use hardly more than four centuries ago.

"In the beginning of the Middle Ages," says Maître

Minvielle,[1] "there was a veritable flowering of architecture, but it is likewise the time when it is most difficult to know the rôle played by the architect. Much has been written of the master builder. What was he exactly? Was he really an architect? If not, what were his attributes? Did he belong to the corporations (guilds)? Was he also a contractor? Did he buy in the markets for his own account or for that of the owner? What were his relations with the owner? We have read quantities of monographs, articles, commentaries, but have never found any work that presented a synthesis of the functions of an architect in the Middle Ages. This may be because the functions were not uniformly regulated by principles that obtained throughout France, and that each acted according to conditions and circumstances."

Maître Minvielle, after the most minute and patient research, concludes there was a master of the work, but no architect in anything resembling the modern sense, and no contractor. "In such a social and rigidly controlled organization as that of the Middle Ages, where would architect or contractor have found a place? For the contractor, there was none; one was either mason, carpenter or locksmith. The existence of a general contractor having oversight over different parts of the work has no basis in common sense.

"As for the architect, by whatever name he was called, and there is a wide number from which to choose, he was not the artist-maker of plans, directing the work on behalf of the owner, and practising a liberal profession, as today. He who is called architect, in the Middle Ages, was a simple workman, almost always a mason, who, by his intelligence, capacity, skill, had perfected himself beyond his comrades and risen a little above his modest rôle, but who remained a

[1] *Histoire Juridique de la Profession d'Architecture.*

workman, a master mason belonging to his guild and submitting to its statutes and rules. Having passed through all the degrees of his craft, he worked mostly with his hands, generally with the comrades whom he directed, whose life he shared, with whom he lived in the lodgings that were part of the workyard, and like them he was paid by the day.

"One should not be astonished at this collaboration of director and executor. In our day, it seems strange, but in the Middle Ages manual labor was not thought degrading. In the doorways of our cathedrals that so well reflect the life of the day that is gone, the liberal arts and trades are sculptured on a footing of equality, and in the language of that day they were often designated by the same words."

In returning to church-building and the reasons that led to the almost profligate profusion of Gothic fabrics, large and small, one may guess that there was rivalry, as wherever numbers, power and wealth are at stake. When, says Maître Minvielle, Jean Labas was engaged as master of the work by the chapter of Saint-Michel of Bordeaux, in 1464, he not only promised to stay on the job until death but also to reside within the limits of the parish and never to absent himself therefrom, save once a year when he might go to visit his family. Colin Trenchant, master of the work on the cathedral of Saint-André, in Bordeaux, agreed not only to live in the lodgings on the work but to sleep there. Gautier de Varinfoy, in charge of the restoration of the cathedral of Meaux, in 1253, agreed not to leave the work for more than two months a year and to accept no other work. Maître Thomas, chosen in 1369 as master of the work at Troyes, promised to "take no other work without permission from the dean and chapter." Jean de Damas became master of the work on the cathedral of Troyes, in 1517, on condition that

[128]

he would hire himself to no one and "to the end of his life would not leave the job."

In 1505, the chapter of Beauvais gave their master Chambiges a holiday of several days in which to visit Troyes, where the chapter of that cathedral had asked him to come for a consultation, but when they asked again in 1511, Beauvais demurred. Troyes sent Canon Jaquotti to urge the loan, but he failed. Then they sent Jean de Damas, son-in-law of Chambiges, telling him not to come back without his father-in-law. He brought him. At another time they sent presents to the wife of Chambiges in the hope that she would urge her husband to leave Beauvais and help at Troyes. Then they sent Chambiges two purses each of thirty sous, one for his wife and one for his daughter, and again a little present of thirty-seven sous to his son. In 1514, when he couldn't go, he sent some plans by his wife, who got "seven livres indemnity and gratifications," in order that "on her return she might persuade her husband to come in person, for he is greatly needed."

Of course there was rivalry! Why not? In the general scheme, all churches were useful in spreading the doctrines, and a little competition kept up a general agitation that had what the modern world knows as "news value." There is no reason why it should not be so, if one believes in empires and knows the way to contrive them, but again one is reminded of the plain fact that when all was done and over, the days of the craftsmen were numbered, and the condition of the multitude was no better, relatively, than it had been when Khufru finished the Great Pyramid.

In the early days, the new religion "transformed society by bringing about a state of things in which human values took precedence over economic values. Little by little this

[129]

changed spirit came to affect the arts. The humble worker began to gain confidence, and to think and feel on his own account. This changed feeling, combined with the communal spirit which Christianity everywhere fostered, tended to bring into existence those communal traditions of handicraft which reached their most consummate expression in Gothic Art. For Gothic Art is just as democratic in spirit as the Greek and Roman is servile. Every line of Gothic Art contradicts the popularly accepted notion that the Middle Ages was a period of gloom and repression. The riot of carving, the gaiety and vigour of the little grotesques that peer out from pillars and cornices, the pure and joyous colour of frescoes and illuminated manuscripts, the delight in work that overflowed in free and beautiful details in the common articles of daily use, tell the tale of a rich and abounding life, just as much as the unanswerable logic of Greek architecture tells of a life oppressed with a sense of fate." [1]

One might be diffident in accepting the Parthenon as a symbol of the sense of fate, without in any way demurring as to the greater freedom of the Gothic builders.

Yes, even with the multitude living in dirt and squalor, it was a golden day for the craftsmen. Yet, once again, one can hardly escape reflecting what might have happened had they been bidden to build, not for a religious empire but for a decent way of life for those who paid for the buildings only by going without a decent roof over their heads.

[1] *A Guildsman's Interpretation of History*, by Arthur J. Penty.

VIII

THE RENAISSANCE

IN THE sixteenth century, early, after some four hundred years of spasmodic building, work at Beauvais ceased. Those who dreamed of it, so long ago, had thought to make it the tallest fane in all the world. When the builders abandoned it, the day of the free creative Gothic craftsman was over. His skill and vigor were spent. The power of money-price trade was rising and the Renaissance, although it had been slow in changing things in France, had now quite altered the rôle of the craftsman. Bidding in terms of price was eating away at the old quality of work done by the day and founded on rightness. In Italy, where the "Rebirth" was now spent in what its admirers think its finest flowering, the Gothic builders had never been highly appreciated. Too playfully free, by far, too hilarious and too risky, they were concerned not so much with the manner of saying something as with what they said. They had no style, the new artists of Florence had said, one fancies, and style was coming to the front again as not since the days of the Parthenon.

The huge cathedral at Milan, one of the largest of all, was finished only a few years before they began putting the dome on the cathedral at Florence, in 1419. The Milan cathedral is a body of muscles and sinews, but as bejewelled as a fop and so done up in gewgaws as utterly to hide the dazzling delight of their interplay. The factors that had produced the Renaissance, which was at the same time a protest, were no doubt at work during the building of this great cathedral. Many cities and towns in Italy were becoming "art conscious" towards the end of the fourteenth century. There had begun to thrive, under the wing of the church and the new wealthy patrons, many skilled callings not directly concerned with buildings. Men were painting as never before, beating gold and silver as beautifully as at Knossos or Mycenæ, carving wood, forging iron, weaving, potting. Finiguerra's work in niello was paving the way for engraving and soon men would be printing from movable types.

Style was being recaptured from that brief period in Athens when the builders tried to do something so perfect that it never need be looked for again. There was not so much thought about the usefulness of what one did as the manner in which one did it, although lovers of the period might protest at such a suggestion and aver that any fine craftsmanship was useful, no matter what the purpose. The answer to that may still lie in purpose, nevertheless, but be that as it may, great wealth had flown into the princely and ducal treasuries and many a tradesman held his head high

[132]

as he counted his ducats. Social life was emerging, classes were forming, distinctions were being arranged, luxury was in the air. To set the stage completely, there had to be display of wealth. It became a matter of renown, and much publicity, to take a rising young man under one's wing and help him to get a chance to use his talents and make a name for himself.

Talents there were, in abundance. It was the moment when men played at work with a fine sense of style. Concern with use was limited, as is plain in many a building. Painters, goldsmiths and sculptors had begun to see building as a field for "art." They would have denied, one guesses, that Romanesque and Gothic had spurred them to do something they thought better, and so to prove the base on which their despite rested. They wouldn't have admitted, very likely, that they didn't like Gothic because they couldn't do it, nor would it be fair to say that they had tried and failed. It simply didn't go in Italy as it had gone in France, whichever of the many offered reasons one may prefer. At its best, in smaller things, it never excited the Italian builders to such a frolic as the French builders had. One can feel that the prelude to *Die Meistersinger* could have been a picture of the French or Flemish craftsmen, in their glorious day, as well as of those who worked in Nuremberg. Its final burst seems to fill one with a sense of craft delight such as no other music has ever made. Would one, however, think of the Italian builders at that moment? Perhaps one would think of the Venetian craftsmen, if one had read those opening pages of Don Byrne's *Messer Marco Polo*, and perhaps the lovers of the Florentine Renaissance think only of Florence when they hear that Prelude, which is as it should be, of

[133]

course, for craftsmen are craftsmen, no matter what their time and place.

Many influences, racial, climatic, geographical, or even the quality of wine, may have been the cause for what appear to be their differences (and they are suggested with no thought of disparagement), but the fact seems to be that the Renaissance artists looked down on both Romanesque and Gothic. One could aver that there was a Gothic trace in Giotto's campanile at Florence, and another could deny it, as Giotto would probably have done. St. Mark's is as Byzantine as well may be, but the Doge's Palace, begun four hundred years later, has a pretty strong Gothic flavor to the two lower stories, although it would not be surprising if someone stoutly denied it.

Has any period in history had such ardent lovers as the Italian Renaissance? Have its historians not vied with one another in fervor and often in idolatry? Its effect upon the student of buildings who happens to feel that what one says is the thing, and that saying nothing with elegant words is a poor way to build, doesn't incline him to either fervor or idolatry. The builders of that day were badly handicapped by "artists" who were not skilled builders. It was, after all, a day not of simple living but of great luxury, and it is not strange that the builders were caught up and carried off on the same stream of wealth that was lapping all the shores of Italy, at the moment. The record, as one looks at it, would appear to indicate that the church had acquired, in the princely and ducal art patrons, rich rivals who at the same time saw to it that the church got plenty of glory in its buildings.

Symonds gives great praise to Arnolfo del Cambio, for example, as one of the foremost of Italian architects. If I

[134]

dared to speak in such a presence, I would say that Arnolfo was a fair stylist, with a certain sense of relationship, yet who made a very bad guess in his plan for the Duomo. Even though he had lived to achieve the dome that Brunelleschi later added, he could hardly have retrieved the error in plan. He had been intoxicated with the idea of scale, as many before him and more since. The story of how Brunelleschi won the dome competition (even competing on equal terms with the carpenter who made his models) has been told to all readers. He had been studying goldsmithing, but buildings intrigued him, and the chance to enter the competition at Florence was a grand one. In the actual building, however, he was often dependent on the advice or opinion of the builders, precisely as most architects today could not direct the simplest building but must depend upon a skilled builder to tell them how to build what they have designed. Whether they would take to their bed, in order to get rid of a rival, as Brunelleschi took to his in order to get rid of Ghiberti, is another matter, but I happen to have known some pretty clever rival-extinguishers, as late as the twentieth century in America.

The Renaissance class distinctions, among builders as among others, were pushing aside the camaraderie of the earlier days. The artist-architect was coming and the builder-architect was going. The road was becoming clearly marked to the point where it was to split and diverge until at last the architect would be no builder and the builder no architect. Under the craft freedom of Gothic days, nothing more than a rude sketch or a spoken direction was necessary, as between master and craftsman. The time was now to come when no workman would be able to build without a drawing and some writing before him. Creative impulse was to be taken

[135]

over and mingled with the rules and formulas of the architect.

One could hardly say the Renaissance caused this sad separation, or that it never would have taken place had there been no Renaissance. Landlordism and usury were really at the bottom of it, would be my guess, while the steady rise to power of the money-price profit-making method of buying and selling was like a black death, so far as craftsmanship was concerned.

Thus it was that Brunelleschi, Alberti, Arnolfo, Lombardo, Palladio, Peruzzi, Bramante, the Sangallos, Michelangelo, Vignola and Bernini, the men who filled Florence, Padua, Mantua, Verona, Pisa, Venice and Rome with their work as artist-architects, were men who dissected the work of past builders. Not for reasons related to their own life, times or building needs that suited new ways, habits of living, and changed uses, but just as a paleontologist might arrange old bones in a search for some possible variety of animal that Nature had overlooked.

Worse was to happen. The quality of rightness that had set craftsmen to seeking ways to do things well and beautifully was now to become separated from the day's work. As men built and hammered, carved and wrought, the result was to be called "art." What had been so largely unconscious was to become conscious. The childish wonder that questioned only the right way was now to become all mixed up with rules that had nothing to do with inner rightness but with outward looks. It was the rape of craftsmanship by the new white-collar artists. One cannot call it anything else, and it had a profound pecuniary basis, for henceforth the men who had built things so well that they are still standing in this day and age, and so lovely that people from all lands

[136]

go in millions to look at them, were to be forced to divide their wages with the new men who worked with paper and ink, and who were to call their work "architecture."

Up to that time, it had needed no name. Up to that time, men had been building well and beautifully. But the invention of printing was beginning to displace the knowledge based upon the craftsman's inner communion with rightness, and sow in its place the new half-knowledge of those who did not intend to work with their hands, but to be paid for using their wits. The printed word was so astonishing that it has taken five hundred years to find that printing presses do not of necessity speak the truth. Neither do men, but craftsmen could not long deceive each other, even if they set out to, for what they said and did had to pass a test. But a world that began to learn to read began also to think more of words than of a craftsman's ways, and to transfer its respect to those who were so clever as to call buildings "architecture." Dear me, how wonderful! Think of it! We used to call it "the work," or the "cathedral," and it is really "architecture!" "All these years, I've been talking prose and never knew it," said Monsieur Jourdain.

This would not be to deny the charm of some of the things designed by the new artists, but merely to suggest that they added nothing to building knowledge or skill, and that while some of them had a dawning glimpse of what it meant to make a fine city, their sense of fineness was not concerned with something that would be fine all through and for everybody. They were interested in fineness that would satisfy princes and dukes, in whose graces they found themselves, even as they lived very well on the crumbs from their tables. They were never asked to bother their heads about such things as sunless alleys or damp slums. Italy was a land of

[137]

little empires. There were reasons why the lower stories of palaces were of solid masonry.

One can go much farther than this, if one starts peering and prying below the surface of Florentine luxury and patronage just as one can go farther, no matter where one pries and peers. The figures that strut the stage are seldom more than shadows of what goes on behind the scenes. Men are moved a good deal by they know not what, and wise is he who knows exactly why anything ever happened.

One thing seems true: The architect, in the Renaissance, may be said to have got his name in the cast. He was no longer the person who would have been called "master builder" or "master-of-the-work," or squeezed in under "the builders," as the program writers would have managed him a few centuries back. Whether he began to put on airs, or they were thrust upon him, would be quite impossible to say. He had arrived. He was known to those who knew what was going on and were always glad to pick up someone in the spot-light, on the chance that a few rays might fall on the patron as well. Craftsmen, one guesses, and history seems to affirm, didn't like the new building designer. He had ideas of style but he knew nothing about bones, muscles or nerves. It's one thing to make a picture of a building, and how the roof ought to sit, doors open, windows be arranged, and stairs planned so that one can climb them, but quite another thing to build it.

That was where the split came. Quite naturally, too, for men who knew about bones and nerves disliked to be asked to put a lion's paw on the leg of an antelope, precisely as Arnolfo, in the cathedral at Florence, had the idea of combining a vast space conceived in classical terms, within the fabric of a Gothic skeleton. The builders knew this was wrong, just as they knew the wrongness of any work to which they applied their simple tests of rightness, but the boss of the show was now an outsider, not an insider. As time went on, this process was to continue until true building craftsmanship passed out of existence, and in its place there grew up only bitter class warfare.

Dare one think of Michelangelo as having feet of clay? His architecture, at all events, is the stuff of a dilettante and not the wholesome nourishing fare of a craftsman builder. Whatever he was, sculptor, painter, or what not, he looked at building as a job in decoration. He wanted spots here, shadows there, high lights, accents, profiles somewhere else, and patterns arranged without regard to good building procedure or the purpose for which the building was to be used. His group of palaces at Rome made an imposing trio, balanced and harmonious, but one knows at once that Michelangelo was not designing them primarily for the use and convenience of the occupants. He was after an external effect based upon rules set forth by Vitruvius, and those who used his buildings could make the best of it. As for St. Peter's, which finally fell into his hands after four other architects had worked forty years on it, all this chronicler can say is that unhappily it became the example for many large and small imitations.

Medieval craftsmen, working simply to bring purpose into right relation with method of building, got their rhythms, accents and profiles where they belonged because that was where they belonged. It was as simple as that, but no artist of the Renaissance would have deigned to think of a building as a thing merely to be used. To make the lower stories of a palace fort-like, was as far as they got in that direction. Art was the thing, and so, to many, all Renaissance building has a rank smell of pedantry. Often very delicate, sometimes faintly fragrant, but hardly more than a boudoir with a demi-monde aroma. One can imagine a robust Romanesque builder, or even a more delicate but still lusty Gothic artisan, ill at ease in a Florentine palace where they took wine in virginal stemmed glasses rather than swigging it heartily from a leathern bottle.

That, roughly, was the difference. One lived for the sheer joy of the journey; the other played at living by stimulated sensation. Everything became "art," and even though a little poison was a good way of getting rid of a rival or a creditor, there had to be a touch of the theater in the deed. The silken life has that tendency, of course, or at least to avoid a good rough and tumble where the best man wins and the loser has the sense to know that he wasn't the best man, and bear no malice. Craftsmen have a natural respect for those who are really more skilled than themselves. Did the men of the Renaissance have that, one wonders? Vasari says that Brunelleschi "admitted that he (Ghiberti) was a better master in casting" than either himself or Donato, but Vasari excels in salves and ointments and, after reading many historians, one might still wonder.

As for "architecture"—the word was about to be established, in the sixteenth century—a withering palsy was henceforth to fall upon many builders and most buildings. The new word was to make vague and obscure what had heretofore been simple and plain. People had been using folkwords that meant what they said. Now, there were to be bastard words, coined from other tongues and with their own home meanings changed. The Greeks didn't talk about

[140]

architecture. An *architekton* was a master worker. In Italy, people had long spoken of a great building in process as *l'opera*—the work. In France, a *batiment* was a building, straight from the folkword *batir*, to build. In Germany, a building was a *gebaude,* from their plain folkword *bauen,* to build. No definitions were needed. Everyone knew what the words meant.

Henceforth, the word "architecture" was to indicate that the days of creative craftsmanship were numbered. That the creative skill with which craftsmen had met and overcome the obstacles that stood between them and the thing they wanted to do, in order to create afresh, was slowly to be embalmed in books and drawings, from which it would be copied by architects as servers of the "art conscious," who have never been better set forth than in Moliere's *Le Bourgeois Gentilhomme.* The Renaissance happened to be the moment when the change began. It would have come anyhow. Nothing could have stopped it. If one likes to think that an old Roman builder, by name Marcus Vitruvius Pollio, was the cause, it makes a good story, and unless one is interested in the real sequence of events that brought the word "architecture" into the language and moved the craftsmen "below the salt," Vitruvius serves as well as any other fiction.

He was, so far as one knows, a Roman builder. Having retired, somewhere in the early part of the Christian era— say, between the year 1 and 200—he sat down to put his notes and observations in order. He knew Roman building and had seen some Greek temples, and so far as building is concerned (his ten books contain a great variety of technical and archæological information) he saw it as something to be formulated. The right things had been found.

It was now necessary to explain them to all. Then there would be no further need to experiment or investigate. Building could be done by merely continuing.

Cataloguers and pigeon-holers had to come. The world could not be spared from them, for they are a part of the methods by which men live without working. To many, they are symptoms of race fatigue, of that wish to turn backwards rather than face the future that looks desperate and bewildering. Others would answer that the Renaissance architects, who looked upon Vitruvius (his ten books had been dug up after a long burial) as the last word in authority, were certainly not tired men. They were as active as a modern "live wire" and for their day might well have been known as hustlers. Nothing tired about them—and yet there was. There was fatigue in plenty, as there had been a thousand years before in Rome. Of what other period could Goldsmith's lines be a more faithful picture?

> "Ill fares the land, to hastening ills a prey,
> Where wealth accumulates and men decay."

There was a future for Florence to face, as always for all men, but where was the will to face it?

Vitruvius had traced the principles of purity in Greek building. He had no interest in that form of rightness that guides the true craftsman into the making of the thing for the purpose. Foreseeing nothing and guessing little, Vitruvius was a faithful recorder. His poor ability with words is a fair indication that he was more concerned with what he said than with how he said it, and one feels a bit ashamed at dragging the old gentleman into public gaze, in this manner, yet the fact remains that he had a greater influence on the art of building than any other one man. He might

[142]

well be called the Father of Building Humbug, and he was certainly one of the world's most expensive historians. The amount of waste and debt piled up by his disciples, as they sold architecture as a mess of antique pottage, would have paid all the national debts on earth. The mantle falls upon Vitruvius, however, merely because he happened to be the first pigeon-holer of his kind. They had to come. He fitted well into the empire theory, for just as the church had learned how to use the Inquisition and put Savonarola to the rack, so were the empire makers learning that an empire cannot be built if people are allowed to go about saying whatever they think, as Savonarola was to learn in that very Florence of the Rebirth! How far the part of the church was dictated, not by fiendishness but by having to compromise and make terms with all the big and little empire makers is another question. One compromise, like one lie, leads ever to another.

The works of Vitruvius, however, were deemed classics, right down to the time of the World's Fair in Chicago, in 1893. One can have no quarrel with the old gentleman. His name might have been Pontius Pilate or Nebuchadnezzar. He reflected what was going on. The classifying and dissecting of buildings had to begin somewhere. Up to the year 1900, a good five centuries after the Renaissance architects came upon the stage, their followers spoke reverently of "precedent," which denied the right to use any building form or pattern unless one could prove that it had already been used. In my own apprenticeship, to one of the kindliest men I have ever known, the word "precedent" was as sacred as I then thought the Litany or the Catechism. He would no sooner have thought of inventing, or of letting a form grow naturally out of a new arrangement, than he would have

[143]

thought it dishonest to take a present from a contractor. That's the way ideas become confused, when the craft feeling for rightness is overlaid with art-consciousness.

"Architecture," says Penty, in writing of the Renaissance, "from being something vital and organic in the nature of a growth, became a matter of external rules and proportions, applied more or less indifferently to any type of building, quite regardless either of internal convenience or structural necessity. When this point of development was reached, any co-operation among the crafts which had survived from the Middle Ages came to an end. Henceforth painting and sculpture became entirely separated from architecture and continued an independent existence in studios and galleries, while the minor crafts degenerated solely into matters of trade and commerce." This statement would be plainer if its writer, an architect, had used the word "building" instead of the word "architecture." It was the new type of building, arrived at by a reversal of the craft process, that was henceforth to be known as architecture, and the point is not without significance.

If one looked for examples of the long influence of Vitruvius and the Renaissance, in buildings of the present day, one may look no farther than the Public Library in New York City. This unworkmanlike perversion is due wholly to the point of view just related. Libraries are houses for books. Why, in planning a library, should one begin with a palace?

It is a pity to cite single examples, for they exist by the thousand, and tell one only that their designers were well versed in the Renaissance. So, to plan a library where heaps

[144]

of books were to be stored for daily use by hosts of readers, one sought the form of a library by going back to buildings built five hundred years before, when the first book had not been printed. The designers of all such buildings were showing off their Renaissance, wasting vast sums on grand staircases that no one climbs, and on vast corridors that lead to inadequate spaces. Strangely enough, the rear of the New York Public Library is a good straightforward façade that tells the story of books, simply and truly, while the front is a costly attempt at stage setting. As for the Library of Congress, the pity is even greater, for this dreadful medley of waste and maudlin virtuosity is accepted, by Americans on a visit to their national Capital, as a triumphant piece of architecture!

Among the group of Italians who paved the way for this nonsense and humbug, there was Palladio, who studied with ceaseless vigilance. He put some arcades on the medieval basilica at Vicenza that are really delightful. The purpose is served by a series of small arches, balanced with a nice amount of wall. This gives light and shade without such clumsiness as would have resulted from larger arches, or the monotonous messiness of twice as many little ones. This use of arch and column, with a window-like opening on either side, became known as Palladian. One may see examples of it, in America, all the way from Maine, if I remember right, to Charleston. Indeed, Palladio is still a factor in teaching the young, for not long ago, while visiting a well-known school of architecture, I found one class had just finished a problem that was stated about like this: "It is proposed to build a bridge across a canal in Venice, using the Palladian motive, and connecting a monastery with a church." It occurred to me, at the time, that one might have developed a

[145]

more interesting problem by having the bridge connect a monastery and a nunnery, but having blushed at the thought, I quickly forgot it. Probably the Renaissance architects would not have blushed, which would be something in their favor.

In Venice, life had a different gaiety from that of Florence. It was lighter and more playful. Windows were used as craftsmen would use them, to give light rather than to make spots in a design. Balconies overhung the water and gave great charm to the long frontages of palaces that Ruskin could draw as few others have done. As for Santa Maria del Salute, one remembers its pleasant mass, its incomparable site, and the glory of its image when the haze of the sea still partly enfolds it, or when, by starlight, its dark outlines add a great serenity to an aged city where memories abound and where the sounds of voices and footsteps—the only sounds once to be heard—made the spot blessed indeed.

As for the builders of Italy, they were still as helpless as all others had been. They could do no less than serve emperors, princes, priests and the new landlords who collected and spent huge sums. But in respect to the freedom of their craft they had, at the end of the sixteenth century, lost heavily rather than won, although they were not going down without a bitter struggle, as the history of Italian craft guilds and rebellions plainly tells. One has to remember these things even in roaming Florence or riding in gondolas in the canals of Venice, for these were veritable battle-grounds where the craftsmen were being slowly defeated by the rising tide of landlordism, usury and the money-price value that now began to govern all interchange of goods and sale of services.

What had the craftsmen learned? Very much, so far as

tools and ways were concerned, but largely in the manner of speeding up. They could build no better than their ancestors, so far as quality of work was concerned, but they took less time, and that was beginning to be a very great factor. Speed was not yet driving the whole world into the frenzy of four centuries later, but it had definitely become a factor. The honor of the craft was being assailed by the hunt for profits, which would have been all right if the profits had been evenly distributed. But they weren't. Indeed, new means of profits, through rent and interest, had entered the lists. Men wanted to be paid for not working, which only meant that the wages of those who worked would have to be less. There isn't any other way to pay people for not working, and while that too might be all right, if the people who were so paid would circulate their wages and keep the stream constantly flowing, that wasn't what happened. Such people preferred to invest their rents and interest in fresh debts that would pay them more and more for not working, and that led to difficulties indeed, as the question of debt now makes plain to everybody.

At first, these things brought not too great hardships, although as the standard of life rose for the non-workers, it declined for the workers. The craftsmen—and there were practically no other kind of workers—had plenty to do, while wealth was flowing freely, and for a long time the demand for their goods, at home and in foreign lands, kept them from sinking too deeply. But in order to contribute to the non-workers, it was necessary to do more work in a shorter time, and so labor-saving and skimping in quality were resorted to. That process was never to cease. The better the tools grew, the more machines were invented, the more of them there had to be. For a long time it was supposed that

[147]

machines would make it possible for everybody to have plenty, and that illusion led men on. It seems strange that so few noticed that buildings were beginning to grow poorer, and that the chance for everyone to have a decent house to live in—which doesn't appear to be an unfair benefit to ask of and for all workers and craftsmen—began to recede rather than to grow nearer.

"Since first the dominion of men was asserted over the ocean, three thrones of mark beyond all others have been set upon its sands: the thrones of Tyre, Venice and England. On the First of these great powers, only the memory remains; of the Second, the ruin; the Third, which inherits their greatness if it forget their example, may be led through prouder eminence to less pitied destruction."

There is the story, told by Ruskin, as over Venice he poured out his heart in chanting such praise as craftsmen have seldom known. He then spent the rest of his life in a futile effort to restore them to their domain of rightness, but he failed, as did Carlyle, his master, and Morris, his disciple. None of them could guess what had really happened. They all rebelled at the ugliness that was creeping in and the palsy that was overtaking the crafts they so loved, but they could not get to the bottom of the empire business and method, and the price that had to be paid. Ruskin, however, hung an affectionate wreath on the tomb of Venetian craftsmen, in language that is immortal.

For a moment, about this time, Moorish craftsmen were building in Spain. Were they the most skilled civilization builders that had yet appeared? One can hardly say, without discussing the meaning of words, but the fact seems true

[148]

that while the Moors were building Alhambra, Alcazar and Giralda—the last two having much influenced many a tower in America—they were also seeing their task as one of human concerns. In one costly fling, they built the mosque at Cordoba, but this great forest of columns clings closely to the ground and makes one feel that here was a feeling for man, the creature whose feet were set upon earth, no matter how high his spirit might soar.

The mosque, sadly altered by Christian changes, was barely more than an accent in a great social land program by which an arid land might yield the abundance that could come only with water. Beginning where Rome left off, the Moors had notions about civilization. Their era came to an end just as Columbus was peering ahead at what turned out to be the Bahamas. Moorish towns, held tightly within walls, made space precious. Narrow streets and alleys were all; but, even so, what is left of these towns has a craft flavor that few others have ever matched. Ronda, for example, still exhales the fragrance of a superb craftsmanship, and though now relapsed into pleasant contemplative apathy, it rose some centuries after the Moors, to build one of the most glorious bridges with which men have ever spanned a gorge. It is even one of the cleanest pieces of building rightness that can be found, though one search the earth over.

The Renaissance overflowed to other lands, in time. In France, it was modified according to the French builders' traditions, and was thus more vigorous than in Italy. Wealth again was flowing, this time from landlordism, in France, and the princes and nobles were calling for their chateaux. They were bigger, more ostentatious and more luxurious than had been the dwellings of princes and nobles before them. Fontainebleau arose, Versailles, the Luxembourg, the

[149]

Louvre was expanded in the new style, the Tuileries, Pantheon and many a minor church was built, and the dome put on the Invalides. St. Etienne du Mont and St. Eustache, two of the famous churches of Paris, were built in that day, yet seem also to mark the reluctance with which the Gothic was being overthrown by the artists who were no builders.

For this was the day of such as Mansard, made famous by the ugly roof that bears his name. He was one of the first mass-production architect-contractor-speculators that rose out of the crushing of the craftsmen. "The fifteenth century was, for the arts and for architecture in particular, an epoch of very marked decadence," says Maître Minvielle. "In the Middle Ages, when one began a building, it was the custom to treat directly with the different trades; among them there was a certain liberal collaboration and a tacit recognition of the master mason as playing the leading part and thus called the master of the work. In the fifteenth century a new spirit began to be manifest, quite as much among masters as among craftsmen. Up to this point the master of the work had been a veritable artist, in love with his work and laboring with conscience and a sense of dignity. The esquire or the chapter, about to build, chose him carefully because of his known ability and probity. Then, under his guidance, were called in the masters of the other crafts. Almost always, they were known by the master of the work. He had suggested them because of his confidence in them, and it was in an atmosphere of perfect harmony that the building arose.

"The master of the work was now changing. He was bothered about many things that had never before troubled him. Often, he now had to engage his own craftsmen and buy the materials, and these cares absorbed much of the time that he had formerly been able to give to the building. And alas,

[150]

the lure of lucre came to trouble him. To the modest honorariums to which he had been used, he now sought to add a bit in gratuities from those who sold materials. The masters of other crafts did the same. On the other hand, the esquire or chapter, also sought to save, and no longer chose a constructor merely because of his ability. They looked about for the one who made the lowest offer. In consequence, the different crafts grew less intimate, each being interested only in its own welfare and careless of what happened to the rest. The authority of the master of the work, hitherto freely acknowledged, disappeared. Each sought to do his work as quickly and as profitably as possible, with no care for the other craftsmen. That is why their work had no longer that grand character of unity the work of earlier days had shown. Each builder was interested in details, but not in the whole! Such are the reasons that seem most characteristic of the decadence of architecture towards the end of the Middle Ages.

"In the time of the Renaissance, the word 'architect' was currently used. When, for the first time? Certainly before the first half of the sixteenth century, and variously as *architecque, architecteur, maître d'architecture*. Its prior use had been denied, but the word was known before the beginning of the fifteenth century. (The oldest document in which the word is mentioned, according to Vacquier in a Bulletin of the Société Historique de Paris, is a letter from Jean Lemaire to Margaret of Austria, in 1510, concerning the church at Brou.) . . . The characteristic fact in the history of architecture, at this time, however, is the appearance of the true architect, wholly differing from the master of the work, because wholly independent of the (guilds) craft corporations.

"We have seen how the master of the work was only a workman who had risen above his fellows, yet still a member of his guild. Henceforth, a certain number of artists were to invade the field, quite outside the guilds to which they never belonged, never having studied except in theory and privately, and without having learned their art by practising a craft. These new artists, who took the name of architect, had their origin in functions wholly unrelated to those of the master of the work. He, born a worker, continuing to live with workers, even after his elevation, had never had to give more than summary instructions in order to build a *chef d' œuvre*. The architects of the Renaissance, on the contrary, were born bourgeois, and often with such an education and instruction as to permit them to bask in royal favor and in the esteem of the esquires. They were the lettered ones who knew the classic, who had read Vitruvius, and were themselves capable of writing treatises on architecture.

"As to the architect's functions, one has but to turn to the writing of Philbert de l'Orme, who was one of them. The architect, for him, was the grand director of the work, head of the workyard with absolute authority over all the crafts, and seeing that his plans were executed to his taste. He had nothing to do with accounts, could not receive the usual *pots-de-vin*, since their acceptance would asperse his probity, and could give no more than his opinion on prices. One must not believe, however, that such architects were to be found in any numbers. The care with which de l'Orme describes the ideal architect is the best proof that he was a rarity. Actually, many true architects did the whole job, speculating in materials and the labor they were charged to buy, as did masters of the work, contractors and even the city corporations.

"Whoever could hold a pencil called himself architect.

Everyone thought himself able to make a plan—priests, princes, esquires, the plain bourgeois artists of all sorts. Those who were too timorous to design for themselves hailed the first architect handy, as de l'Orme so laments. Not only were the plan-makers so chosen, but the builders as well. No wonder there were mistakes!

"This situation was due to the influence of Italy. There also the whole world wanted to be an architect and when the amateur Italian artists were summoned by the kings of France and began to arrive on French soil, they all called themselves architects, whether they were gardeners, mosaic-workers or locksmiths.

"The seventeenth century saw the continuation of these movements and the triumph of the profession of architecture. The word was definitely consecrated. One knew that architects were artists who had done the necessary studying and had a general knowledge of all the branches of art. Their functions began to be sharply defined. It was the time of absolute monarchy and France was about to embellish itself riotously. Kings, seeing the necessity for protecting the artists, attached them to the court. The queen, the princes and also the towns had their own architects and honored them with the greatest consideration. Celebrated families of architects arose—Mansard, Perrault, Blondel, Le Vau. Finally the art of architecture was officially consecrated by the creation, at the instigation of Colbert in 1671, of the Royal Academy of Architecture.

"One talks of the triumph of the profession of architecture, but what a fiction! If one takes one's eyes for a moment from the pleiades of great artists who revolved around the Court magnet and in the light of high personages, we shall see that the greatest confusion reigned in the building busi-

[153]

ness. First of all, the architects were in business, even those of the highest talent. . . . For example, it is certain that Salomon de Brosse, one of the most renowned artists of the day, was not only the architect of the Luxembourg but also the contractor. He grew so rich out of the operation that he was suspected of fraud, although there were no profits that held in law. His son, *'architecte ordinaire des bastimens du roi,'* was also a contractor, with his shops on the right bank of the Seine. We could also cite Mansard, the great Mansard, author of the dome of the Invalides, who altered Saint Germain and finished Versailles. His artistic ideas did not prevent him from buttering his fingers rather handsomely and from speculating in lands and buildings. He inherited some tendencies from his father, no doubt, an architect hardly less celebrated. Was it not he who had the idea of getting from the Chancellor, in 1651, the monopoly of the sale of all engravings published in the kingdom? It took a stern intervention on the part of the Academy of painting to get rid of this concession.

"The example of Mansard is the more striking because he was a member of the new Academy of Architecture. One will be less astonished, therefore, to learn that the Academy did not exclude contractors. It was really composed of two classes of architects. 'Those of the first could not be contractors; those of the second could contract only on the king's buildings.'

"One fact (in the eighteenth century) is worth noting, the almost complete use of the lump-sum bid. The owner, now grown suspicious and fearful of what the cost of his building might total, under such a situation as has been disclosed, adopted the lump-sum bid without hesitation, seduced by the thought that he would know exactly what his building would cost. If the lump-sum were exceeded, the contractor would have to pay. The contractor, on the other hand, was willing, because he hoped to make a profit through all sorts of economies and even, if he were not too honest, by fraud or substitution. He disliked the presence of the architect and used all his eloquence to persuade the owner of his uselessness. He merely added expense, said the contractor.

"Vainly, since the preceding century, and precisely for abolishing the abuses under the lump-sum contract, there were Royal Acts forbidding it, but nothing could head it off. Royal authority had to bow to business, and in 1782 the lump-sum contract was formally authorized. The real architect did not disappear, but he was rarely employed on private or on great monumental work. In Paris, he could pick up a practice, but not in the provinces."

This piece of history, from a lawyer who undertook the most patient research in order to learn why the architect in France had so anomalous a legal status, makes plain what was happening. It wasn't all Vitruvius; it was business. The craft idea could not stand against the price-bidding system that cared only for profit. Whittling and paring of materials and skimping of workmanship were the only answer, for landlordism and usury had to have their nippings.

The tale of the French builders cannot be kept within the limits of architects and contractors, nor of palaces and churches. In spite of landlordism and the coming ruin of exhausted tenants, the builders got free, here and there, to build the little manors and mansions that are strung from Calais to Provence. In Normandy, the tale was almost as pastoral as the one the English builders were telling across

[155]

the Channel, for here was a land of noble trees, water-fed with winding streams, full of contours. The builders were craftsmen, of the first water, and they had a knowledge of what belonged. That's a good word, be it remembered, for it comes not from the need for distinguishing property, but from the feeling for rhythm or fittingness, and so from the will to find and know rightness.

French towns were still walled, and streets and alleys still narrow. Many of them are still there, just as they were five centuries ago, and many of the houses of that day are still being lived in. I have climbed long flights of spiral stone stairs, in Montpellier, hanging on to a rope, to seek a *stoppeur*, in the house where Jean Jacques Rousseau once lived. I have walked miles in old towns where, as in the fifteenth-century house in Montpellier, all water had to be carried up the dark stairs, and where the sun made a patch of light for a few minutes, in some rarely favored room, when it shone. The builders also built those houses, thousands upon thousands of them, but no craftsman ever thought them to be right. In the walled towns, there was no escape, but although the walls are now gone, the builders are still no freer than they were then. Empire building makes queer history, when one studies it in terms of human beings.

In Germany, Spain and the Low Countries, the influence of Vitruvius made itself felt. There's the Rathhaus at Cologne, the Castle at Heidelberg and many a minor building in the lesser towns, although Nuremberg, Stuttgart, Leipzig have examples, while everyone knows the Zwinger at Dresden. But in Germany, as in all the other countries, from now on, it is the smaller houses in the towns and cities that display the charms of the building craftsmen. What an array of towns! Once they were filled with the savor of the day

[156]

when craftsmanship was in its glory, all the way from
Bordeaux to Amsterdam and Lübeck, from Bruges to Roth-
enburg, from Brunswick to the Eiffel, from Strasbourg to
Le Puy, from Perpignan to Ronda. One can almost feel that
these little towns and lesser cities were really the beginnings
of civilization, that some blight fell upon them and withered
the tree before it could get its roots into the soil. Here the
builders were beginning to settle down to the real work of
making a world, and here they were pounced upon and
slowly swept into the vortex of empire and battlefield, of
landlordism and usury, and of the rising tide of inequality
that had to be, so long as men could find no way to check
the lust of empire seekers. They, in their turn, grew more
and more skilled in gaining their ends under the mask of a
republic or a democracy, but they were the same aims that
moved all the others, from Memphis on.

Vitruvius, in Germany, Spain and to a limited extent
elsewhere, ran off into the Rococo or Baroque, which one
can see at its best in Bamberg and Naples. At its best? Well,
the Baroque was merely the result of setting craftsmen to
work on things that had no innate rightness. Whether it
began at Rome, or at Florence, does not matter. It was not
primarily a change that grew out of building. It came from
a series of pecuniary consequences, just as much as came
the modern slums, or the ancient ones. People have often
said, in my presence: "Yes, but think of how the people
lived in the Middle Ages! They may have been craftsmen,
but they certainly didn't know much about sanitation."
Well, it's all true, but one would like to ask the commenta-
tors to follow one through parts of Pittsburgh, Chicago or
New York, and see neither sanitation nor craftsmanship.
There is no reason why there can't be both. The builders

[157]

could be at it in no time, if given a chance. It's just the matter of deciding whether individuals are to be allowed to build their big and little empires, or whether we would like to have a civilization. One can't have both.

IX

BUILDING MANORIAL

ENGLAND

ONE cannot name two dates and say that Gothic began and ended with them, either in England or France. Running through the period of some three hundred years, there was a continual trying, testing, playing, daring with this new form. A new freedom had been born to craftsmen. Where they had before plodded steadily and stoutly, now they could leap and dance and frolic. This new building body was full of creative delights such as all previous craftsmen had been denied. They may have seen them in the distance, as they learned to center arch loads and thrusts, but not until the rib-vaulted roof were they to revel in the freedom of lightness.

That was the starting-point of Gothic, although the actual moment is neither known nor important. It came, as all other things came to men who loved tools and materials and rightness. The end of Gothic, sadly enough, was a gaudy sham, but that was not the fault of the craftsmen. Someone was trying to show off, and inasmuch as the church had long been using the builders to advertise itself, just as the Romans had used them for empire, and as it had found the glory of Gothic one of the best advertisements the builders had ever offered, a good guess would be that there was not only rivalry between bishops in England, as in France, but as between the church in both countries. Each sought power and income. The church, in both lands, was seeking an empire. Each was also tightly bound up in the national quest of empire, with which each had to keep in step. The church was never to get free of compromising with the schemes of men, once it had given in. Its power and income were dependent upon dancing to the tune that continually led it farther and farther into the maze of politics and finance. If that did not lead to the decline of the Gothic, what did?

Enormous sums were spent upon churches and cathedrals, in both countries, from the tenth century on, and these sums rose to fabulous heights after the builders got on the track of the rib-vaulted roof, say in the middle of the twelfth century. From then until the end of the sixteenth century in England, and perhaps some fifty years earlier in France, was the day of the great cathedrals that were to advertise and fix permanently in men's minds—what?

It is usual to classify Gothic and mark the various changes as the builders gained in skill, grew more daring, and then fell into sheer advertising stunts. As heights rose, windows grew higher and wider, carving more ornate. The tendency was towards height and away from simplicity, with a growing loss of feeling for the beauty of the live Gothic form and a desire to excel in embroidery. Between the days when the English builders were feeling their way out of the Norman (such as the small church at Iffley, and great parts of the early cathedrals of Durham, Norwich, Exeter, Ely, and many others) and the time of Henry VII's Chapel, at the end of the fifteenth century, English Gothic had passed through changes that may be classified roughly, if one is so disposed. One can even pick out spots where the changes are acutely visible, yet it is almost impossible to point to any single building and say that it is purely in any single class. If one delights in noting how the English builders played with their new-found freedom, and what they did with the rib-vault and the flying buttress, one can begin at Durham and end up at Henry VII's Chapel in London, or vice versa.

That last building is said to mark what is known as the Tudor style of English building (corresponding roughly to that known as François Premier in France). Here the pointed arch suddenly flattens down below the semi-circle, while the tendency is to treat the whole stone fabric as a field for ornament. Historians usually refer to this change as having been caused by the entrance into England (the same reason is assigned for the change from Gothic to François Premier in France) of the ideas of the new men in Italy. These artists, as we have noticed, were looking at buildings from a new point of view, from the outside in rather than from the inside out. They were not interested in how a building grew, but in beginning with the wall as a decoration and proceeding, from that point, just as a painter proceeds with a composition. It wasn't building at all. It was "art."

Tudor architecture was Gothic pushed to the extreme limit of florid embroidery. It was what was needed to express the stage of power to which the favored class was rising. The Chapel of Henry VII, in London, is a veritable *tour de force,* in which all semblance of straightforward building is gone. The whole is a gewgaw, a desperate flourish such as might have been imagined by a church that knew wherein it had not only failed to stay the greed and avarice of men, but had actually taken money for its silence. It wasn't a pretty record, as all people now know, but the effect upon craftsmen was as blighting, in so far as their effort was to be put to the building of a civilization, as well might be.

Other blighting factors were also at work. The rise of the manor in England had more and more sharply marked the ways of sharing wealth. Trade had begun, and the wealthy landlords and merchants in the cities, wanting to spread their wings gaudily, knew but one way: to follow the wealthy Italian princes and nobles who had been spreading theirs. Because of all this rising landlordism and trade, the British Empire was taking form, classes were sharpening, and the idea of advertising royalty and nobility by building showy palaces fell in very well with the ideas of both landlords and church. That institution had now to stand by as a staunch supporter of the whole empire idea as avowed in the palace and hovel plan upon which all empires have to rest.

In this, England was to commit no breach. Palace and hovel were rising side by side, for there was no way to get palaces save by putting the multitude in hovels. Up to the sixteenth century (and long after, for many) the English worker lived in huts made of turf, or of wattled branches or rushes daubed with clay. Histories of architecture usually ignore this part of the story, save to refer to the picturesqueness of the mud-walled thatch-roofed dwellings still to be seen. They are prone to touch this part of the building story but lightly, until the moment when a layer of bourgeois tradesmen or renters manage to get enough money to have a house that would at least have a faint flavor of the aristocracy that is architecture's. King and priest, however, were at the same old game in England. Their ways had not changed. The vast class of peasants and workers were slowly being dispossessed of land, although the manorial system still left them some common rights. In the end, they were to become payers of rent and nothing more.

"The proprietary and economic aspect of manorial organization is ruled by the main consideration that it is directed towards two distinct aims: It represents and formulates the interests of the villages and it acts as the machinery for the collection of duties and enforcement of services on behalf of the lord. In this way it is a standing combination between the township and the home farm or domain, and it would be wrong to lose sight either of one or of the other element of this combination. The manor does not exist for the exclusive use of the lord any more than it exists for the exclusive use of the tenantry; it has to reckon with both.

"The Domesday Survey, with its two lines of entries representing the state of things before and after the Conquest, not only enables us to notice the variations of social condition within the class of freemen to be replaced by a process of subjugation to lordship, but gives copious evidence as to the gradual stages of the process. There can be

[163]

no doubt about its general direction. The number of free-men steadily decreases, and their position gets worse. . . . The absorption of free holdings by manors is mostly achieved in one of two ways. Domesday is full of encroachments or invasions, weak freemen being reduced to subjugation by the strong hand of powerful neighbors. The formation of manors becomes from this point of view a kind of social integration—the swallowing up of small units, unfit for the political struggle, by more resisting and aggressive units." [1]

"The economic development of medieval rural life is to be accounted for by the formation in Old English society of a village community of shareholders which cultivated the land on the open-field system, and treated all other requisites of rural life as appendant to it. The evolution of individualistic husbandry and of political protection produced the growth of lordships which culminated after the Conquest in the arrangement of the manor, a complex institution partaking of the character of an estate and of a unit of local government. The influence of the Conquest and of the subsequent formation of common law was decisive in submitting society to a system of personal rights and relations; but underneath this system the ancient principles of communal action and communal responsibility were fully alive." [2]

If one views the decline of Gothic with the rise of the manorial system, one is likely to see more than is seen by those who look at architecture as a flower without roots or other nourishment than the ambrosia it sucks from art. If one then traces the decline of the manor, with its vestige of common rights, into landlordism, one may be able to see

[1] *English Society in the Eleventh Century.* Sir Paul Vinogradoff.
[2] *The Growth of the Manor.* Sir Paul Vinogradoff.

still further, and so come to have a real grasp of the relation of buildings to society as a whole.

If one then looks at Gothic with no fear of facing the tale as a whole, one finds it pretty hard to make out a case for a glorious day of religious faith. Faith in what? Faith in the gains of the manorial system, and faith that one day there would be nothing but landlordism and comfortable living, for owners, from rents? It was a day of great advertising by the church. The part played by the craftsmen was sublime. They denied nothing in their quest of building rightness. The Sermon on the Mount, however, was now completely denied by the church. How could it be reconciled to the plain truth that the many would have to live in wattled huts, while lord and priest robbed them at every turn? If taxes to build palaces and tithes to build churches were not robbery, what were they?

About 1600, when the Renaissance had spent itself on the Continent and the little empires were being swallowed by the bigger ones, England's industrial era was still slumbering in the tea-kettle that was one day to whisper its secret to Watt. Landlordism and usury were well in the saddle, and England's kings and ministers, reflecting the general feelings of the growing nobility and landed aristocracy, had already sensed the fact that sea power was the only key to an empire on which the sun would never set. In grasping landlordism as a tool of empire, England was far to surpass the Roman scheme of tribute. It was one hundred and fifty years later that Sir John Dalrymple wrote, in his Memoirs, what had long been true: "To all nations their empire will

[165]

be dreadful, because their ships will sail wherever billows roll or sails can waft them."

Spain was forcing England's hand, no doubt. Her galleons brought back treasure from America with which to keep up the running quarrel, but the landlords of England knew a thing or two, and they had power. So English builders were set upon another quest, more alluring than that which led to Canterbury and York, and which one day led to the building of America. That quest was a ship! Perhaps it was the most honest quest, so far as form and skill played a part, on which builders ever were set. A ship had to be alive as no building ever was. Resist? Yes, but it had also to yield and be swift in courting winds, as it had defiantly to dare the thwarting ones. Were craftsmen ever happier in their work than in the building of the ships of those days? The end of their labor, alas, was to be an empire and not a civilization founded on peace and justice; and the men who sailed their handiwork were for years to be the victims of such horrors of food and slavery as to make one of the ghastliest pages in the story of empires. But for the craftsmen, there was the delight of playing with oak and deal, keel and rib, spar and yard, prow and strake, and with such curves and contours as the makers of buildings were never to know.

Who made the ships that would round the grim forbidding Horn? Who so beautifully mastered the secrets of form as the men who built, rigged and trimmed the stolid merchantmen that went from the ports of England to everywhere a ship could go? Who made possible the birdlike flight of the clippers? Even a history of architecture cannot forget these men!

Four things have come from the builders, three so perfect, and yet so dimmed by the fourth and more loudly shouted. Of all that men have built, however, what has been so rhythmic, so straightforward, so cleanly in tune with the flow of earth and life as bridges, canals and ships? Buildings that fittingly match these handiworks are far and few!

Elizabeth, one day, was called "Restorer of the Navy and Sovereign of the Northern Seas," but it was not until half a century later that the *Sovereign of the Seas* was launched and christened. The name was full of meaning. It meant the flinging of the challenge, publicly, at last. Henceforth, English builders were to know no respite in their pursuit of the sun. The monasteries had been broken up. The last of the common land was slowly slipping into private hands. In trade, England had been reaching out rather than drawing in. Her people were insular, too, and slow to change a way or a method, but they had a dogged will and they meant to make an empire that would pay—some of them.

Craftsmen, however, were still having a fairly good time. They were not much given to travel, and took their pleasure in writing one of the loveliest building records that ever was. They looked gruffly at the foreigners who strayed over from the Continent, or who were hired to come across as the rising princes, nobles, esquires and gentlemen got to wanting some novelty in their dwellings. All in all, English landlords and traders were growing rich, and it was very likely that fact that finally brought the ten books of Vitruvius across the Channel, some two centuries after they had been exhumed, to become the building style-book of the Italians.

English builders, as a result, were so to alter their Gothic, that in spite of the manner by which the cataloguers have marked the various stages, one is hard put to find much more than some pedantic divisions, useful to teachers. French,

[167]

Italian and Dutch workmen had been offering their labor in England, and angering the English workers to protests and even riots. Books about buildings had begun to appear and to be read by the rising bourgeois tradesmen, and even by the nobles and esquires. It is a good guess that it was the rise of the kind of wealth that believes in showing off, and in advertising the virtues of its possessors, that finally obliged English builders to pass from Tudor to what is called Elizabethan. The Renaissance artists were pushing and crowding them, and fussing up all their hard-won knowledge of how to make a building grow out of a natural way of doing and arranging things.

But they managed to keep a good English flavor to the Elizabethan halls and palaces. They gave a great romantic charm to the oak-panelled Great Hall where hung the family portraits, trophies and heirlooms, with the minstrel's gallery above and facing the big mullioned bow windows. There was flavor, too, in the second-story Long Gallery, with its "upholstered depths of velvets and damasks, like ripe fruits, heavily fringed and tasselled; the fairy-tale background of the tapestry, and the reflections of the cloudy mirrors." The gallery connected, upstairs, the two wings of the mansion, and was reached by a lusty oaken staircase, heavily railed and balustered. With its sturdy carved newel posts it rounded out the savor of spacious hospitality that great lords and esquires could dispense so lavishly.

Every visitor to London remembers Staple Inn, which is of the period, just as everyone who goes to Oxford can hardly forget the Court of St. John's, the Library at Merton, or the Quadrangle at Clare. At Haddon Hall, Tudor and Elizabethan come together, the cataloguers say, as they also refer one to Burghley House, Wollaton Hall, Charlecote

[168]

(the scene of that memorable frolic of Shakespeare so well narrated by Douglas Jerrold), Montacute House, Knole, Penshurst, Longleat and Kingston House. Charming places to visit, with the savor and flavor of something that sets one to musing and wondering, indeed.

But the artists were pushing, and the architect was getting his foot over the threshold. The ten books of Vitruvius had a mighty salesmanship value. France and Italy were getting reputations for smartness, and although the stubborn English builders resented these continual attacks on their craft traditions and its ideas of rightness, they had to give way. They wanted to build straightforwardly, and while they were keen about looks, as all their work testifies, they wanted looks to grow naturally out of use and materials. But the Jacobean had to come. The forms of ancient builders were to be demanded as an avowal of the rise of culture. Men with money had now to appear cultured. It wasn't so important to be so, but one must look so, and builders were believed to have a great deal to do with the front that a man exposed to the world. Wealth from trade was pouring in. The profits from voyaging, based upon buying for a penny and selling for a shilling, gave a great fillip to architecture. If one cares to trace the result, as shown in what is known as the Jacobean style, there is Holland House in London, and Audley End in Suffolk, said to have been based on a model brought from Italy at a cost of some five hundred pounds.

Still, these borrowed plumes had not yielded the full cachet of Italy, nor yet of France. News of Florence was coming, now, by report and in books, for travel was growing easier. The day of the grand tour for young noblemen had hardly arrived, but business was increasing the number of visitors, to and fro. Why couldn't England be done with

[169]

these old-fashioned styles? After all, they'd been used now for some time, and there was no longer great distinction in an Elizabethan Hall or Jacobean ceilings. With a new palace or mansion, in a new style, one could offer something novel and gain not only prestige and publicity, but the obeisance that good master empire makers know so well how to foster and use; and so, after having struggled as gamely as any builders ever did, in an effort to hold on to their craft traditions of what belonged and what didn't, the English builders were driven to think seriously about something that didn't belong, and never would belong: the elegant palaces of Florence and the imposing French chateaux.

Inigo Jones, with a feeling for buildings, went to Vicenza to study under Palladio, whom he greatly admired. He returned to London in 1604 and went back to Italy in 1612. He ought, for his own sake, to have stayed at home, for so might he have built a good deal more of the great Royal Palace he designed and which was to outshine all others, with its roof a hundred feet above the pavement of Whitehall and the rooms thirty feet high. He had the true Vitruvian sense of empire, but the palace was not to be. The great Banqueting House was built, and still stands, and every visitor to London remembers its aged and mellow façade, with a faint flavor of Vicenza and Palladio. Jones built many other less ambitious country houses and town buildings, but the star of his fame was dimmed by the squabbles of kings and parliaments, and the tightening of purse-strings that led to the Commonwealth.

Christopher Wren, mathematician and professor of astronomy at Oxford, was to inherit the halo that might have fallen on Jones. It fell on Wren, however, and there has rested for going on three centuries. Rightly? That depends on whom one asks.

One owns up at once to the fine romantic flavor of Wren's London churches, of which he built more than fifty. They have a real atmosphere, with their tapering spires, and make pleasant buildings to live with. One used to feel, before London began to hide them amongst the clutter of growth, that they must at one time have seemed like the forerunners of civilization rather than empire, which never could have been said of St. Paul's cathedral, a greatly overestimated piece of inferior engineering, decked out with a meaningless jumble of gewgaws.

"In the exterior design," says Waterhouse, "we see two stories of the Corinthian order, but the upper story is a sham, for it is merely a screen with nothing behind it. A deceit such as this detracts from the architectural merit of the design, though it adds a dignity which would otherwise be lacking in the composition." The dome, one admits, sounds the usual trumpet note of empire, but: "The inner cupola is carried up in brickwork almost in the form of a hemisphere, with an opening twenty feet wide at the top. The dome, as we see it from the outside, is constructed on a much more imposing scale, in woodwork covered with lead; a brick core, built up between these two, carries the heavy stone lantern. Thus the 'dome', which forms so conspicuous a feature is, in reality, merely a sham." [1]

Wren was a genius such as the Romans would have exalted. He was not creative, but had a knack at combining such forms as the craftsmen had fashioned out of their centuries spent in searching for rightness. These he put to-

[1] *The Story of Architecture.* By P. Leslie Waterhouse.

gether in ways that were novel and that perfectly fitted the temper of that moment when the Renaissance was getting its feet firmly planted on English soil. The empire tradition was ready to be advertised, and Wren was a great help. Craftsmanship was being twisted into formalism. "Houses were built to be looked at, not to be lived in." Still, to get the savor of Wren at his best, one must go to Hampton Court or to the old Orangery at Kensington. There one finds brickwork worthy of the best that craftsmen ever laid.

In the histories of architecture, Wren has been likened to a saint, and in order to exalt and keep him in such a niche, his buildings have been cited as great works. It is not unlikely that the real reason for the saintship is that Wren was the first shining English example of the rise of the architect to dominance. Wren had a large and profitable practice before he got through, and there can be no doubt that he fitted well into the new theory of both building and design that had swept the designer in and the craftsman out. As an apostle of the new profession of architecture, Wren might well be classed about as McKim would be in his similarly brilliant rise some two centuries later.

Some of the craftsmen of Wren's day could cheerfully have murdered him, no doubt, for he was not above letting his contempt for them be known. In a letter to the Master of Trinity College, Cambridge, Wren wrote, for example:

"I suppose you have good masons; however, I would willingly take further pains to give all the mouldings in great (full size) ; we are scrupulous in small matters; and you must pardon us; architects are as great pedants as critics or heralds. Let the mason take his measures and transmit the drawings to me again, and I shall copy out parts of them at large more proper for the use of workmen, and give you a careful estimate of the changes, and return you again the original designs, for in the hands of workmen they will soon be defaced."

Nothing could more plainly reveal the state into which the craftsmen were being pushed. The quiet murmurs were growing into the feeling that there was brewing a conflict, as between the crafts and the new designing-architects. If one has the faintest appreciation of what it means to be a craftsman—to handle tools and materials with a freedom that seeks only how to find the right answer to the problem—one can understand how the craftsmen of that day were beginning to feel. Slowly rising above them, in both a pecuniary and a commanding sense, were men who had never been builders, and who took a patronizing attitude towards their craft. To the masons, especially, it was an insult impossible to forgive. A man who had learned the theory of the historic styles was challenging the competence of those who belonged to a craft that went back five thousand years and embraced all the fine masonry that had been built!

What turned out to be a retribution for Wren, so far as the craftsmen were concerned, was discovered many years later, when it came to be seen that a good deal of St. Paul's was not very well built. There was of course a shortage of money, in the first place, and Wren's ambitions exceeded the supply. He was no laggard in watching, as his letter to the Master of Trinity suggests, but he was not a trained builder who could both feel as well as see when work was being rightly done.

At all events, it turned out that there was some pretty shoddy work in the rubble piers that were to carry the dome. We cannot possibly believe that this was due to any other cause than to Wren's ambition to do more than could be paid for. On the other hand, neither can we refuse to believe that the craftsmen may have been a little less careful than was their wont under the new regime. They saw everything being taken away from them by a rising profession, the members of which had never done a stroke of building, and who were merely appropriating their skill and knowledge in order to sell it at a far greater profit than they had ever been able to get.

The arrival of the ten books of Vitruvius, backed by Jones and Wren, did not convert the English builders by any means. They had, nevertheless, to serve those who had the money to pay, and the rising wealth of England led to plenty of demand for sumptuous official buildings, such as Somerset House in London, as well as for luxurious country houses, halls, palaces and the minor houses of the esquires and lords of the manor. In these last, no builders ever wrote a fairer record, in the rhythmic blending of man and the land, than that which rose in one of the loveliest of earth's pastoral areas. Traditionally, that record has a place in the affections, not only of the English but of all who have that blood in their veins, no matter how far the land in which they dwell. Nor has any tradition so greatly borne upon what the builders did, for many a long year, in the United States.

All England was to be sprinkled with the work of the builders, as they used stone so simply and truly in the Cotswolds, or brick wherever clay was handy, or half-timber, where the wooden frame was filled in with a kind of rubble and then whitewashed. Except for the palaces, halls and great manors, much of this was more picturesque than comfortably habitable. There was wealth enough, as time went on, to have given everyone in England a good comfortable house,

[174]

but that wealth went not only into the England of the Ding-ley Dells and Bleak Houses, but of Coketown and the Marshalsea. It was the usual empire route of palace and hovel. Yet so well did craftsmen fulfil their part that no one can forget the England of the end of the nineteenth century, when many a hovel had a charm as it nestled close, seeming to belong to the earth that gave life and to be rooted in her ways of seed-time and harvest. Who can ever forget their long journeys afoot or awheel, over winding roads between hedgerows, with an endless array of spires, towers, chimneys, gables, roofs and gardens? To classify this record has been the object of many a building cataloguer. The tale is better left as a record of a people who were betrayed by empire builders, but whose first love was the land, and who thus had a sense of the rhythm of its hills and vales and contours, of its woods and glades and leas, of what belonged and what didn't, of the set of a chimney, the hang of an eave, the peace of a lane, the wind of a path, the delight of a garden. They built of materials that were at hand, varying form and pattern now and then, but clinging close to simple things and the way of life in their corner. One can scarcely think of a finer tradition than this, or of a sadder blight than when it went helpless down the yawning maw of landlordism and usury. Here were the beginnings of a civilization. Here was the knowledge of that earth kinship that men destroyed so carelessly, in order to make an empire.

Naturally there rose great palaces, halls and manors, at which one now looks in studying architecture. The land system compelled them, even as empire makers used the law of primogeniture and entail to keep landlordism forever fixed on the backs of those who had to pay someone for doing no more than owning. These palaces, halls and manors became celebrated, in and out of literature, and were much sought after as a hall-mark of social position, until debt and taxes made land-owning less profitable than business and usury.

Not so many years ago I walked in the rooms of one of the proudest of the old palaces. Built from royalties paid for mining coal in the very land on which the palace stood, the galleries underneath were falling in, walls were cracking and settling, and it was to be broken up and sold. It was nothing great as a piece of building, but in thinking of the miners who had sweated out the millions to pay for it and its luxuries, one could hardly call it a very intelligent use of craftsmen, either in making a building or delving in a coal mine—especially if one happened to be wondering just how a civilization might some day be built.

The long march of the builders wound its way from one empire to another, from one land to another. One can fancy the talk, as men set themselves the task of finding a way to surmount and do better. Over five thousand years one can observe the changing forms and the growth of skill, but even finer was the unflagging responses to the everlasting challenge.

One can, if one has a flair for imagining, make a mental picture of the day when the first chimney was built. One can call up the people that came to see smoke going out the new-fangled flue. No doubt the old folks had never believed it would work, and yet there was the smoke going out of it. Fancy, again, the scene of fifty years later, when some mason was probably saying to his son: "Aye, lad, I've another chimney to do at the squire's. People do like 'em, I can tell ye. The day's a-coming when no one will believe what I can mind so well. No, indeed, there wont be a soul who'll believe that the smoke used to go out through a hole in the roof! Aye, it did, for the fire was made on a great stone that sat in the middle of the room. We all sat in a great group around it, when I was a boy, and that's why we still talk about sitting 'around the hearth', though now we only sit in front of the fireplace. It isn't so homely, I'm thinking, for the old group in a circle had plenty of room. It was more neighborly, too, and there wasn't a draft on the back.

"The chimney is better, though, in lots of ways. The smoke doesn't come in the room any more. My, I mind well how my eyes used to smart and fill with water, as a boy, when the wind blew the smoke all back in the room, some days. But I've seen chimneys where it still does it, though. There's some trick to building a chimney so that the smoke will always go out. If I were a young man, I tell you, my lad, I'd be learning that very trick, I would. The day's a-coming when a chimney builder will have to know his job, he will, and if he does, there'll be a-plenty of work for him."

The Romans called their hearthplace the "focus," which is why we still use the word—in the sense of drawing things towards a center—of "focussing" attention. As has so often happened, the word that meant the place fell to being used to tell what went on at the place. At the "focus" people got their news and there met for talking over the world and its ways and what was best to do. One is often doubtful as to whether the news that travelled slowly in the days of the hearth was not more accurate and more useful than that which now speeds to the ends of the earth in a few seconds. So does one also wonder whether there has ever been so good a meeting-place as that around the central fire on the floor,

[177]

in the days when the smoke went out through the hole in the roof. It may be significant that men have now invented the word "smoke-screen."

One day a man invented a stove, and then another followed with a radiator. Around the stove one could sit and talk, even though one missed the sparks and the glow of the open wood fire. There was a glimpse of flame when the door was opened, and the light of it could be seen in joint or crack. When the radiator came, fire disappeared from human companionship. When something comes, something always goes!

Again, imagine how craftsmen stared when came the first pane of glass. Not first in England, to be sure, for other craftsmen had long used windows, but never with quite the delightful feeling for them that the English craftsmen acquired. Rome had certainly known glazed windows early in the Christian era, and their use spread slowly in the centuries that followed. When the first pane arrived in England, it was very likely a cloudy green in color, was probably at least a quarter of an inch thick and some ten or twelve inches square. It wasn't cheap, by any means, and although there is no record of when the first pane crossed the Channel, it is known that one Benedict Biscop sent to France for glass for the windows in Wearmouth church, late in the seventh century. The word window was about to have a new meaning. Heretofore it had meant a "wind's eye," and described the small hole bored in the wooden shutters that closed openings against wind and rain, and out of which one might peer at strangers.

But then, having the panes of glass, what to do with them? French glass masters came, says Bede, "and not only did the work needed of them but taught the Angles how to do it."

[178]

From that point, imagine the long effort that made glass not only thin and clear, but of all the shades and hues that now light the great windows at Chartres! It was the Gothic builders, as has been noted, who wanted big windows and who gave a great push to glass making and the work of the glasswrights, as they were at one time known. The problem was not alone to find the right sand, but to get enough fuel. Great forests were cut down by glass makers. Parts of Lorraine, for example, were denuded, and, even in England, the use of wood for firing glass pots had to be forbidden.

Slowly and surely, the window came under control. The glaziers learned to set the panes in lead, to devise the sash (from the French *chassis*, now known by all who drive a motor car), to fill it with delicate muntins, and finally to make it raisable for letting in air, and ever to study its proportions in relation to the wall into which the frame of glass was to be set. The panes made a lovely pattern and gave the hole in the wall a new meaning as part of the wall pattern itself. Perhaps no single thing had a greater effect on external design than the window. English craftsmen, especially, grew to have a wonderful sense of window arrangement, even though they too suffered, in their studies, from the tax-collectors who had their eye on windows as a source of revenue. In England, the tax bore a little easier than in France, where a house owner thought long and steadily before he ordered more than one window for a room, and that not too large, since the tax was levied at so much per square foot. One can hardly think of a stupider tax than one that forced people to shut out sun and air, but tax-collectors have always been just a little stupider than tax-payers. At all events, whether a difference in method of taxing windows in England will explain why the English craftsmen got to

[179]

making mullions, oriels and fanlights, for example, the fact remains that they gave a charming quality to windows. There is still something about throwing open a casement in England that isn't quite the same thing elsewhere!

The multitude, in England, living in huts, was lucky to get as much as wooden shutters. Even the well-to-do were not too well off for glass, for many a long day, for it wasn't even made in England for nearly a thousand years after Rome had it. So scarce it was, in early days, that when English gentlemen went travelling they were known to carry their glass windows with them, just as the boats from Dover to Calais once carried private bathtubs as luggage.

There came a day when English craftsmen saw that they must have brick, and as no sun offered it to them as in Egypt, they learned to shape it and bake it in wood fires. There was plenty of clay all the way from East Anglia to Hampshire. It was gathered in autumn, the kilns were made in the winter and fired in the spring. Both the craft of making and laying bricks probably came to England through the Low Countries where brick was a chief material, but the great fire in London put English brick-craft stoutly on its feet. One saw that it wasn't safe to have a great city of wooden houses.

Craftsmen had been playing with brick for many a long day, by that time. In Italy there had been a delightful tradition of brickwork, in Holland another, and in France and Germany still others. There were so many things one could do with brick, so many little tricks of giving texture and pattern to a wall. It made all the difference which way bricks were laid, not only as to looks but as to strength. Thickness of wall varied with height, and walls more than one brick wide had to have their vertical surfaces tied together. In Italy there was one way, in Holland another, and in England

[180]

still one more, where there was also a pleasant pastoral quality to the greater part of the brickwork. The Continent had grown up in walled towns. England had been freer to build in the open country. On the Continent one therefore got fine façades, but in England more all-round four-sided buildings, where walls, chimneys, gables, cornices and roofs were worked out as a merging of form, pattern and texture into a whole.

On the walls of many an old brick building in England, one may still see the work of the plumber. He played with the very material whence came his name, for the man we now call plumber should be named the "iron piper." He knows nothing of the leadwork that went into old buildings in the days of the craftsmen plumbers who harked back at least to Roman days. They knew about it, as did the mineral-hunting Phoenicians. Voyaging to England in search of lead they may even have carried the knowledge of it. One can never know how news travelled in those days or how a craft-way spread from land to land, but in England, lead has a most pleasant building tradition connected with roofs, gutters and downspouts.

The ornamental boxes, many shaped, joining gutter and downspout, were no doubt a relic from the gargoyle, but they made agreeable additions, none the less, and carried water away from the building to a cistern or reservoir rather than pouring it in a splashing stream (as gargoyles still do, in many places) that damaged walls and cellars. Lead was then cast in sheets, fairly thick. The forms had a bed of damp sand, in which one could trace patterns of one's fancy or names and dates connected with the building, and these then appeared in relief on the cast sheets. The sheets could also be rolled into pipes that were soldered together to take

[181]

water in and out of houses, as well as away from roofs. There were all sorts of things to be done with lead, for it was ductile and easily shaped to fit odd jointings of wood with stone where one wanted to keep out the wet.

Yet care must be taken also to let out the wet! Many a lead-covered spire was lost because of the moisture. Drawn by the sun from the wood underneath, it stayed there and rotted the timbers, so the plumbers found they must not only learn how to keep out the wet but also how to let it out. As with all other crafts, rightness had to be won by trying. Workers on the Continent knew a deal about leadwork long before the English, and did it very well, but the English craftsman liked to find things out for himself and to get at the way of use that was right for his way of building in his climate. He was never cordial to his fellow-workers across the Channel, as has been already observed, which may have been a natural craft fear for his livelihood, or, after the sixteenth century, a well-defined fear of the new-fangled architect who went to France and Italy in order to get ideas that he brought back and too often was able to force on the workers. They didn't like them, for they felt them to be un-craftlike, as they generally were. But it was these English craftsmen, by their stubborn resistance to the men who built on paper, that prepared the advance guard of the little army that would later set out to write a chapter in building such as had never been written before. The time was nearer than they thought!

What of the carpenter? The history of building, for fifty centuries, gave him the minor rôle. When wooden houses were first built, no one knows. No very old ones have survived, as centuries go. History records their use at Byzantium, early in the Christian era, and no doubt they were very

[182]

much used in all lands where timber was plentiful. The
carpenter, however, comes down through known history, up
to the Gothic period, as a builder of roofs, very largely. His
the task of making the frame that would carry the covering,
whatever it might be. At just what moment he began the series

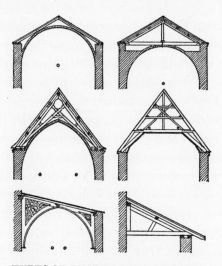

TYPES OF TIMBER ROOF FRAMING

of roof-frames that finally led to the trussed roof that supported itself and looked after its own thrust, no one knows.

Tie-beams were used as far back as the Romanesque. They
were bedded in the walls and helped to give stability under
roof pressure and thrust. From that simple beginning there
were developed all the forms that followed: kingpost, queen-
post, cross-brace, collar-brace and the hammer-beam, both
single and double. This last one became common in England,
in churches and halls, for it did away with the row of flat
tie-beams. These shut out the fine sweep of space as one
looked down the church nave, or the great hall, such as in

[183]

Westminster. Where there were rose-windows in the apse, or high ones in the end of a great room, tie-beams quite ruined the view. The hammer-beam not only gave the look of height to the roof, but offered a great chance for the flourishes of the wood-carver, who often gave far too much rein to his fancy.

When the half-timber house came to be used, the carpenter had a chance to let his work be seen on the outside of a building. His fancy could have a fling, as he played with patterns of timbers and bracings and gave an air of gaiety to the romantic contrast of white plaster and dark timbers. These he could hew to give them a pleasant unevenness of surface, and then tie them together so deftly that one would never guess the neat tricks of mortise and tenon, as he built up the pattern that grew so cleanly out of the knowledge of stoutness and the feeling for grace. This was no purely English craft, as is known to anyone who has travelled in Normandy or Lorraine or Germany, for many races of craftsmen saw that the half-timber house was a good way to build well and quickly. It was sparing of timber, and the plaster was easy to make and apply. The timbers would rot out, in time, but they were good for some centuries, and that no doubt seemed long enough.

When the day came for panelled walls and wainscoting, for balustrades and galleries, the carpenter had his chance again, but this time he was called a joiner. That was a good name, for the chief labor in such work was the making of joints. Roof-frames were joined, it is true, but when it came to putting an oak panelling on a great hall, the joining was quite another matter. Unless one has tried to do such work, one can have but little idea of what it means to make a joint —not a good one nor a fair one, but a joint! The prince of all building joiners was he who worked on a ship where nothing was square. Then it was joining indeed! So it was with the cabinet-maker, who followed the joiner, but he belongs in the tale of furniture rather than in that of building.

Among all the tales of carpenters, perhaps none is more interesting than such a one as some father might have been telling his son, sometime in the fifteenth century in England. The father's name would be Herland. He was a carpenter, descended from a long line of carpenters, and he would be turning over some of his tools to his son, who was also to be a carpenter. The tools had belonged to Herland's father, and had been made to serve for generations. His tale would be more or less as follows:

"There's a chisel I had from my father and he had it from his. Some day, maybe, you'll be handing it to your son. Keep it whetted and away from stone and iron. There's no harm can come to a chisel that's kept at cutting wood, as your grandfather once told me. He was a grand carpenter, was old Hugh Herland. Them as could match him are getting scarce, I can tell you. Did you know he worked for King Richard? He was on the King's own rolls and worked on the Tower of London. The King thought so highly of him that when he was through with the job he gave him a pension of ten marks a year for as long as he lived.

"Do you think old Hugh Herland would stop working just because he had a pension? What would he do with himself? No, indeed, he got another job and went over to Brittany and taught those people how to do some of the things they'd never seen before. Oh, and have I ever told you that he had the right, every winter, to ask for a winter robe out of the suite of the Esquires of the Household, and they had to give it to him. That was because he was such a Master

[185]

Carpenter! And when he came back from Brittany he went down to Winchester Castle, where they had a job for him, doing some repairs that they wanted just right.

"But the best job he ever had was at London. Do you remember the great hall at Westminster? Did your uncle explain to you, when he took you there, about the hammer-beam roof? Well, it was your grandfather, old Hugh Herland, that built that roof and there isn't a finer hammer-beam in England. It was the King that would have him to do the job, and he had a place made for him so that he could live right in the palace yard, and another place where he could keep his tools and models. There wasn't an Officer of the Household, nor any Officer of the King could put your grandfather out of that yard. He finished the job in 1397, and before it was done the King made him an Esquire, and King's Chief Carpenter, and gave him a new grant of money for as long as he lived. A good sum it was, I can tell you—almost twenty pounds a year.

"Did your grandfather stop working? Not a bit of it. The next year he was down at Great Yarmouth, working on a dock or a pier, and he kept working in the King's service until he died. He loved a tool as though it were his nearest and dearest kin and there was never a carpenter who knew what he did about a piece of wood, once he had set eyes on it. You might have thought he had once been a young sapling himself and was turned into a man, such a feeling he had for wood. I tell you it went hard with a man, if he was about, who mauled or mishandled a timber. He'd be like to cry, as though someone were hurting a fellow creature. Never mind what tool he was using, you'd 'a' thought he was a-making love with it!"

The language is my own, but the story of Hugh Herland is

[186]

a matter of record in the archives of England. Plainly, and with all due allowances for the palace and hovel way of life, it was something to be a craftsman. One wrestled with jobs, seeking to do them well, and basing one's effort on an inner

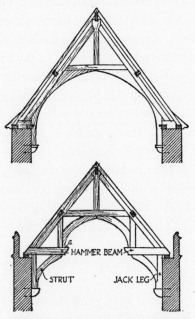

Above: CURVED BRACE ROOF
Below: HAMMER-BEAM ROOF

feeling of wanting to do it in the right way. The work of that day still stands because of its rightness, even though we may well question the purpose itself. As for rewards, they were twofold. One had pay in money, and one had satisfaction in craft freedom. That was enough. Common land was still plentiful, although landlordism was bearing down swiftly. There were taxes and there was the relentless tithe, taken by the church under royal sanction. It was as stupid as almost all other forms of collecting money by taxation and tribute, for tithes, in the end, came out of craftsman's and worker's pockets. Some were spent on abbeys, to be sure, but that also meant they were not spent on good houses. Indeed, under tax and tithe, and the new profits beginning to be taken by the middleman under the money-price method of buying and selling, workers and craftsmen got less and less. It was a slow sinking, for the multitude, hovelwards and slumwards.

If one believes in compensations, one might say: "Bless the tithe-takers! If it hadn't been for them, we wouldn't have had the abbeys and the tithe-barns." Probably so, yet we might have had something better! That's always possible! I once knew an old tithe-barn on the edge of the Cotswolds. It was as fine a building as I can remember—a great long stone-walled barn sitting on the ground as though it had sprung from it. It used to make me think of the longness of Winchester Cathedral, and had a pointed roof of stone slabs laid over a timber framing. What a framing it was! Beautiful oaken timbers knitting themselves together like a wooden cobweb of the greatest simplicity and seeming far too fragile to carry those tons of roof stones. All brown and gray and green with moss, they were, and wall-flowers had taken timid root in cracks and crevices all over the great tapestry of roof expanse. In the great elms that stood guard over all, rooks were chattering like mad about their spring building plans, the last time I saw it. The land all about was grass-carpeted and divided by hedgerows, but the farmer who now used the barn could never begin to fill it, so huge had it been made to shelter the wagon-loads of tithes that once came rumbling in at harvest-time. It was a craftsman's job, in which one felt,

[188]

like the stab of a sharp spear in the side, the feeling for building rightness that once was and is no more.

But there were other barns, built two centuries later, on untithed land, of which there will presently be something to be said, for craftsman rightness had a rebirth, one day, in a new land. Things were happening. There was talk of freedom in the air, and while the old history writers used to tell us that men were after religious freedom, along about 1600 in England, my guess is that they were far more concerned with land freedom, and land speculation. Taxes, tithes and tribute were then taking so much of a workman's wage that life was growing hard, so hard that men talked boldly about leaving and going across a sea to build themselves homes where they would be free of tax-taking kings and tithe-taking priests, in all of which they were presently to be both encouraged and driven by the landlords who had been sharp enough to get there before them.

In the end, we know the story. Jamestown and Plymouth, the Colonies, and then the United States of America. In remembering the story, however, this chronicler avers that the magic in the name "America," for nearly three centuries, was in money to be made out of land! It may have been that people wanted to worship as they chose, and that landlords in Europe were interfering with that right, but free land, or land that can be bought cheap and sold dear, is a call that men have listened to from the day when landlordism set its temptations before men.

One cannot give any serious study to the history of buildings and builders without seeing the effect of this departure from common to private land. The change was slow, insidious and began to crystallize in the time of the American migration, as a sign and a principle, while the French Revolution was the violent blowing-up of a landless peasantry who came to the end of their endurance. But it was in the new America, curiously enough, that the principle was to work itself out to complete disaster, although it took three hundred years, a complete revolution in building methods, and the masterful rise of banking and money-price-trade to get all the cards laid on the table where people could see them—if they wanted to.

One might choose other than English craftsmen to whom to say *au revoir*, as one prepared to leave the story of building in Europe. There is here no intent to single them out as the most perfect, or the most stubborn. Certain craft traditions in France have persisted, almost with ferocity, until this very day, for although the French craftsmen were no more friendly to outsiders than were the English—they often bitterly resented the calling in of the Italians, during the progress of the Renaissance—they have perhaps more skillfully resisted the whole idea of bigness and mass production. To live in a small town in France is to know the joy of being able to get anything mended by a competent craftsman, which is a joy one seldom knows any longer in the United States.

English craftsmen, however, are more directly related to building in America. Their traditions and those of the people they served in the new land, together with the English printed books about buildings that began to appear in the seventeenth century, were to set a heavier impress than that of any other land or people on building in the Colonies. The books were mostly manuals, compiled a good deal after the manner of Vitruvius, by retired craftsmen and amateur archi-

[190]

tects and builders. One supposes they were prepared for a people who had been cut off from the source of direct supply and who might easily forget how things had been done. Fancy, if you please, those people who had gone to a land where there were no buildings! Everything had to be built and—one must not underestimate this point—there might have been a smouldering hope in the bosom of many an English tradesman that the new builders would have to buy a heap of things in England—even more than a smouldering hope, as we shall soon see. One couldn't go so far as to say that this was a reason for making the books, although such things have been done in the most modern of times. Still, the books were no doubt useful, and while their influence may be traced, if one is in the mood to prowl a bit with a seventeenth-century carpenter's manual in one's hand, there was to be printed, in the latter half of the next century, a book that had a much greater influence on both English and American building; its impress can be traced by anyone with as much as a vague notion of what a Greek temple looks like.

The Renaissance that had such an influence in Europe was now to have a parallel. The rebirth was to be even purer than before, although the name of the leader was not Vitruvius. This time he bore a no less kingly name than James Stuart. He wasn't a king, however, nor even distantly connected with royalty, at least so far as his birth and estate are matters upon which to found a guess. He had no easy time of it, taking care of a widowed mother and a family, in London, along about 1740 or so. One might wonder why his thoughts never turned to America, until one learned that he liked to paint fans. America, certainly, was not yet a place for fan-painters. It seems that young Stuart had a wish to learn. He wanted to cross the Channel and see what could be seen, how they painted and what scenes they had that might be put on fans in England to make them more salable.

One of the amusing aspects of Stuart's journey and what came of it is that he was not interested in buildings except in a romantic way. It is even said that he was seeking for old castles, since these made good subjects for fan-painting, and the flavor of English castles was beginning to pall in those circles where painted fans still had a vogue. What he collected, one doesn't know (his sketch-book may be in some museum), for when he got back to London a new vocation had fallen in his lap, so to speak.

To leave London, however, he somehow got a little money together, perhaps hardly more than enough to pay his boat fare across the Channel, for he walked to the English Channel port and intended to walk, from the landing place in France, all the way to Rome. If he were after castles, he perhaps went by way of the Rhine and there took an occasional boat. Otherwise, he went afoot. He eked out the costs of inns and food by painting portraits, as he travelled. There was then no other way of getting a portrait. No doubt his terms were reasonable, and he could probably turn one out fairly fast, while he was making notes in his sketch-book of future material for fans. He got to Rome, and there made the acquaintance of young Revett, a lad who had a sound feeling for measuring with a rule and drawing with a pencil and who was making some studies of Roman buildings.

Some time during their stay they fell in with people who had lately been in Athens, and were greatly impressed with the Greek temples, almost forgotten for fifteen centuries or more. These travellers may have brought back some sketches, but at all events, their enthusiasm greatly affected young Stuart and Revett. Rome was a bit overdone, after all, but Greece was a new field. Why not go to Athens and make such drawings as would enable English builders to use the Greek temple form for palaces, country houses, halls, schools, theaters and what not? But how to get there? How to stay there long enough to do the job?

It came to pass, then, by just what events we know not, that the Dilettanti Society grew interested. This was a group of mostly English people, living in Rome. They were interested in seeing that England had the best sort of art possible, the tried and true art that had been developed by artists who worked in studios, and not with their hands as building craftsmen. These Dilettantists were a sort of Renaissance nuisance, such as still prevails to a tiresome degree, who believed that perfections had been won and now only needed to be copied. The Greek temple was one of these perfections and could safely be offered to a land that was seeking novelty, under the leadership of artists. The craft idea by that time had been pretty well shot to pieces, so far as building was concerned. The Renaissance had done its work so well that more renaissances were wanted, and the Dilettanti Society existed for the purpose of bringing them to pass.

So they backed Stuart and Revett with money. They went to Athens, drew and measured the temples and other remains, and in the course of some seventy years, their work was published in four volumes, under the title *Antiquities of Athens*. Stuart and Revett quarrelled, early after their return to England, and Stuart became the sole proprietor. He died, however, long before the second volume saw the light, although he had, before his death, been much sought after by those who were able to afford a building in the new Greek style, and who wanted his advice. He even became known as "Athenian Stuart," and while one cannot possibly imagine a method of building more unsuited to England than was the Greek temple form, under Stuart's guidance, it took very well. No traveller can forget the old Greek entrance to Euston station, in London, or St. George's Hall, Liverpool, although the theme for this was borrowed from the granite-columned Great Hall of the Baths of Caracalla at Rome. The "Classic form," as it is usually referred to by English writers, was quite as ridiculous as the Renaissance, in so far as there was anything about it that was related to the English way of life or the ways of their craftsmen. It was a form by which one could show off—exhibit one's knowledge of Greece and stand for purity—that impeccable purity of Victoria, in whose reign the London and North Western built the Greek railway station at Euston.

As events turned out, it would have been better to have left the job to the craftsmen. It is true that they, like the architect, had never had to do a building where people, carefully sorted into three classes, arrived and departed in trains, with luggage to be handled, carriages to be served and provision made for the thirsty, the hungry and the sleepy. Never, however, could they have imagined anything quite so absurd as that which came from the architect's dream of using a Greek propylea to start off the new business of steam hauling. It wouldn't be surprising to find that the Dilettanti Society had a special celebration for that crowning touch to its labors!

What had the English craftsmen learned when the coming, first of Vitruvius, disguised as the Renaissance, and then of Stuart, whose influence was called a Revival, at last toppled them from their domain? Rightness had been theirs for so long that wherever the ships of England sailed, people

[194]

had a regard for their wares. There never was a finer tradition of workmanship and quality than that passed on by the English builders. Even after several centuries, when machine industry had enriched England as never empire before was enriched, English wares had a reputation that no others could match. In time, that too was to be swallowed up in the competitive race, as elsewhere, but never was a vantage ground so stoutly defended as that where English builders fought to keep out the new-fangled ideas that were being talked about as "art." They hadn't known such a word, or ever heard of "architecture." Their gospel was rightness.

The builders might have talked of that, somewhat, as things began to go against them, but mostly they talked, one imagines, at least while at work, of the job. The word still remains, for even the architect of today still uses it. He never tells one that he has some architecture to do, but a job. That, for the craftsman, was his school and his philosophy. How to do something well! How to do it better! How to change his methods as the other craftsmen bettered their ways of making brick, glass, iron, copper and plaster, or as a new tool made easier that which had before been hard or even impossible!

Towards the end of the sixteenth and the beginning of the seventeenth centuries, there were murmurs and protests all over the world, wherever people were building, and to the results of some of them we shall presently arrive. The moment has come to slip away from the lands where craftsmanship had been slowly crippled and robbed, and take a look at it under new skies, new ways and new hopes. The chance had come. The day had dawned. An old world was being deserted by bands of emigrants. A new one was being born. To none was it some day to hold out a fairer prospect than to the craftsmen who believed that the way to rightness was through respect for men, for tools and for materials. There was no other way to rightness, one can hear them saying. Without it, no new world would be worth the making. So, at least, thought many a craftsman, as he sailed from Bristol or Plymouth, and saw the shores of England fade forever from sight.

X

EARLY AMERICAN

BUILDING

I. THE LAND

FORESTS! Nothing but sea and forests! Forests primeval, deep, stately, endless! Not a highway, not a roof, not a steeple, not a sound! Over all, the stillness of the forest primeval, the languorous seductive silence of sandy-shored Virginia, the proud and solemn silence of the land of Massasoit.

With clang of anchor and hawsepipe came cries of startled birds, lowering of boats, excited talk and plash of oars. If for a moment these sounds ceased as they neared the shore, and the newcomers sat in thought that peered and strained with an intensity that only the migrant know, a vast cloak

[197]

seemed to come down and wrap one in that unspeakable silence of Nature, brooding, watching, waiting, unhurrying, as life and death passed by in sea and sky and forest, where no time was. No pilgrim had known silences like these, nor any mariner. Their end was at hand. Into this untouched land men were to pour by millions, shattering the silences with such a clatter of building as not even Rome had known. The World of Noise was coming to birth. The symphony of silence was to be swallowed by the cacophony of melting-pots, machinery and salesmanship. No, never was there a silence like that—not even in pastoral England.

Pastoral England! Did the newcomers think about that? How could they help it? Why had they left it? The question must have surged like a flood, sudden and terrifying, as they looked at the dark forests of America, and thought of the moors and downs of home. Did they know what they were to begin building? Had anyone thought about buildings? No doubt, but the first thing to be done was to clear and break land for food. Everyone knew that. Buildings would come later. Wood was plentiful and with it one could make a shelter that would serve until afterwards. In the meantime, to the land with axe and spade.

To whose land? The destiny of uncountable millions lay in the answer to that question, but the answer had already been made. Whatever may have been in the minds of those who landed from the *Susan Constant* at the place to be called Jamestown, the answer had all been settled. Where? In the counting-houses of Bristol, Plymouth and London, where the old well-hardened rent-receivers had quietly mused, and laid their plans, one may be sure. Nothing much would be said, for never to betray one's feelings was the first pass-word to gentility and the corner-stone of Empire. Back in

[198]

one's own private premises, one could make inquiry and see what was to be done to get hold of some of this new country. If one showed interest publicly, the price of land in America would rise as sure as fate, and everybody would begin ogling for patents and grants.

Martin Frobisher had been to Labrador in the *Gabriel*, in 1576, just a year before Drake began the first all-English voyage around the world. There must be a lot of land if it took almost three years to make the journey, but Frobisher had brought back some "black earth" from Labrador, and that, they said, meant gold! It was already a magic word, casting its spells and whispering its witcheries to men, but to the wise ones who knew a thing or two, it was not yet a topmost excitement. In case there were gold, the land would be worth a lot and the gain got quickly, but even without gold, one would still have the land, or a company share in it. One might have to wait, but land wouldn't run away.

When Shakespeare got money and retired to Stratford, he would buy nothing but land. The wise playwright had learned where to put money and have it safe. With a foresight for which landlords could never be too thankful, Nature had seen to it that man could not live without land. Men and women would love or desire each other, and the world would keep filling up with children. They came faster than they went. There was bound to be crowding, some day. It was so simple.

To ignore the land game is to fail utterly to understand the building of the United States, or the architecture that followed. It was the men in the sombre counting-houses of London, Bristol and Plymouth (to which were later added those of Amsterdam and Stockholm) who set their hard inhuman impress upon the whole United States, from that day to this. The pattern, ever since the beginning, and right up to the last line of it—to the now debt-ridden towns and cities, struggling with taxes and "economies"—the harassed and tumbling-down villages and farms—the alleys, slums and "blighted areas" (last word in the lingo of Tweedledum and Tweedledee)—came from these old counting-houses. The pattern has grown, been swollen and bloated by new ways of building high and fast, by profligate use of debt in order to pass on to the future what the present cannot afford, but it is the same basic pattern. Talk about it in the House of Parliament, today, is the same that is heard in the House of Representatives. Men fled from the slow creeping mesh of it in England, in the seventeenth century. Now motherland and the land of refuge are caught in the same ominous web. This time there can be no running away. There are no more unowned lands.

The planning of America was by anarchy. It was no more in the hands of such craftsmen builders as at least wove charm and serenity into the beauty of pastoral England than heaven is in the hands of the priests. The general pattern was decided and settled by the ways and usages of English land owners. Pilgrim and emigrant escaped them, for a moment only, just as the Daniel Boones escaped many years later, and just as pioneer and backwoodsman have always managed to elude landlordism, up to the moment when it caught up with them. In that it has never failed. In the new land, the landlords were soon swarming. Change in government changed nothing save the manner of talk. Whether one called it democracy or monarchy made no difference to landlordism. Whether the men in the English counting-houses would have gone in for that sort of thing if they could have looked as far as 1776, or 1812, or 1914, or 1929, or if they could have let their affections reach out to embrace their unborn great-great-grandchildren, or theirs, no one knows.

From the record, one can't guess much good about them. They were bent on empire, and the process and effect are ever the same, on men and on things. Choosing landlordism as the basis of the colonial efforts for which the great Companies were founded, there was no alternative. Land derives its price-value from people. It has no money price until it is needed by people. With land in possession, one has to get people to it, or in need of it, before one can cash in. The history of the colonial land companies has all been written. The story of how people were indented into white servitude, by thousands, and kidnapped by more thousands, and then got to America in order to fill up the land and give it a selling price-value, is no longer concealed from anyone.

The record is clear and has been turned up and laid bare by many competent students who have wanted to look beneath the platitudes of history as taught. The English colonial program was made quite clear by young Richard Hakluyt, in the manuscript he wrote and that was handed to Elizabeth in 1584.[1] It set forth, in twenty-one ways, the benefits that would come from planting colonies in North America. Chief of these were: Clearing out the Spaniards from the fisheries of Newfoundland, and capturing their galleons on the way from Mexico to Spain; their use as stations on a possible sea highway to Cathay; as a market for English wares and manufactures; as a means of adding customs to the Royal revenue, especially in wool and linen cloth, and as a way of getting rid of the idlers and vagrants in England.

[1] *Old Virginia and her Neighbors.* By John Fiske.

It was perhaps as a result of this document that the throne and its ministers and courtiers were later made aware that things were not going so very well in England. In fact, the situation turned out, as a result of the inquiry that was one day set in motion, that: "There was in many quarters a feeling that, with its population of 5,000,000, England was getting to be over-peopled. This was probably because for some time past the supply of food and the supply of work had both been diminishing relatively to the number of people. For more than a century the wool trade had been waxing so profitable that great tracts of land which had formerly been subject to tillage were year by year turned into pastures for sheep. This process not only tended to raise the price of food, but it deprived many people of employment, since sheep-farming requires fewer hands than tilling the soil." [1] (If one likes here to substitute machines for sheep, one can get a picture of twentieth-century America.)

"In the London Company, incorporated to develop Virginia, were, besides earls, bishops, knights and gentlemen, plain commoners, merchant tailors, stationers, grocers, ironmongers, cutlers, leather sellers, saddlers, cordwainers, weavers, carpenters. . . . Its stock was advertised in the pulpit as well as in the market places and subscriptions were made in the interest of religion, patriotism and profit." [2] The general plan was to enlarge England for the benefit of the English, and very little less, although in all the charters and instructions there was much talk about God. Fear of Him was the best selling talk for landlordism. Of those who went to the Massachusetts Colony, the Beards say: "Beyond question, their leaders desired to reproduce in America the

[1] *Old Virginia and her Neighbors.* By John Fiske.
[2] *The Rise of American Civilization.* By Charles A. and Mary Beard.

[202]

stratified society they had known in England, excepting the titled aristocracy which stood above them in rank and in the affections of the king. If they had not encountered obstacles they would have made Massachusetts a land of estates tilled by renters and laborers, with yeomen freeholders interspersed and the home of an Established Church directed by a learned clergy according to English forms." [1] In Virginia, this was possible, for a time and to a degree, probably because of the natural resources and climate.[2]

Plainly, as one now looks back, it was the beginning of the empire game all over again, although few guessed what was really going on or where it would lead. Wealth may be made to pour in a torrent, for a time. Debt may keep the

---

[1] *Idem.*

[2] " 'The Renowned Noble Lady Armina', amid the luxuries of her ancestral hall in old Lincolnshire, meditating upon the lost condition of the heathen in the New World, putting up her prayers and sending her gold across the seas for their redemption, represented a deeply seated sentiment of the time. It was her aim that the occupancy of New England should result not only in the accumulation of earthly riches by the adventurers, but should redound to the glory of God in a large harvest of souls through the conversion of the barbarian inhabitants. Capt. George Weymouth, a historian of the times, active in promoting the settlement of our shores, testifies that the main end of all these undertakings was to plant the gospel in those dark regions of America.

"The sagacious John Smith, warrior and trader, tired with his rough experience in Virginia, and looking to the settlement of new colonies as fields for profitable commerce, declares that he is 'not so simple to thinke that any other motiue than wealth will euer erect there a commonweale', but hopes that 'gaine will make them affect that which Religion, Charity, and the Common Good cannot,' and he shrewdly urges the grasping Prince Charles to send settlers to the coast, pointing out a way in which he could serve both God and Mammon at the same time. 'Nothing', he says, 'could be more agreeable to God than to seeke to conuert these poor Saluages to know Christ and humanitie, whose labours there with discresion will triple requite thy charge and paines.' In the closing paragraph of this message Capt. Smith struck a theme which caught the popular ear, and sent hosts of adventurers across the wide waters, seeking the gold of another Mexico or Peru."
History of Deerfield. By George Sheldon.

torrent pouring for a time. England, looking towards America, saw vaguely a sort of loophole by which to save the situation at home and make a little on the side. Men of affairs looked at least as far as that. But first, the land had to be taken into possession. Nothing could be done if people got away from the landlord method of owning and renting.

One might hardly say that the first main idea was wholly based on land exploitation, for something had to be done about getting the jobless English vagrants to some spot where they might be able to buy goods from England. They couldn't do it at home. They surely ought to be able to do it in America. But the big Companies had not been long in existence before the profits of landlordism were too obvious to be passed by. The record of all effort to get people to America, and to keep them at their labor after they got there, tells the story very plainly. The passion for land and exploitation had taken its hold. No one wanted to work. Everyone wanted to own land and get indented white servants to work it. The record is as plain as daylight.

To fill up the colonies, the English Companies sent not only the idle and the good-for-nothing, but such a constant stream of criminals that the colonists protested vigorously. "When a man convicted of manslaughter and sentenced to be hanged was reprieved, 'because he was a carpenter and the plantation needed carpenters,' " [1] in 1618, it was plainly a hard task to get good workers to go to the Colonies. As late as the early eighteenth century, England softened her criminal laws, so that a death sentence might be commuted to seven years in the Colonies. Criminals serving a life term could have it commuted for fourteen years of such service,

[1] *White Servitude in the Colony of Virginia.* By James Curtis Ballagh.

if they were workers.[1] The colonists fought this loving caress of the motherland, tooth and nail, but, "Between 1717 and 1775, the number sent from the Old Bailey alone is thought to have been 10,000, and the whole number from various places in Great Britain and Ireland at least 50,000."[2]

Maryland, a special "dumping ground for English jails, received more convicts than any other plantation on the continent. A contemporary, in 1767, estimates the number imported into Maryland for the preceding thirty years at six hundred per annum."[3] The custom of indenturing pauper and orphan children, together with the practice of promiscuous kidnapping children for transportation as servants, resulted in the presence in the colonies of a very considerable number of young people. "So great was the demand for these youthful laborers that in one year alone, 1627, fourteen or fifteen hundred children who had been gathered up in different parts of England were sent to Virginia."[4] Even after Parliament made kidnapping punishable by death, it still went on. "Ten years after this act . . . it was said that 10,000 persons were annually spirited away from the kingdom by the arts of the kidnappers."[5]

Only by filling the land, however, could any money be made. First, land owners wanted workers. Second, only people could give a money price-value to land wanted for building purposes. From this starting point, and wholly on that basis, the United States began to grow. Land was at first so plentiful that no one thought of congestion, subways,

[1] *White Servitude in Pennsylvania.* By Cheesman A. Herrick.
[2] *White Servitude in Maryland.* By Eugene Irving McCormac.
[3] McCormac.
[4] *Economic History of Virginia in the Seventeenth Century.* By Philip A. Bruce.
[5] Bruce.

[205]

skyscrapers, slums and millions of people herded in swinish disorder, while millions of acres lay barren. Building a house that could be filled with light and air was so simple and easy, as soon as the craftsmen came, that no one dreamed of what landlordism would at last lead to. Yet the basic system of dealing with land, as worked out in those English counting-houses, was what settled how the United States should grow, not in order, but in one vast and costly disorder, as buildings became nothing but pawns in the great gamble of land.

This is not to ignore Watt and his engine and the mass-production it led to, or the vast cobweb of paper-money inflation, or the rise of the competitive system based on money-price alone, or the train of adulteration and substitution that followed, or the decline of quality and workmanship. The result is plain. What the United States might have been without landlordism, no one can say. Hardly, one guesses, could there have been piled up the present mountain of debt, if land had been made the basis of a social order headed towards civilization, rather than one headed towards the anarchy of a host of big and little empires, fighting with each other for the right to own, control and loot the natural resources of what people said was a "free country."

Nothing is more striking in the story of settlement than the moment on the *Mayflower* when it was seen that the land in sight was not that for which the voyagers had aimed. They had sailed three thousand miles of watery waste, and yet a landlord had got there before them. They had a patent allowing them to found a settlement in land of the Virginia Company, but the land now in sight belonged to another company. They had not even the right to land there. If they did, said some of the company, they would consider themselves free from all the terms of their own patent from the Plymouth Company. It was then, in the cabin of the *Mayflower*, that was drawn and signed the historic document that bound them together "for ye generall good of ye colonie, unto which we promise all due submission and obedience." [1]

Nothing was said, specifically, as to social and economic arrangements. Things were evidently a good deal mixed in their minds, for in declaring to "ye glorie of God and advancement of ye Christian faith, and honour of our king and countrie," there is a note of fear that takes a good deal of lustre from the exploit. People who had exiled themselves in Holland for eight years and then were swearing to the honor of their king and country, and to Christ in the same breath, were plainly a good deal mixed in their minds.

At all events, and to their everlasting credit: "The Pilgrim Company, from the time of breaking up their homes in Holland, like those of the primitive church, 'had all things in common'. Each family sold all that it had and put the proceeds of the sale into a common fund. . . . At the outset, then, the division of lands into homestead lots was made only for present use and not for inheritance." [2]

In Virginia, "One of the most serious difficulties under which the colony labored was the communistic plan upon which it had been started. The settlers had come without wives and children, and each man worked not to acquire property for himself and his family but to further the general purposes of the colony. . . . The strongest kind of premium was thus at once put upon idleness, and the skill-

[1] *The Pilgrims and Their Story.* Roland G. Usher.
[2] *Idem.*

[207]

ful and industrious fared no better than the stupid and lazy." [1]

In no other words did Fiske so plainly betray his failure to understand the forces at work in those days of settlement. The manorial system of England was being transported to the Colonies, later to emerge as a landlordism as lawless and defiant as any the world had ever known. For long, however, the disasters ahead were too remote to give much concern to a people who saw before them land unlimited. In New England, especially, over a period of a hundred years or more, there was a concerted intelligent effort to create a natural type of community based on the use of land. First, there was the need for growing food and of so disposing the land that it might be best used to that end. As the need followed, for land on which to build, there was also the natural instinct to make such a plan as would give each householder a fair chance to be a part of the community and partake of its social life and amenities.

It was therefore a general principle that when a group had grown so large that additions would require the use of land so far away that the householder could not get easily and quickly to the general center of things, a new grouping was necessary. It is plain that in the minds of the majority there must have been a clear concept of the relation of land to a normal life for men. One used it to the best advantage. Life was carried on by that direct use that produced food, clothing and shelter. No one was to live merely by owning land.

A history of the various types of community that were set up and tried in the United States, from the New England villages with their admirable tree-shaded commons, many

[1] *Old Virginia and her Neighbors.* By John Fiske.

[208]

of which still remain, to the Missions of California, the trading post and the religious groups that have tried a balanced mixture of social, agricultural and industrial life shows only too plainly, even up to the present day, that a sense of land use is instinctive to people in search of rightness. The thought of forcing land to a high monetary price and the idea of passing people through turnstiles—back and forth and round and round—for no other purpose than to give higher monetary values to land, was for long no more than a seed lying dormant in the great land paradise of the United States.

II. THE CRAFTSMEN

It seems fair to guess that every colonist had an idea of what sort of houses ought to be built. Ideas would derive naturally from memories of home and old ways of life. Those "gentlemen" who first came to Virginia had lived in houses with fires, windows and a garden outside. The peasant class came largely from wattled or turfed huts. The criminals that followed later on, in swarms (one ought not to be too hard on them as a class, for there were in the England of those days some three hundred crimes punishable by death), came very likely from town alleys and slums. Still, all had known some form of communal life, and few there were who were insensible to some general arrangement of houses, gardens, fields, lanes, hedgerows, and the manors and halls, of the rising tradesmen, landlords and nobles.

Settlements, at home, had grown by a river ford, ferry or bridge; or by a castle, or an abbey where the church took tithes; or in an area good for growing wool, corn, hops or fruit. The first workshops were already urging people into

[209]

towns, as they were later to be driven first by water-wheel and then by steam. Still, most of what had been built grew straightforwardly out of land use and human needs. Things were being changed by rising factories, all making steady inroads on home industry.

English building had settled down, in the sixteenth century, to a tacit acceptance of the palace and hovel basis. The builders had learned much. They were ready to carry their skill overseas. They were skillful with all woods, and knew how to lay brick to get fine patterns and textures and rosy lights flicked with dancing shadows; how to mould and diaper plaster, while the window had been turned from a clumsy wooden shutter into a thing of exquisite grace and comfort. These things, of course, were for the palaces. The multitude had to get on with their lore of wattles and turf.

What the builders had learned was by trying and testing, letting each trial be the touchstone. They had gained a vast knowledge of materials and got hold of better and better tools. There was no end to building lore and learning, for those who could pay for their services didn't all want the same kind of a house. Some wanted one longer or wider or higher or with more windows, larger stairways, bigger fireplaces or what not. It was an endless game of searching for rightness, for each change in size or arrangement of the parts of a house changed the outside look of it. There was always the way to get harmony and proportion, if one had the feeling for those things. The test of a craftsman was not merely one of skill with a tool. He had to have that feeling for rightness in which looks was as vital a factor as was the way he set his tool to deal with the material before him. Such were the craftsmen who made the Europe that men have so loved.

[210]

They did not come to the new land for some time. One can be pretty certain that no decent craftsman wanted to indent himself, for a term of years, to some plantation owner. Nor did he care to take passage on a ship and then be auctioned off in the colonies to whoever would pay the price of his passage to the captain, and then let him work it out at meagre wages. Nothing but utter penury would drive a craftsman to such a bondage. Living conditions were hard enough in England, by that time, but less so for the building craftsmen than for many others. Money was flowing in from foreign trade. The new master and landlord class were spending it for buildings. That process was to continue for a long time. How then could craftsmen be tempted to go to America? The newly rich landlords and tobacco planters also wanted some fine houses. Indentured white servants and criminals (many of them were merely mild protesters at workless starvation) got to be landlords and exploiters, in time, and wanted to be rid of their social tags as quickly as possible. A fine house was a good way to begin.

Where were the craftsmen that were to build the houses? Agents of the British colonial Companies and some of the early Governors were much wrought up over the "exorbitant demands" of craftsmen and skilled laborers. A colonial treasurer of the Virginia Colony declared, in 1625, that the wages paid there were intolerable and "much in excess of the sum paid to the same class in England." [1] In 1633, Governor Winthrop noted that the "excessive rates" charged by workmen "grew to a general complaint which called for legislation." [2] Gabriel Thomas wrote a history of the "Province and Countrey of Pensilvania" in 1698. It was hoped,

[1] Bruce.
[2] Governor Winthrop's *Journal*.

one guesses, to get landless and workless paupers from England to come and swell the price of land in America, for it points out that the "encouragements are very greate and inviting, for Poor People (both Men and Women) of all kinds can here get three times the wages for their Labour they can in England or Wales." [1] William Penn said in a letter that "all provisions are reasonable but Labour dear, which makes it a good poor Man's country." [2] What Penn was after, everyone now knows, but the general opinion uttered in these references is that of landlordism. To operate it there must be people, and the time was at hand when colonial landlords needed something better than the riff-raff and scum of jails and kidnapping.

John Smith, in that fearless letter of 1608, in which he exposed the avarice of the Company in London, had also begged: "When you send again I entreat you (to) send but 30 carpenters, husbandmen, gardeners, fishermen, blacksmiths, masons, and diggers up of trees roots, well provided (rather) than 1000 of such as we have; for except we be able both to lodge them and feed them, the most will consume with want of necessaries before they can be made good for anything." [3] The record is so plain that he who runs may read. The dominating thought was land exploitation for the benefit of shareholders in England. The craftsmen were not thought to be a part of plans that were concerned with dividends. Only when the colonists themselves began to imitate the English shareholding landlords was it possible to get good builders to cross the ocean. In the end, they had to be offered land, but when they got their hands on a good piece, they

[1] *An Historical and Geographical Account of the Province and Countrey of Pensilvania.* By Gabriel Thomas.
[2] *British Empire in America.* By John Oldmixon.
[3] *Old Virginia and her Neighbors.* By John Fiske.

had a tendency to work more for themselves than for others. Laws were passed, at one time, to prevent a craftsman from working for himself or from cutting down the amount of time he might put in on his own land.

The New England Colonies tried many plans to overcome the shortage of skilled craftsmen. "Both Boston and Charlestown in 1640 waived certain of the citizenship requirements to obtain carpenters. As early as 1635, Lynn voted to admit a landless blacksmith, and later granted him twenty acres of land, thus keeping both the blacksmith and the letter of the law requiring that residents be landholders. These concessions as a rule had strings to them. When twenty citizens of Haverhill raised a subscription among themselves to purchase a house and land in order that a blacksmith could come into the settlement, they required that the smith agree to remain for seven years, and did not permit him to work for any person other than the twenty subscribers. The town of Windsor, Connecticut, presented a currier with house and land, and 'something for a shop', but it was to belong to him and his heirs only on condition that 'he lives and dies with us and affords us use of his trade.' " [1]

For long, craftsmen were far from free to sell their services as they chose. Over them lay the heavy hand of a growing centralized government that believed it "could legislate prosperity and well-being for everyone, rich and poor" and that "either public need or demands of private business could enforce" impressment of labor.[2]

New England was first to give up the idea of holding craftsmen and workers well in leash, but Virginia carried

[1] *Economic and Social History of New England, 1620-1789.* By William B. Weeden.
[2] *Idem.*

[213]

on for some time after. Bruce says that both by impressment and wage-fixing, it merely drove the good mechanics out of the colony. They gave a lot of trouble, did the craftsmen. They were too independent, by far. A man who could do fine things with tools had those who wanted his services where they could hardly do more than pay what he asked. No doubt it was for some time a craftsman's market. That he was greedier than the rest is doubtful. His good work is so evident after two and a half centuries as to be beyond question. He came to see chances in land, as did everyone who had money to buy some, in which respect he was like all the rest. The only way to be out from under landlordism, so far as paying rent was concerned, was to own land. To escape the ultimate consequence of landlordism, as it bore down on society as a whole, was impossible.

Little by little, craftsmen began to arrive. By the end of the seventeenth century, one could build what one pleased. The builders were ready and able. Money to pay for the colonial palaces was piling up, from all sorts of sources. The country was still amply supplied with land. There was almost a halcyon day, as in the Middle Ages, when one might have said: "This is the beginning of a civilization!" Craftsmen were still fairly free. The architect-contractor-trades-union set-up of today was still far in the distance.

One can trace the story of the American craftsman, not only in buildings, but in newspaper advertisements that began to appear in the eighteenth century. These show very clearly that the architect, as a non-building planner and designer, was emerging. Craftsmen were using the new title in an effort to keep up with the times, and quite naturally.

[214]

They knew, or sensed, the new architect as one likely to cut down their wages and destroy their freedom. The Carpenter's Company of Philadelphia, whose guild hall was used by the Continental Congress, may have been the first of the thousands of defensive groups that were to grow out of the splitting-up of the building industry. More than that, the books that came from Europe were finding their way into private libraries and those who had attained to the station of "gentleman" were finding it worth while to appear well informed on the past of Europe. America had no past, and one had to have one from somewhere. Altogether, the simple relationship of the man who wanted a house and the craftsman who could build it without any help from European books was in such a state of flux as these advertisements indicate:

"DAVID BURN, will begin to teach, as soon as sufficient numbers of scholars shall offer, the five orders of architecture, planning and shading in the modern taste. Any gentleman may be attended at his own lodgings; likewise any gentleman may be furnished with plans, elevations, and sections for buildings. Apply at No. 19 Bereford's Alley." SOUTH CAROLINA GAZETTE. July 18, 1785.

"THOMAS CARSTAIRS, architect and house carpenter, lately arrived in this city from London, begs leave to inform the Public that he intends to follow his profession in all its various branches. Being regularly bred to it, and well acquainted with all its modern improvements, he flatters himself he will give satisfaction to such gentlemen as please to employ him. He is to be spoke with at his lodgings, etc." PENNSYLVANIA PACKET. May 6, 1784.

"DUDLEY INMAN, carpenter and joyner, lately arrived from London in Capt. Crosthwaite, who now lives next door to Mrs. Finley's in Church Street, Charles-Town, undertakes all sorts of carpenter's and joyner's work, particularly buildings of all kinds, etc." SOUTH CAROLINA GAZETTE. May 6, 1781.

[215]

These four advertisements are mere examples. They fix no dates, for none can be fixed. The passing of the craftsman and the advent of the architect, contractor and trades union ran over a long period of time. It has not by any means come to an end, for the modern cheap house, generally built as a speculation, and handled as a commodity along with coal, shoes and clothing, cannot stand any expense for either craftsmen or skilled guidance. The rise of the architect, in America as in Europe, came by clinging closely to the well-founded precedent of palace and hovel. In the beginning, a majority of the colonists could at least get a decent house, although the proportion grew steadily smaller and smaller.

As time went on, the gap between the palace and hovel became ever more marked. To say that this was due to the passing of the craftsman and the rise of the architect would be wholly untrue. To say that those forces that approved and made compulsory the passing of the craftsman were at fault would be to put it more rightly.

I well remember, in Rhode Island, where I was born and spent my boyhood, how men pointed to houses "built by the day" in comparison with the shoddy contract work then beginning to appear in all directions. The new lump-sum competitive contract had, by that time, made a great inroad on the craftsman. Neither architect nor contractor set out deliberately on any such task. Both were agents for a so-ciety that cared nothing about craftsmen. Woodworking mills had forced many craftsmen to daily watching of band-

[216]

saws or lathes that made things by the thousand—the same thing, over and over again.

Buildings, however, could not be put together by machines. Not yet! The craftsman still had that vantage ground. To hold it, he fought, with unions, wage scales, hours of work, just as society fought him without knowing or caring. Society wanted its building done by contract, on a money-price basis. Between society and the craftsman stood architect and contractor. The latter used his power to beat down prices by playing off manufacturers and workers against each other. He finally drove the manufacturers into agreements, combines, trusts, and all sorts of tricks for controlling price. He likewise drove the craftsmen into unions. Society applauded, as buildings got bigger and bigger and profits swelled. Society was interested only in buying cheap and selling dear. Everyone hoped to live by owning, and out of rents, interest and dividends.

The architect, helpless, and busy with his fight to get work, encouraged the system. It was easy for him to take a percentage of the cost and let it go at that. The more things cost, the more he got. He was dependent on the crumbs that fell from the tables of the successful, who alone could pay for good work. All unnoticed, America was going in for the empire game, and with a vengeance indeed.

Only a Ruskin could write the tale of the vanished American building craftsman. His passing was unnoted. The quality of work done by union-card men became poor indeed, but by that time building had become so much a gamble that the hardest thing to do in the United States was to get anything either properly built or repaired. Having known many intimately and watched them at work, I look back on their honest day's labor as I look back on the woods and

[217]

fields, gardens and orchards, highways and lanes where I roamed as a lad. All are gone. The craftsmen are now so pitifully few that one might say they too are gone. I remember their houses, their yards, gardens, barns, fences, gates, the neatness and tidiness of them and the manner in which the grass was cut and the roses trimmed. I remember tools and tool-boxes, their pride and joy, a very part of their dignity of soul and their love of the rightness of good work. I remember the razor-like edge on which they looked with real affection, as they picked up a tool, even as I remember how they eyed a piece of old timber. It was likely to hide the end of a broken nail, and long they eyed and turned it before they set tool to it. A bit of nail meant a ruined edge in saw or chisel, and hours of labor to regain it. I remember the pocket-knife that was used, over and over again in a day's work, to mark a saw cut for a fine matching, to tease a joint or true a shingle. I can see them now as they whittled and paired a threshold to make it snug, even and creakless. I can see them, always remembering the drop of oil that saved the tool.

Once, some years ago, when building a small house in Massachusetts, three such men came to work with me. Two were over seventy, and the other in the sixties. There was no contractor. Their best was expected and they meant to give it. They belonged to no union, earned three dollars a day, lived in the country and had a garden and some animals. Their situation was growing precarious. Their craftsman sense had been a good deal blighted by ready-made cheap wood-work, unseasoned and tasteless. They were the last stragglers of the vanishing army.

For a brief moment in the new land, craftsmen had recaptured that craft freedom that began to go with the Renaissance. Five thousand years of craftsmanship lay behind them, during which there had been built up, always by the workers, the skill and knowledge that led to the glorious record of building rightness. Yet in all that five thousand years, the craftsmen never got free to begin the building of a civilization. How to build—they knew. What to build— they might have known, save for king and priest, always bent on empire, changing their robes as new forms of government came and went.

For a moment, due to William Morris, the Arts and Crafts movement came creeping in. It was too late, by far, and had no relationship to the labor of life. It was a dilettante movement and while it fostered and kept alive some struggling craftsmen, the wares and output had little or nothing to do with arresting the general decay in building craftsmanship.

From Memphis on the Nile to Washington on the Potomac, there has been but one way of using the building craftsmen. Palaces and temples, manors and mansions. Straggling on behind, somehow manageable yet always growing more ominous, followed the hovels and huts, tenements and slums.

What a tragic use to make of the finest thing in a man!

III. THE BUILDINGS

The men from the *Susan Constant*, going ashore, built round wigwams of wattled rush and branch, just as on the banks of the Nile five thousand years before. In the company were four carpenters, but it was a long day before trees could be turned into houses. Later on, "The gentlemen, compelled by stern necessity, could wield the axe like accomplished woodmen, for after two years of disaster, it was enacted as a law, 'that if a man would not work, neither

[219]

should he eat.' " Jamestown, in 1611, had "two rows of houses of framed timber, and some of them two stories and a garret higher, and three large store-houses joined together in length." [1] It was about as far as Jamestown ever got, in spite of entreaty and command from London.

Henrico, the new town built by Governor Gates, was said to boast, in 1611, "three streets of well-framed houses, a handsome church, and the foundation of a better laid, to be built of brick, besides store-houses, watch-houses, and the like." [2] The picture has a flavor of real-estate boosting, one fears, for since Smith, in 1608, sent his burning letter to London, nothing indicates any rapid flow of skilled builders into Virginia.

In New England, "Particular pathos attaches to the landing of the Pilgrims at Plymouth, when winter was already ahead, their hasty building of their humble homes (wigwams and burrowed holes in banks) and the prolonged suffering from cold, scant food, and sickness until summer came. But the settlement of the towns of the Massachusetts Bay Colony, Salem, Ipswich, and the rest, presents no such frightful picture. To these points came an orderly migration of gentle folk and artisans, direct from their comfortable English homes, with much of their belongings, no doubt." [3] The arrival of the ships was so timed that "The long days of summer afforded an opportunity for building complete houses, and settling themselves into their new life, before the ordeal of winter came." [4]

Again, as ever before, none can say where and when the

[1] *History of Architecture From the Earliest Times.* Mrs. L. C. Tuthill, 1848.
[2] *Idem.*
[3] *Early Homes of the Pilgrims and Some Old Ipswich Houses.* By Thomas Franklin Foster.
[4] *Idem.*

[220]

first house arose in America. In another half century, the Atlantic seaboard, and the rich lands inward on the river valleys, were dotted with them. The story has been faithfully and copiously told, both as a whole and in detail, in any number of books. It is one of the very pleasantest the builders ever wrote in any land. One can spend a lifetime in tracing and pigeon-holing the works of American craftsman builders, for minor variations are as endless as the lives that went into the making of them.

One writer says: "The geographical differences in Colonial architecture are so few that they may be listed in a single paragraph; a great fondness for wood in New England, the use of field stone in Pennsylvania, a preference for brick in the South on account of the omnipresent clay." [1] But lest one think the subject too simple, one must attend upon another writer, who points out that: "Colonial America had two varieties of architecture, one of which is correctly called Colonial, and the other is not. The one is entirely distinct from the other and it is mischievous to confound them. The second variety is Georgian and it is illogical and indefensible to call it anything but Georgian. The Colonial architecture evolved its distinctive forms in America subject to the dictates of local necessity while the Georgian was directly transplanted from England, and although it shows marked tendencies to differentiation in the Colonies, preserved its unmistakable likeness in every instance to the parent stock from which it sprang." [2]

"Georgian architecture echoed the spirit of the Renaissance. Its whole fundamental principles afforded a direct antithesis to the conceptions on which Colonial architecture

[1] *The Story of Architecture in America.* By T. E. Tallmadge.
[2] *The Architecture of Colonial America.* By Harold Donaldson Eberlein.

WALLER HOUSE, WILLIAMSBURG, VA.

was based. It breathed the atmosphere of the well-ordered
classicism that had spread over the Continent and over
England in the train of the New Learning and had its outward concomitant in the stately creations inspired by the
masterpieces of Greek and Roman antiquity. However modified by the successive media of its transference from the
original springs of inspiration, it still voiced the measured
formality and easy restraint inherent in the ancient models.
It was essentially the architecture of the well-to-do, polished
and, if you will, somewhat artificial state of society." [1]

This will give the reader warning, one hopes, if he plans
to devote his life to tracing the "marked tendencies to differentiation." The men who built both Colonial and Georgian were masters of craft. They had the same sense of
fitness—the "belonging" of things—that the manorial craftsmen of England had. Natural materials were abundant and

[1] *Idem.*

of the best. Only perhaps in the North of Europe have carpenters ever known such a wealth and variety of workable woods as lay in the American primeval forests. Stone was less plentifully distributed, but the builders, in time, learned to make brick for chimneys and fireplaces, and later for houses, because good clay happened to be handy and because brick was far more fireproof than wood. They even learned to "bootleg" the locally made brick and pass it off for "made in England," when the motherland forbade brick making in the Colonies, since it took profits away from English brickmakers. No doubt, many a house was said to be built of brick made in England! Nor were these the only defiances the colonists had to utter, as they presently discovered why they were colonists.

The true story of the building of America can never be written. One can guess from the skeleton record, and no more. Flesh and blood are gone and with them the myriad

PEYTON RANDOLPH HOUSE, WILLIAMSBURG, VA.

[223]

secrets and uncountable whims, caprices, plans, hopes, vanities, desires, greeds, showing-offs, and keeping-up-with-the-Joneses, that for three hundred years led many millions of Americans to build what they did. A large part of it is still standing, supposedly as evidence of civilization. As to the very early part now left, there is no disagreement. It looks like the act of a people out to find a decent way of living together peacefully and equally. The old houses of Salem as of Charleston, of Kingston as of Williamsburgh, of Enfield as of Bayou St. John, have an air that arouses one's affection, even though we know now they were the advance guard of a landlordism that made the spread of justice and security utterly impossible. Palace and hovel were hard on their heels.

Nevertheless, there is scarcely a finer pageant of old buildings than from Exeter, New Hampshire, let us say, to Vicksburg, Mississippi, following the Atlantic Coast generally but not too closely, and skipping from St. Augustine

ST. JOHN'S CHURCH, HAMPTON, VIRGINIA

[224]

BRUTON PARISH CHURCH, WILLIAMSBURG, VIRGINIA

to Mobile and New Orleans. Then to the Bayou Teche country before going up the river. The complete story can be
read only by following El Camino Real, from San Diego to
San Francisco. Now much modernized, the old Mission
settlements have quite as delightful a flavor of peace as anything to be found anywhere. Both journeys are quite as romantic to lovers of craftsmen's buildings—to things that
belonged in the scene where they were placed and that came
so near to being the key to a decent way of life—and as
satisfying to the tourist who doesn't care about the kind of
hotel labels that are pasted on his luggage as anything in
Europe. Over there, looked at calmly, even though one murmurs one's delight at what the craftsman did, most of the
great architecture stands only to record man's failure to
found the human order for which he still professes to be
groping. For a moment, in some forgotten backwater such
as I have found behind Toulouse, or near Bayeux, or in

[225]

A BARN NEAR CARLISLE, PA.

Luxembourg, or the Moselle Valley, even as today in some remote Kentucky upland, one savors the day when peace, justice and security must have seemed just around the corner. Today, in the busy places, where debt hangs like a pall, the buildings tell only the story of the missed chance.

How strange, also, is it not, that in a land sworn to the gospel of a decent life for all, the throw-back, when it came to wanting to build something that would show off the growing wealth of the colonists, was to the very forms that were rooted in a denial of the decent life to all! At first, as craftsmen began to arrive and as raw materials could be converted by indented workers, the houses of the colonists were as simple in form and pattern as one might have hoped that life would be. They were of that rightness that relates to a healthy life of work and the scene of it. Straightforward craftsmanship in the very finest sense of the word, whether one goes to Yorktown or Salem, Wickford or Charleston, or to any

[226]

one of a hundred old towns within the rough limits of those four.

As income mounted, by looting the land and exploiting the laborer, there came the porticoed and pillared houses of the plantations, with a mint-bed near the back door; the more English-flavored manors of Maryland; the stately mansions in and about Philadelphia, and the less pretentious houses of New England where the Colonial tradition held on fairly strong. In New Amsterdam another type of good substantial *burgherhaus*, and in New Orleans and the French parishes, something quite different. Some built against the cold, others against the heat.

The story in churches parallels that of the houses. The history of the various land grants and charters fairly reeks with the pious injunctions of kings, priests and landlords. The church, as a bulwark of landlordism, must not be neglected in the Colonies, not by any means, said the men in

A BARN NEAR EPHRATA, PA.

[227]

the counting-houses, and while there need be no question of the genuine piety of many an emigrant, it is now equally well known that the church was helpless, in America as elsewhere, when it came to infusing society with a love of justice. Throughout, it was used as a primary agent of landlordism and in that respect it has never budged. The sin of the original compromise still rests squarely on its head, which is not to deny the beauty of the craftsmen churches nor to deny the serene and simple faith of many worshippers. They are a part of the pilgrimage, when one goes to look at old buildings, for even more eloquently than all the others do they tell the story of how near men were to founding a human order based upon that rightness that the craftsmen poured into the buildings themselves.

The Colonial pilgrimage is a pageant of varying ways of life and manners that grew out of bringing a wilderness into something that satisfied landlordism. Nowhere is there finer evidence of the homely stages of this labor than in the

YORKTOWN TAVERN, YORKTOWN, VA.

[228]

A VIRGINIA FARM-HOUSE

stone barns (almost always much finer than the farm-houses in which one probably wished to show off) of Eastern Pennsylvania. They are models of clean straight craftsmanship, working out usefulness in a barn where hay goes in at the top, cattle below, and whence manure is disgorged at the bottom; where, also, the interior wanted the least possible framework, since it was in the way when it came to storing hay. In the vicinity of Ephrata, with its quaint old *saal*, one can still see plenty of these barns in their original stout and homely beauty.

Suddenly the content in simple buildings seemed to vanish overnight. With a fever that may best be explained by guessing that wealth had so turned all heads as completely to bury the early gospel of freedom and equality—the ideal had already been somewhat tarnished by the stately porticoes and noble manorial domains—the wealthy turned to

Europe, to Europe of the kings, priests and landlords, for building forms that would make the United States look up-to-date, and enable one to vie with England in putting on a front. Many social and economic factors were involved, no doubt, for boosting the price of land became a feverish occupation as soon as the new owners, such as William Penn, saw how to make the pickings fat and juicy. Neither was it unnatural that the showy splendors of the old land should have been turned to when a restless society, full of idle people, growing bourgeois and artificial, was ready to show off. One might imagine that European forms of building would have been so obnoxious, since they derived from a state of society which the bulk of the colonists were professing to have done with and be damned to it, that the choosers would have had some pricks of conscience. But by this time, one guesses the story of the Colonial migration to be more a romantic factor in history as it is told to the young than a solemn and serious quest of the Good Life.

At all events, before the hunt was over, Europe was ransacked, measured, drawn, copied, imitated and, later on, imported in shiploads. Samuel McIntyre, the Salem shipwright, made himself famous by playing with the delicate and rarefied details invented by the Adam brothers and quickly clamored for by the *nouveaux riches* of the day. The later influence of Athenian Stuart, for example, was even greater in America than in England. The tale of it can be plainly traced, from the moment when the second volume of the *Antiquities* reached American shores, for that volume was needed in order that the Greek revival might get well under way. (The four volumes were published in London in 1761, 1784, 1794, 1816.)

Curiously enough—in fact, it is one of the most paradoxical events in the story of American building—Thomas Jefferson fell hard and aggressively for the Roman style! In his day, it is true, native forms were growing outmoded to a society so bored with idleness that it sought novelty as a gambler craves a green table. Jefferson had been in France, seen some Roman ruins—especially the Maison Carrée at Nîmes—and the visit convinced him that America was an artless, childish land. It needed a vigorous polishing with something that made a noise like a man! Pooh, pooh for the ladylike squeaks of the Adam brothers! As for the simple grace of Mount Vernon—that was schoolboy stuff! Yes—it was Thomas Jefferson, one of the few genuine spokesmen that democracy has had, who chose the ruins of the Roman empire as the building medium by which to symbolize and echo the quest of freedom and the pursuit of happiness.

He had his way, too, in several public buildings in Virginia, in others at the University, and in his own Monticello that no more belongs to a Virginia landscape than the form of Karnak could belong in Rhode Island. More than that, he sold the Roman idea to General Washington, who was no doubt much impressed by Jefferson's plea that America needed some art, when they cantered with L'Enfant over the present site of the Capital. The Frenchman was to introduce democracy to the aristocratic glories of Versailles, and so help to make people think they were getting something for their money as the government sold the historic ten square miles to the clamoring landlords and taxed the citizens to pay for L'Enfant's ideas. The capitol city became Roman, and Jefferson is often called an architect, though many prefer to think of him as a good man who went astray because of some silly bookishness, as others have done. In 1781, writing about the buildings of his native land (the

[231]

very Colonial heritage that we now cherish), he said: "The first principles of the art are unknown, and there exists scarcely a model among us sufficiently chaste to give us an idea of them." That's a tough piece of snobbish bookishness to reconcile, and although the Commission of Fine Arts was later to be equally silly over keeping Washington pure Roman, one is perplexed to think of Jefferson as belonging to this little band of personally conducted Vitruvians.

What a pity there are not some comfortable and kindly inns, all the way from Exeter to Vicksburg! One might then enjoy the journey as one may still enjoy one in France. There, if one knows how to escape the beaten track of the tripper, one may come intimately to know the simple array of human buildings, all the way from Mont St. Michel to little Olette in the Pyrenees. It is indeed a pity—a sad and tremendous pity—that instead of flying to look at the work

A VIRGINIA FARM-HOUSE

[232]

ST. GEORGE TUCKER HOUSE, WILLIAMSBURG, VA.

of building craftsmen in far-away lands, Americans cannot
be brought face to face with the history of craftsman building in their own land, get to understand why it was and what
destroyed it, and why we have what we have. The answer is,
of course, that no sensitive person could endure the series
of syndicated hotels, gawkily aping New York, and with as
much local flavor as beer at a soda-fountain counter has the
leisurely savor of a *brauhaus* in Munich. Otherwise, the
pleasure of a journey in craftsman America would be a
delight hardly to be matched in any land.

As a part of the Colonial scene, distant though it now be, a
group of out-of-work architects and draughtsmen, in 1933,
were set to work at making a book about old Georgian houses.
They were paid from funds given in small amounts by many
who wanted to help keep them in food, clothing and shelter.
They made a very lovely book, full of fine drawings and
such detailed studies that with them anyone who could pay
the price could get a very good imitation of a Georgian

[233]

house, if he could find the craftsmen to do the work. As the book did not occupy all those who needed help, others made models of Mayan temples, and still others modelled old theaters and bridges.

The whole method of administering architecture to the American people has hardly been more than dosing them with the opiate of debt. Debt, they have been made to believe, is the way by which they are to realize those human aspirations to which so many simple people still cling in what they call the "faith of their fathers."

In the meantime, it may be, all in due course, when men begin to move towards peace and justice, security and a pleasant life all round, they will use the history of buildings not to glorify and cater to their emotions, but to save themselves from the pains and agonies that grow more acute and even desperate as time goes on. That's a speculation on which each is entitled to his own guess. In looking at the record, though, one must scan the whole. It's a damnably accurate record when one looks at the whole of it, which is why, one infers, so few look at it, although events in the United States, since 1929, have laid many a corner bare, and vividly. It is far easier and pleasanter to look at what is called the architecture and forget the rest, as do the historians, but that merely confuses, unless it be true that all the architecture any people can ever have is what comes from the palace and hovel method. If that be so, then there's nothing to be said; but is there no better method?

In any case, the farther one searches with open mind, the more one is driven back to the counting-houses of seventeenth-century England and Holland. The men who sat in them and planned their "Companies" were in control of the American pattern that was to follow and that has been called by many names, none of which is very truly descriptive. The men in the counting-houses had their minds on land. They were the forerunners of the Forsytes and the Jarrolds, who were merely the invented likenesses of the dogged empire makers of England. Miss Sackville-West says, in that fiery protest of old Jarrold, that they hardly "could be expected to know that by nineteen thirty-one, it would have become an unmanageable monster."

Why couldn't they? What else has ever happened to an empire?

XI

THE

RISE OF THE ARCHITECT

IN AMERICA

FOR some forty or fifty centuries, buildings grew out of craftsmanship. Building form thus grew out of the kind of building craftsmen happened to be making. The Renaissance changed all this. As a result, what long had been one, now became two. The architect was to claim all knowledge of building form and use it to design buildings. The building craftsman was to do what he was told.

This was no mere selfish act by the architect. He followed the law of class, for money-making purposes, that ended in dividing and subdividing all work into a host of classes, each fighting all others and society as a whole, which also fought all classes without mercy.

The true building craftsman disappeared. The effect is plain if one but compare the Victorian period with Colonial America. The architect-architecture of the Civil War period, for example, is a series of horrors—city halls, opera houses, schools, monuments and jig-sawed houses. Not only in looks is that era agonizing. When the new building designers, intent on doing the very best they could with knowledge from their copy-books, were floating somewhat foggily on a sea of paper and ink, there was a competition in New York in the nineties, for a "solution of the housing problem." It was won by an architect who did it by placing a windowless room between the back and front rooms of houses placed side-walls to side-walls in a block. Architecture was got by giving the middle room an imitation window that opened—into the next room! "Dumb-bells" these slums came to be called.

The new architect-designer, who began to get a foothold in America in the eighteenth century, looked backwards. Where else could he look? Building workmen had to look forward. They were beset by men making all sorts of new materials and devices, and by people who wanted these new things in their buildings. Left to themselves, the workers would have gone on as before, letting the form of the building grow out of the new things and their uses. But so to go on was out of their hands. The great river of knowledge, used by builders for centuries and out of which had flowed the wealth of building rightness, was divided. Knowledge, instead of being one, was two.

Designers were driven to learn about the rising flood of

new things in a new way. Old intimate craftsman contacts were gone. The priceless experience that came to them alone and that master builders deemed their most precious asset slipped away from the architect and was replaced by the advertising and salesmanship that finally became games by themselves. To the architect, the salesman repeated the formula he had committed to memory. He had learned it from the sales manager who had it from the advertising manager who probably got it from the advertising agency. In fact, it was by advertising agencies that an incredible amount of misinformation known as "copy" was distributed to all and sundry.

Designers were never to know the field of labor as the craftsmen had known it. The feel and touch and ways of tools and materials, that wonderful play of craft and manners, passed out of the hands of the working class, as they came to be known, until they were all dumped into the group known as Labor, finally to emerge as the Unemployed. In the change, workers had no longer anything to say about how a thing was to look. They were to follow drawings made by men who had taken over half of their craft heritage. Thus, working only to produce what the designer drew, they ended by losing their craft skill, the other half of their craft heritage. It is a fact that in the twentieth century architects held classes where the bricklayers could learn to lay bricks, and nobody laughed! Likewise, by every means in their power, including rewards of medals and diplomas, were architects trying to restore life to a dying craftmanship.

The information given by salesmen and advertising, whose efforts were directed towards sales rather than towards accuracy, slowly became nothing more than formulas. Manufacturers' competition gave way to price-fixing in gentle-

[238]

men's agreements, combines, trusts. The phrase "or equal" crept into all architect's specifications. It meant that the architect either did not know what was best for the purpose, or that when he did he had to say "or equal," lest any single bidder, with a monopoly, seize the chance to boost his price. The "or equal" clause ended by filling the mails with tons upon tons of printed matter, most of which went direct to the waste basket. It was junk as soon as printed, but it went into the cost of building just the same.

Under the whip and spur of town and city "boosters," landlords trying to cash in and building speculators, the gap between architect and worker widened. Those who gained actual structural knowledge kept it as a business asset. Contractor consorted with architect, under the lump-sum bid, and generously allowed the architect to fall back on him for the mistakes in plans and specifications, filled as they were with such phrases as "or equal," or "in the best manner," or "satisfactory to the architect." The contractor, having to pay for these mistakes, naturally fell back on the client. He learned to add to his bid a sum to cover the architect's blunders, just as he later learned to add other sums to cover the cost of bribing public officials to let him use street and sidewalk for his trade.

That part of the story is hardly worth the telling. It is but a part of the general rugged individualism theory of class rights and class hunting grounds. In one form or another men group themselves to get the best pay they can. Architect and hod-carrier, in that respect, are exactly alike. One can point no finger at any man, in any trade, as he struggles to save himself by guarding what he calls the rights of his calling. It is a mercenary and merciless warfare, but nowhere did it more sadly affect the quality of output than in the building industry. Allied with debt, it led steadily slum-wards for the multitude. In the early days, before the struggle became acute and pressure of debt so ominous, good buildings could still be had at not too great cost. Many early architects were carpenters by trade and had not lost their craft knowledge.

The story of individual American architects and their work has been well told. Since both history and teaching of architecture have been based on the palace and hovel method, all effort to gain a following for architecture as art has gone into persuading people to look for the art in separate specimens of the outside of buildings, and thus to ignore the vital relationship of all buildings to the wholeness of the community and to the manner of life that individuals have to live, endure and pay for. A few escape and enjoy the separate specimens as sky-line effects (few city buildings can now be seen in any other way) when there is a pleasant sunset, but the great majority must live in tightly herded runways of subway, street and so many rooms with bath.

From the early days when settlement was still going on and the frontiers were still open, one can pick out a few architects and some of the historic buildings that marked those days. There was Robert Mills, for example, who much resembled Inigo Jones but was luckier. He grew to be a favorite in government circles, quite deservedly, and so got to build a series of custom-houses all the way up and down the Atlantic Coast. He put the row of columns on the Treasury Building in Washington (the present row is a replacement), thereby shutting out much light from offices where people had to work. It was part of the dreadful influence of Athenian Stuart and the theory about precedent.

Then Mills did as glorious a thing as mortal ever did. He laid out the simple lines of the Washington Monument, the most superb piece of pure masonry to be found in all America, and exceeded in its majesty and purity of line by nothing built anywhere. It was, after all, a natural design for a man who began by building locks, canals and bridges. Nowhere was the effect of craftsmanship ever made clearer. When Mills took to buildings, because he really liked them, he fell a victim to the current idea that the Greek ruins were the perfection of all art. In the Washington Monument, his natural craft taste reasserted itself, for, as he faced a temptation that hardly another designer of his day could have resisted, he left the surface of the monument clean and flawless. Up it goes, five hundred and fifty feet in the air, a soaring majesty of craftsman simplicity, rising from the earth, like a noble bole of genius.

Had Mills been the complete craftsman of Khufru's days, he would have known that the crushing weight of his obelisk form was more than the lower stones could bear. The corners, at the base of the Washington Monument, will one day need a treatment such as no one knows how to give them, if the monument is to be saved, and such as the pyramids of Khufru do not yet require. It was not for nothing that a pyramid builder referred to his work as a "firm thing."

There was Bulfinch of Boston, with his State House and dome. A careful student of the bygone, he took to the work of the brothers Adam in England just as did Samuel McIntyre of Salem fame. There was Latrobe, who rebuilt the Capitol at Washington, sticking pretty close to the original design by Dr. William Thornton, one of the best of the

[241]

classical dabblers. There were any number who won major or minor places, entirely by the borrowing process. No purely creative architect was to appear in the scene until Louis Sullivan, late in the nineteenth century, threw down the gauntlet. Boldly he challenged the whole theory of copying and imitating, and the catchword of "precedent," declaring that architecture was naturally a living and creative art.

Before that came Henry Hobson Richardson. He, too, might be called a copyist, for he adored the genuine craftsman splendors of the Romanesque. The story of his life is one of the pure romances in the history of American building, for Sullivan's was nipped in its prime. Richardson, born in Louisiana, with a talent for drawing, although he was never a great draughtsman, went to Paris and in the Ecole des Beaux Arts learned the classic thoroughly. He got back to Boston just when men were making the choice between Union and Confederacy. To save him from jail, since his choice was for the South where he was born, his friends got him to go back to Paris. There he worked in the office of Labrouste, another great French copyist, and after a while came back to Boston, got into practice and won a competition that gave him a start.

To say that he borrowed from the Romanesque is hardly to put the matter in the light of Richardson's point of view. He had the creative instinct of a full-blooded craftsman, had Richardson, and loved the feeling of aliveness in a building. Not the wayward daring spring of the Gothic, but the solid substantial dependable aliveness of the Romanesque. He would have restored craftsmanship in America, had it been possible. He would have worked on the job like a true master builder (it is said that he often did), and so

[242]

would have got a huge and lusty joy out of dressing a stone or cutting a grotesque. He infused life into the dull and deadly stuff that architects of his day were palming off on the public. He gave a meaning to building that had not been known since the decline of Colonial craftsmanship. If he went back to the tenth century for his ideas, he threw something into his work that no architect had ever done—not even the more exalted Wren—and that no architect has been able to do since his day.[1]

His most famous work is Trinity Church, in Boston, which led to a succession of buildings as far west as Chicago, but by one of those paradoxes that seem peculiarly ironical (Richardson once said: "Wait till they see my jail!")—his finest building is the Pittsburgh County Jail. There one finds true masonry, flawless in the rhythm of all its parts. In the jumble of modern Pittsburgh, with its dull and pompous pseudo-Roman, at Schenley Square, and its miles on miles of shabby streets and sprawling fringes of sheer and utter ugliness, Richardson's jail stands out like a finger of shame. As for the later additions—both Gothic and Classic—to the University precincts, one can hardly say more than that the

---

[1] Wren might have managed a thin wan smile, but Richardson would have roared at the tale of what happened to an architect friend of mine, not so very long ago. Having undertaken some changes in an old house in the country for which he had made the most careful measurements and drawings, he went one morning to see how the work was going on. The house was in the neighborhood where he was born and had grown up, and where he had learned to have a great respect for the old craftsmen and their ways. What he observed was the old carpenter with rule in hand and with the blue-print spread out on his work bench. From it he took a careful measurement. Then he moved over to the stairway that was to be changed and there appeared to use the measurement in some occult calculations. He patiently repeated the operation, a number of times. At last he seemed to be satisfied. He paused, looked up as though addressing the universe, and said: "By gosh, the drawings are right!"

city is still an easy mark for good architectural salesmen.

With Richardson there passed a moment when it would be easy to say that the fate of architecture in America hung by a thread. So it did, but not in the hands of any architect. Many other forces were shaping it, just as many other interests were to use it whenever it would serve to push on the general scheme of herding more humans in areas selected by the herders as a means of cashing in on land prices and congestion. American towns and cities were not to grow in an orderly way towards a serene and tranquil setting for an agreeable life. They were to become—as the energetic, practical and pushing landlords and bond-floaters, aided by politicians and boosting publicity, got on with their schemes of bigger and better—what have been so aptly described as human corrals of "highly organized discomfort."

With growing demand for more—for bigger and bigger —for ever more dramatic buildings that would give publicity and advertise people into further congestion, the final separation of craftsmen and designer seemed to prove the need for some quicker way of training designers. This was the moment for the architectural school to appear, as it did, satisfying, as historians put it, a long-felt want.

The schools, founded on the idea of teaching students to copy rather than to study and create, could, like the floundering architects, cast their eyes only backwards. For them, isolated from the actual work of building, there was nowhere else to look. Out of what had been done in old buildings they had to evolve a method of making façades. They could do nothing else, and they merely widened the gap they might have been intended to lessen. If they are accused of having

[244]

made little appreciable gain, it may be that swiftness of change in these days leaves all schools at a tremendous disadvantage. Schools, it also seems, are not places for prodding and pushing inquiry into anything basic, and thus it is not to be wondered at if schools of architecture generally do not teach the relation and cost of buildings to society as a whole, or the truth about palaces and hovels. Whether reality, so much swifter than theory, may some day be caught up with by the schools is another speculation.

Ah, you will say, but what of the Ecole des Beaux Arts? What would have happened had not young Americans been able to get a training in architecture at that old Parisian school? It was one of the most brilliant students of building history who put the question to me, as we sat in his study not a thousand miles from Paris. But there was a twinkle in his eye, for he has so long faced the dreary effect of the Ecole on the buildings of his own France that he was quite able to evaluate its influence in America.

The youth of that land, lacking any school of architecture, began to go to Paris. There was nowhere else to go; it was a pleasant place, and the Ecole had a good name in pedantic circles. Unfortunately, even with its well-founded ideas of scholarship and training, it was caught in the toils of the pecuniary process without knowing it. Just as two hundred years earlier, a French king had finally approved the demoralizing lump-sum contract (*contrat à forfait*), so now had come the day when old notions of structure and building methods were being swept away like chaff. The Ecole was based on a study of the Past, and of relating Past to Present. Future? Well, not much thought about that. The school was thus quite unequipped to deal with the modern building process under the lash of landlordism, debt, rent, interest,

[245]

profits and dividends. It was no better off, in that respect, than were the generals of Europe in 1914. All the graduates of Aldershot, Potsdam and St. Cyr were suddenly confronted with a technique for killing that had not been in the books. That, to use the figure of speech, was the position of the Ecole. Its strength and usefulness lay in its insistence on study and thoroughness, for which many a man owes the school a good deal. But these precious factors were limited in their application. They embraced the past, were based on such principles as plan and axis, sorted from the craftsman's work and declared to be good, although if there was any emphasis, it was probably on the Renaissance.

Thus the influence of the Ecole on American architecture was about what might have been expected in a world that was separating life from work, life from art, life from reality, and substituting the academic process of theory, correlation and pretending—even as teaching was by memorizing and simulating. In so far as design was concerned, one supposes that America had to pass through a Beaux Arts period. It could hardly have been escaped, even though it had borne some other name. Backwards was where men had been taught to look (Will history ever be taught by looking at the future?). Across the Atlantic was nearest in distance, and France has always had a good publicity.

The Ecole, it is said, much retarded the coming of a purely American architectural style—one that spoke the tongue of the new world and lauded its aims and accomplishments—but a fair guess is that no one is much longer concerned over that. In its buildings, the United States long borrowed and parroted galore, learned style names and spoke them with unction, and bowed down to them and the imported goods that Europe was never slow in selling to

America. The episode had no more meaning than that. Underneath it all there was growing a heap of debt and the means that would help to pile debt as never before. The day was coming when the buildings of the United States were to make the whole world gasp—for a moment!

In Boston, near the end of the nineteenth century, the owners of the land at the corner of Court and Washington Streets decided to do something that had never before been done. The corner was what real estate men would call a juicy one. It was fairly bursting with juice but it had in some way to be squeezed out. Here were two main thoroughfares, abutting a third (State Street), and carrying people in increasing numbers. The land, as a consequence, was rated as very valuable. To get the value out, however, one must make people pay for using it. There lay the problem. Something must be built, on that corner, that would make people pay. The usual height for a building was then four to six stories. The elevator had arrived, at least in principle, but while buildings could thereby be made higher (four flights was about the limit for stair-climbers), no one felt very sure about the higher buildings.

Doubt rose naturally over the amount of rentable floor space, and its value, in the lower stories. All floors were then carried by the walls which also had to support themselves. It was the problem faced by the Romanesque builders and solved by those of the Gothic period. To go ten or twelve stories, instead of six, the lower stories must have very heavy walls. The Gothic builders had no floors to bother with. They dealt only with walls and a roof. To solve the problem that faced owners of juicy land, in Boston and in all cities everywhere, one must contrive floors, divided up in rooms and served with elevators and corridors.

The Ames Building resulted. It was an excellent building with a good Roman flavor as masonry goes. Land owners everywhere watched it with bated breath. Well they knew that all that makes land valuable is people and a way of making them pay! One must, in playing this game, herd the largest possible number of people and then charge them for being there. If one knows the business, one can do very well at it. One's fellow-citizens will admire one very much, wish they had the same ability, pay the higher taxes and prices that follow, until insolvency is reached, and not grumble too much while waiting for red to change to green. At any rate, they won't get into a fury and begin revoluting about it; so the game is still full of tempting possibilities.

Very likely these were not exactly the thoughts in the minds of those who owned the corner of Court and Washington Streets, nor would I pretend to do more than hazard a guess as to what they were thinking about. They certainly wanted the highest building they could get, within what was then called reason, and to collect as much rent as could be got. They may have wanted to be the first to build a twelve-story office building, just as someone is always wanting to be the first to do all sorts of socially devilish things, and the Ames Building was just as devilish, from every point of view, at that time in Boston, as the silliest things that someone is always doing because no one has done them before. There was no more need for a twelve-story office building in Boston than for an escalator up Beacon Hill to the State House.

If Bostonians had been asked what would happen if all narrow Washington Street, with Tremont, West, Winter,

Temple Place, Bromfield and School Streets, or the area from Atlantic Avenue to the Back Bay, was to be covered with twelve-story buildings, they might have sought to prevent the Ames Building, as they ought to have done. Or would history indicate that too many cannily saw that if the Ames Building worked, and by it a thousand people could be herded where only a hundred had been corralled before, there were juicy pickings ahead for land owners? I suspect there was a silent battle and that manners were defeated. I do not remember much opposition, although I saw the Ames Building built and, as a youth, marvelled with the rest.

The idea, however, did not work. The masonry walls were so thick at the base that loss of rentable area in the lower stories was not offset by gain in height. The total rentals showed no result that excited other land owners. The building yielded a lot of advertising, of course, and a good deal of pleasure for those who had offices in the upper stories, for they could look out on Bunker Hill, the Harbor, and far away to Boston Light, where the old Cunarders—*Carpathia, Carinthia, Catalonia* and *Cephalonia*—with their red funnels, came romantically in from Liverpool each week. I could see them from my bedroom window in Dorchester, so the Ames Building was of no use to me.

That was all there was to it. Architect and contractor had solved the structural problem, in masonry, for a twelve-story office building, but that wasn't enough. Views of Boston Harbor were not thought such a help to health and the higher life that land owners would present them to hirers of offices, just by way of being friendly. Owners want to be paid for such things—and usually a view is used to collect a little more than where there is none—but the answer was,

[249]

when the Ames Building was done, that not all the architects and contractors on earth knew how to build a high building that would pay taxes, its keep, and give a profit out of rentals.

When Trinity Church was finished, in 1877—the porch was added some years later and after Richardson's death— the profession of architecture had taken organized form. The American Institute of Architects was then some twenty years old. Its members were scattered about the country, mostly fighting the skirmishes that usually fall to an advance guard. The United States was not yet arrived at the "architecture-conscious" stage. Its citizens had gone on with their building, in the usual and customary way, none very good and much very bad, for the craftsmen, after a moment of freedom in the new world, were again being pushed to one side and the fine flavor of Colonial and Georgian days was disappearing. Now and then there was a flourish, as some wealthy citizen built himself a mansion, or an opera house or an Odd Fellows Hall for his town, or as some community was inspired to memorialize in granite the youth that fell in the Civil War.

The contractor had hardly made his appearance. Craftsmen were not yet corrupted into the trade-union stage, and while the influence of European styles and modes had made itself felt anew, in the Greek revival, a lot of plain simple building was being done, punctuated by some groping bid for the new and greater glory that people felt was a part of "God's country" and that ought somehow to be uttered. Palaces and hovels were drifting farther apart, and the

[250]

spread of the slum and that down-at-the-heel disorder, now so plentiful, was well under way.

The greatest public buildings were the capitols, beginning with the big one at Washington and ending, for example, with the little one at Annapolis. Seen, in illustrations, side by side, or looked at chronologically, these capitols made a picture of a fair part of the story of American architecture in the nineteenth century. The usual pattern was the capitol at Washington, and the general appearance smacked of Greece or Rome. The capitol was, of course, a new kind of building. It had no precedent. A new kind of government was being forged. But the method by which a building grew naturally out of the purpose for which it was to be used had been upset by the arrival of the professional designing architect. Not that he was to blame, for he was merely the agent accepted by a society now agreed that one no longer began a building by considering the purpose, but by selecting a design for the outside. What was to go on in the building would then be fitted to the inside, as best could be done. Generally, in the case of a capitol, a dome was thought necessary. Why? No one could have told.

This idea of outside design as the way to begin a building was by no means dominant over the whole field. Farmers still built their barns to hold hay and cattle, and factories were building in order to use machinery. The influence of the idea, however, was growing fast, especially in the larger towns and cities. Even builders and carpenter-architects were beginning to copy. They could hardly help it, for they were being pushed by a people that were, and still are, tremendously imitative, and generally more concerned with looking, acting and talking alike than with thinking in those social directions that lead towards civilization. There began

[251]

to appear a trickling stream of buildings that put on airs and pretended to be a little better, socially, than the general run. On them were stuck some Greek columns or Roman pilasters, or a borrowed frightful roof from Mansard. They began to dot the United States in the more settled parts, and many of them still stand to be looked at.

It was the day of imitating the Louvre and the French chateaux in America—the Post Office and the English High School in Boston, the State Capitol at Albany, the Broad Street Station and City Hall in Philadelphia, and Army and Navy Building in Washington; there were the quaint Victorianisms such as Memorial Hall at Harvard, Mechanics Hall in Boston and the National Museum in Washington; while a study of the general output of the period shows a cacophonous medley. One can hardly believe that good white paper was ever so wasted, or that the stuff was really built. Yet it was—houses, hotels, halls, armories, schools, colleges, clubs and the ghastly cast-iron city building fronts. Everyone believed in America except when it came to whatever was solemnly spoken of as art. Then one ran to Europe, where the accomplished traders were always ready and waiting. The architectural outpouring of the eighties is an amazing medley, pointedly telling the tale of a people who were trying to go in for art but who really had no more taste than the architects who posed as guides among the building styles of Europe.

Suddenly, like a flash in a dark sky, one comes across inklings of architects on whom it had dawned that America was a land of its own, that it had its own moods, landscapes, contours, materials and even a way of life that would perhaps break through the trammels of aping, if given half a chance. If one hunts the periodicals of the day, one may

[252]

find, as I did, "A House in Jamaica Plain for J. Greenough, by W. R. Emerson" (1879). There one will see America, stirring in its European swaddling clothes, and getting ready to burst its cocoon. This house had a new flavor. Unlike Colonial or Georgian, yet not wholly free of memories of things somewhere seen before, as no building is ever free of kinships, if one looks long enough, it still strikes a new note. It is (there may be earlier ones) a birthday, in American building, and the new country-house is born. There is another sketch by the same man, for a "House in Bar Harbor" (1880). A bit theatrical? Yes—but some honest effort to create!

Then the new note becomes a little more frequent. There is a sketch by Thomas Hastings in 1880, free and easy, natural and simple. In 1881, another by C. Howard Walker, and then follow on the names of Bruce Price, John Calvin Stevens and Wilson Eyre, Jr. It is hardly fair to mention any names, for there followed along the band of spirited young men who were thinking, inquiring, creating. It is easy to imagine, as one comes across the "Perspective View of Cottage for a Young Man of Unexceptionable Position" (1883), the sketch of "A House by the Sea" (1885), or "A Winter Hotel for the Seaside," that things were looking up and that American life was to be more outwardly playful and easy-going, all of which was to the good, for the thinking young architects. It was as though the tinkle of "The Maiden's Prayer" and "Monastery Bells" was fading, and the Sea Pieces of McDowell or the new and quivering melodies of Grieg were stirring people out of their dull and stuffy parlors.

In the eighties, one senses—alackaday!—the coming of Gothic to America. St. Patrick's, in New York, was begun

in 1858, but it was some twenty years before it was consecrated. That America would have to pass through that stage
is plainly indicated by the illustrations in the magazines.
The stylistic day was not over and done with, by any means,
just because a group of young pioneers were teaching
Americans how to live in houses, and on porches. The banks
were to take over the Greek temples, just as the churches
were to make a bid for prestige by going in for Gothic,
which was as absurd, as a mirror of dogmatic religion in
America, as a Greek temple was absurd as a place to cash
a check. For the most part, the best that can be said of the
architecture of the period is that much building was first
for show and then for use.

Bertram Grosvenor Goodhue, foremost American designer in Gothic, who came along in the twentieth century,
was quite honest with his clients. He told them frankly that
a real Gothic church could no longer be built. The life that
produced it had gone. He could, however, give as good an
imitation as could be built—and he did, as everyone knows.
He was a great creative designer, who fell into the Gothic
habit quite by chance and died all too soon after such
buildings as the Nebraska State Capitol and the Los Angeles
Public Library had given an inkling of his great creative
powers.

The story of the good and bad work done by American
architects has been told many times. If one can skip the
flattery and get to know the few shining lights—many of
whom are obscure because they worked for firms that took
all the glory, and many who never got the very large work
that might have ruined them as creators—one can get to
understand the mixture of ideas and forces that dictated the
kind and quality of buildings that now make the American

scene. It was almost wholly a battle of individuals, all caught in the same web, by which the bulk of American building was determined by the process of inflating land and debt.

"In the past," says Mr. Charles D. Maginnis, First Vice President of the American Institute of Architects, "the talent of the architect has been restricted to the discriminating patron. It has shaped the domesticities of the well-to-do and the monumentalities of the state and church. It has served the higher forms of commerce, and added occasional drama to the skylines of our cities. In the magnitude of the national scene, however, the architect has been a carver of cherry-stones. . . . In the shaping of the city, the architect's concern until now has been impatiently limited to the minor problems of its articulation. He has punctuated the skylines of New York, for example, with skyscrapers without having anything to say about their rationality. . . . As it is, the perspective from Hoboken reveals what a staggering price the future is to pay for its splendid and engaging dynamics. The community planning of the future will be too scientific to tolerate such chaos. The skyscraper has been a piquant and picturesque episode in the evolution of American architecture but the signs are unmistakable that its irresponsible vogue is near an end." [1]

All through the nineteenth century the little band of architects was pushing away at the frontiers of timidity and suspicion. It was, for long, slow work. People had a horror of tax-assessors. Public buildings, like those at the World's Fair, cost a lot of money. There was not only the original cost but the interest, and that was as much or more. A quarter-million dollar building really cost a half-million, before paying was over. Wise Eastern settlers and Western

[1] *The Octagon.* October, 1933.

frontiersmen could not be fooled with a bond issue. They knew what it meant. They could add, multiply and figure a tax-rate, and they had a deadly fear of a rising one. Well they knew that to add even a small barn or wagon-shed to their premises meant a visit from the tax-assessors. Even a coat of paint was more than likely to show up in a higher tax at the next assessment.

The selling of architecture in the thriving towns began to grow easier as soon as the astute saw the profits to be made out of costly public buildings, if one knew the tricks of landlordism. Costly buildings gave a lot of publicity to a town, and publicity was what people were beginning to want. All were encouraged to develop a noisy pride in their home town. Generally, it was only the envy aroused at the suggestion that one's natal place or present abode wasn't the equal of somewhere else, or that some other town was growing faster. It was mostly a chip-on-the-shoulder kind of pride, but it was just as useful in voting a bond issue as though the town were the fairest domain in all the land.

For an example of what architecture could do, there was Jonesville. What had the new town hall done for land prices in and around the square? Heigh ho! said the smart ones. Architecture pays! Those architects have the right idea. Heigh ho! said the tax-assessors, licking their chops.

So Richardson got a lot of commissions, and thoroughly deserved them. Even the Boston & Albany Railroad, then plying between those two cities, took him on for a series of stations. Richardson was no cheap man. His buildings cost infernally dear. No railroad company had any right to spend so much money on stations, for, as a public utility, it naturally threw the entire cost back on the travellers. The Boston & Albany, however, under its charter, could earn no

[256]

more than a fixed percent (was it eight?). All over that reverted to the State of Massachusetts. Obviously, there was but one thing for the directors to do—spend the excess earnings in something—and why not in architecture? This was a good stroke, especially if a director owned land in a town served by one of the new stations.

To one who saw the stations built, as I did, and who used them a great deal, they were a pleasure indeed. They were nice stations. They gave a friendly and cordial flavor to railroad riding. How much users of railroads can afford to pay for stations is a very serious matter, as is now indicated by the pile of bonded railroad debt, which, one assumes, will now be bought by the government, if the railroads can put it over, or which may have to be bought as a means of saving those fiduciary institutions that have their money in railroad bonds.

But the idea that a fine station added to the selling price of land in the community that used the station was not lost on the smart ones, by any means. Gradually architecture gained headway. Not because people loved it, or craved it for their starved souls, but because it was seen to be good business—for the foxy ones who knew the game.

McKim sold Boston its Public Library in 1895. This is not to disparage the building, but clearly to mark the moment when an aggressive architectural selling campaign was to begin. McKim was a natural salesman. He had the prime gift—an absolute conviction—and he was a man of wide culture. He had learned his architecture in the straight Classic-Renaissance way, although he appears to have started to be an engineer. But he grew interested in the past and studied it devotedly. He came to believe that out of the past there should be developed a form of architecture that

[257]

would look well in America. It never occurred to him that America might be developed in its own original way, or that the building way of the colonists was the better one, as it was. Never was he led astray by imagining that the task of architects, if they were to justify their theft from the craftsman, was to study American life and ways, and the new purposes for which people wanted buildings. He went straight ahead on the Renaissance basis: one chose a design for the outside and then fitted the inside to it as best one could.

McKim was much helped by favorable circumstances. America was growing ripe for the imperial stage. The rank and file did not understand what was going on, but there were those who did, and they saw McKim as their man. They were not interested in the homely simplicity of Faneuil Hall, the White House or even Independence Hall. They were ready for the trappings of the Renaissance and for precisely the same reason that had brought them to Florence, five hundred years before. McKim had the trappings. He found them ready-made in Europe, which had brought them forth under the sway of those kings and potentates that our ancestors had been at some revolutionary pains to be done with. For such trappings, McKim found a ready market. A few rose to object to his wares. They seem to have been those who clung to the belief that architecture was a creative, not an imitative, art.

As for Americans generally, they had by this time become aware of the fact that Europe was filled with art, and that art must have something to do with culture. They did not realize that smart groups in Europe were engaged in a skillful propaganda to sell their art and its forms and ideas to Americans, and that European architectural styles were a big factor in helping to unload the products of other arts, some good, and a lot pretty bad.

If this importing episode be a basis for McKim's fame, let it be so. It really is not important. The facts are, as I read history, that as a nation we had emerged from the silly idea that a civilization was made up of people. We were convinced that it was made of things. We wanted to dramatize the things, in things, and for that purpose we wanted architecture, or at least a good many people of means and power were easily persuaded to want it and to get it. McKim, like Wren before him, added enormously to the prestige of the architect. He was a better salesman than Richardson. His work has thus been very greatly praised. If this be a pleasant way of studying the history of building, there can be no great harm in it, unless it mislead the student into thinking that names (the deadliest opiates in all history) are more important than the great human movements that underlie and bring to pass all variations in the art of building, and that finally drag all societies, unless they keep their wits carefully about them, to the edge of a financial abyss, and a social throw-back.

McKim's idea went more than well. The World's Fair in 1893 had given architecture a big boost. It expressed to an inarticulate people who drew their respect for art from Europe an idea of that greatness of energy and initiative that had been persistently and skillfully capitalized by all American orators, politicians and newspapers. So this was architecture! said the gaping throngs. My word—isn't it wonderful! Yes, said the canny boosters and land speculators, now well in their stride, and we can duplicate it right in our own home town. We can put ourselves on the map—make people talk about us and our buildings—start on the

[259]

right path—and you'll be surprised to see how land prices will go up, once we begin to do some architecture. To all of which the aspiring architects naturally and gleefully assented, for they foresaw no more than the rest. Some of them really cared more, and believed that architecture ought to be a great socially planned endeavor, but their voices were still and small.

Not nearly so loud as the crying of the boosters, or of the skillful architectural salesman. These might be named as McKim, Richard M. Hunt and George B. Post, of New York; Peabody & Stearns of Boston; Van Brunt & Howe of Kansas City; and D. H. Burnham of Chicago. They were the designers of the World's Fair buildings in Chicago, although others were invited in as advisers and co-workers. Burnham was the generalissimo, the driving force behind the Fair. He was a complete Roman, of pure Roman traditions, as far as architecture was concerned.

Louis H. Sullivan was the one vital spark. There he stood, pathetically alone, urging that the World's Fair be made the testing ground for a rebirth of architecture, for a return to the craftsman simplicity of concept and method. A building, said he, was something that should grow honestly and naturally around a purpose. It should be planned first for use, and the form and pattern should then bloom like a flower opening its petals. That was the way all great building had grown. There was no other way to get great building.

He might as well have saved his breath, except that he got one building to design. To understand his idea and what it means, one has but to look at a picture of his Transportation Building, and then at the rest of the imported ideas borrowed from the panorama of a Roman holiday. It wasn't a perfect building, for there never was one. Anyone who

[260]

roams for long about the Parthenon, for example, will very much doubt whether the interior was much to boast about in comparison with the outside.

Louis Sullivan was trying to give utterance to an idea. To say that any of his buildings were perfect would be to ignore their faults. The battle he fought was naturally a losing one. He was impotent to make people believe in his idea, save the few who commissioned him to build those exciting buildings of which there now remain the Auditorium in Chicago, the Wainwright Building in St. Louis, and the Prudential Building in Buffalo. His teachings were eagerly grasped by a host of younger men, but against the old established practitioners and salesmen, he was as helpless to push his idea as George Westinghouse was to make people believe that a freight train could be stopped by an air-brake, or as Richard Strauss was able to have instantly acclaimed that glorious musical picture of the gallant hungering love quest of Don Juan, or the quaint vagaries of Till Eulenspiegel. Today, all freight trains are stopped by opening an air-valve, and the tone poems of Strauss are as accepted as the symphonies of Beethoven. So is it now plainly seen in Northern Europe, as it is beginning to be seen in America, that Louis Sullivan's basic idea is the valid one for all architecture! Westinghouse and Strauss lived to see their victory. Sullivan died just as Europe was beginning to give great heed to his ideas in many a building, and just as America was beginning to cry out for "modern," "functional" architecture. But what a costly process it has been, even to begin the overthrow of the old Romans, and what a struggle is still ahead before men shall realize that the form of a civilization follows its function, and that the United States has been badly off the road for many a long year!

What a debt has been piled up by architecture in the process! It puts Rome to shame, Byzantium in the pinchbeck class, and Thebes under Rameses a puling pigmy. The United States now staggers under something like five hundred billions of dollars of debt (including all public and semi-public debt, and all land "values" held for rent) almost every cent of which (except the few billions spent on wars) has been piled up in buildings, or in schemes that serve buildings. Not even Louis Sullivan foresaw, as he first uttered his challenge, that the pecuniary method of dealing with land and buildings, in the United States, was enough to hamstring any possible development of a sane and ordered architecture. In 1922, when we talked of the debacle then so plainly on the way, he had seen and understood, as the *Autobiography of an Idea* foreshadows.

What tide might have prevailed, in the battle he fought and lost, had anyone been able to make Americans realize the frightful cost and waste involved in their building methods and land gambling, is no more than a dead hypothesis. My guess is that nothing would have changed the course of events. The United States was headed for empire, not only in a big national way, but in the smaller empires that gradually swung into control of all life as the captains (?) of industry and the giants (?) of finance forged, welded and organized their well-entrenched principalities.

As time went on, it grew easier and easier to sell architecture. McKim's fine showmanship and persuasive eloquence, as he set forth the cultural correctness of his selected European styles, formed the basis for an architectural attack, by the encouraged profession, the results of which we

[262]

shall presently consider. If one tried to draw a sharp line, at this point, one might divide the followers of architecture as a profession into two schools. On the one side they ranged about McKim, on the other about Sullivan. To pick out the leaders of the former school would be to recite the names of most of the eminent architects in the United States. They grouped themselves roughly into the Classicists, the Renaissancists, the Gothicists. Sandwiched in among these more notable groups were the Romanesquists, the Tudorists, the Georgianists, the Colonialists. Towards the end of the prosperity era there came a flood of Spanishists, particularly in California and Florida. So great was this latter inundation that I remember receiving a telegram, about 1925, in which I was begged to find and send quickly a book of Swiss chalet designs; for, said the Florida boomster who signed the request, "we are sick to death of the Spanish stuff."

Straggling along, pitifully in the rear, were the followers of Sullivan. They were the veritable outcasts of the profession, men who tried to point out that buildings were for use and that their form and looks should be determined by a rigid adherence to honesty in plan. They were a constant petty annoyance to a profession that had built its whole attack—and planned all its methods of teaching—on the production of guaranteed and recognizable styles, the styles that Americans flocked to Europe to see in their own habitat, without ever suspecting why they were there. The women came home, all too often, with some guide-book patter about apses, buttresses, mullions, corbels, oriels, loggias, fleches and gargoyles, and then wrote papers for their clubs and indulged their stylistic fancies. The men took European architecture with less excitement, paid the bills, and picked their architect because of his social position or his skill

[263]

(or that of his wife) in casting a halo about his reputation.

The magazines began to see buildings and their materials and accessories as a lucrative field for advertising, and their editors proceeded to make the American woman architecture-conscious. Edward Bok, of *Ladies' Home Journal* fame, once boasted to me that single-handed he had destroyed the American parlor. In the same breath he told his plan for putting a quietus on the separate dining-room, but one suspects that the land-speculating apartment-house generals were on the field before he had his forces marshalled. At all events, the kitchenette appeared, and there followed (or preceded) the wall-bed, the Pullman and the convertible bath. Little by little a vast army of Americans sunk tighter and tighter into their sardine-boxes or gold-fish bowls, at steadily mounting rentals.

The era of the Classicists is not yet ended, although the Lincoln Memorial at Washington is now an old building. Into the designing of it the architect threw all his energy and all the knowledge that pottering measures and calculators have been able to extract from the bones of the Greek temples. The result is a heavy handicap, for the emotional content of this skillfully hallowed Greek form has the effect of completely hiding the fact that the Greek builders, were they alive, would never so build. They had a principle and it produced a temple. To imagine that 2,500 years later they would still be clinging to that form is to insult their superb intelligence.

Also, to compare the Lincoln Memorial with the War Memorial in Berlin—the simple and profoundly moving building that the architect, Heinrich Tessenow, succeeded in fashioning from an abandoned guard-house on the Linden —is to realize the lengths to which a maudlin "art" propa-

[264]

ganda has permitted architectural salesmanship to impose on the American people.

McKim's eminent disciple was his partner, Stanford White. Their firm is credited with the Columbia Library in New York, of which it used to be current gossip amongst the profession that the building had a place for everything —except books. But of how many other libraries may not the same thing be said? The list of absurdities is infinite. The pile of arches, columns, cornices and ornaments grew like an ant-hill. The one idea was to put on a front. Consider, for a moment, the art museum. As the first one seems to have been made by stuffing paintings into an abandoned Italian palace, it was taken for granted that an art museum had to look like a palace. To understand this thoroughly, one might read the report prepared for the trustees of the Museum of Fine Arts at Boston before they built the present structure, and then look at the building, which completely ignored the report.

Slowly, the idea of a Greek temple as the fitting form for a bank gave way to the Italian palace, the lower stories of which were practically a fortified enclosure. If the Federal Reserve Bank at New York is a conspicuous example of this change in style, there are countless other examples all over the country. They began to appear as soon as the architectural magazines could feed the photographs and drawings to their subscribers, most of whom used their borrowings as brazenly as a bill-poster looks for the nearest blank wall.

Whether Gothic, pursued so assiduously by a small clique of salesmen and a host of satellites, will die any easier than the Classic, is hard to say. The cathedral of St. John the Divine, in New York, and that in Washington, together with

[265]

many minor edifices, may serve to keep these highly emotional embers bright for a long time. Nothing could today be more absurd than the Gothic style for any kind of building, but it is particularly unsuited to churches where any fair-sized congregation wishes to see and hear what is going on. Structurally, the Gothic methods of building are as antiquated (but never their principles!) as a trireme would be ridiculous in the rôle of a torpedo destroyer. To imitate masonry by encasing the supporting steel members with Gothic-looking stonework, in order to produce an emotional reaction that will save the revenues of the church, hardly seems more than a desperate expedient. It is probably true that man cannot live without a religion, and that never did he more sorely need one than now, but the one he needs cannot be entombed in any style of building.

To use the outward form of a Gothic tower in order to build an advertisement called a "cathedral of learning," merely indicates the paucity of the American imagination or the gullibility of those in whom the last atom of sales resistance has at last collapsed into a complete abdication of both the will or the right to think.

To offset these endless examples of costly sham and skillfully promoted humbug and debt, one turns to such an outstanding example as the new Telephone Building in New York. It is not a pure growth of organic form, for its designers had to work under legal restrictions, and it has not the soaring quality that height should give, but it is a fine example of courage and logic. So enormous a building—minus the enrichment of the interior—might actually belong in a community, for it is a great public service station where there has to be a vast and complex centralization. It is not easy to find a valid reason for other monstrous buildings, but there are countless minor instances, all over the United States, where the plodding faithful have partly or wholly persuaded their clients to look at the art of building as a creative act. Let those who are really interested in such an idea, where the best that lies in man may find a healthy outlet for a worthy social expression, search out these buildings—not with a list or a guide-book, but with their own seeing eye. So may they grow to penetrate and understand and thus add their mite to the weight of intelligence that seeks to restore building to its natural and therefore prime function—a useful and pleasant service to men.

The problem of the architects, as time passed and salesmanship grew more keen, was to keep the field for themselves. Profits, in fees and commissions, paid for the profligate waste set up by bond issues, and land inflations were too tempting to pass unnoticed. As in France, in the early days of the Academy of Architecture, anybody with some skill with a pencil could set up as a building designer. At first, one had to know a little about building construction, but about the time of the World's Fair, the contracting method had come so well to the front that the practice of architecture was fairly easy. The lump-sum contract was a great help, not only to budding architects who had studied at the Ecole in Paris and who knew next to nothing about how a building was actually built, but to the valiant young army that was hanging out its "architect" shingles wherever a town seemed to be growing.

The contractor named his lump-sum for the building. The architect took as his wage a percentage. He called it a fee, naturally, and having multiplied the total bid of the contractor by some number—usually five at that time— there was the amount of his payment. There was no more rhyme or reason to such a method than in paying a surgeon by weight of appendix, but it was so simple! One only needed to know how to draw and multiply. The contractor did the rest and saw the architect through. His profits were not thereby cut down; and as owners were pleased, because they thought they knew just what a building was to cost, the method worked.

It had one fault, as it turned out later, for architects could undercut each other by a half or one percent, and that made a difference in owners' costs that appealed to many people. After a hard fight, the architect was generally able to have the courts regard six percent as the fair fee for an architect, whenever there was a dispute or where there was no more than an oral agreement requiring adjudication. Many timid architects were loth to talk about their fee in advance, or to lay too great stress on it. If one could get the job under way, and if enough work were done, the courts could be relied on to fix the fee. This is not to say that architects generally carried on business in that way, but the record turns up a good deal of carelessness.

In time, straightforward clear-thinking men in the profession set up a right relationship between architect and client. The sum to be paid the architect, for his services, is agreed upon. The client also agrees to pay the general cost of making drawings and looking after the work. Fair enough! It is an honest basis. If a client suddenly decides, after having approved the plans or after the building has been begun, that he wishes to move the stairs or the bathroom, the architect should not be asked to pay the cost of redrawing the plans. Too often has the architect been sponged on by clients, school boards and church committees. On the percentage basis, he was a tool in their hands. On the fee-plus-cost basis, just outlined, he regains his own dignity, and also becomes dignified in the eyes of his clients. He can cheat, of course, under this method, for none will stop that. But an architect intelligent enough to practise on such a basis is unlikely to be the cheating kind. The reason generally offered for failure to adopt this straightforward method of charging, throughout the profession, is the professional fear of upsetting the court standard of six percent!

The fight to preserve the building field for architects has been as keen as that to keep any but a carpenter from using saw or chisel on any union job. To touch wood, a carpenter must be called, just as with all other trades one of its members must be called. The general cry is that this adds to the cost of building, but costs are something about which no one knows very much, in the final summing. To the cost of present trade-union practices must be added the cost of unemployment. Part of it has always had to be added, but now it is plainly something that has come to stay, as long as the United States keeps on with many worn-out ideas of production and distribution. What a real cost is, no one knows. What charges are fair, or when money is saved in a building, no one knows. The whole subject of building—or any other —costs is as blind a guess as the date of the day of judgment. To say that the building industry is in a state of complete chaos is to say no more than can be said of any industry, so far as monetary factors are concerned.

The architect, fighting his own battle, has steadily sought statute laws that would preserve his hunting-grounds. In many States, registration laws of varying degrees of usefulness and severity now make it an offense to practise architecture without taking a State license. Where filing plans with public authorities is compulsory, no permit to build may be issued, in States having registration laws, unless plans are signed by a registered architect. This leads to various tricks by which the law is evaded; so the general gain for the profession has not been very great. It protests, as a matter of form, that it seeks protective laws in order that buildings shall be completely designed and thus be safe, but the pretext is not very convincing. One surmises that once the profession as a whole were given control of licensing, the tendency would be to keep the number of architects at a point where those in control would not be in danger of going workless. Architects are no more to be trusted with such power than are the members of any other class—not yet.

There have been a few sporadic efforts to form guilds in the practice of architecture. Groups have formed in cities and their services have been offered in public work. It was asserted that the city thus got the benefit of the best thought and skill of many architects, rather than the equipment of one, where one was chosen. The idea sounds plausible, and some day, in some civilization, builders will very likely be sensibly organized to build sensible communities. At present, most guild efforts in the United States have suffered from and been complicated by fights between those who joined the guild and those who wouldn't.

Where they were organized frankly to keep out-of-town architects from carrying off home-town work, emphasis has been on the defensive movement rather than the co-operative idea. In Washington, D. C., for example, the guild was undoubtedly a struggle by local architects to keep the one-time members of the Commission of Fine Arts from getting all the Washington public buildings to design. The local talent never got a look-in, and could scarcely be blamed for

thinking that as an architect had first to pass through the
Roman kindergarten conducted by the Commission of Fine
Arts, ere he could be allowed to design a public building
in Washington, and as no Washington architect could get
on the commission, there had to be some sort of defense.
At all events, the Allied Architects of Washington got one
Federal building to design!

The guilds in other cities had another appeal. Any public
authority finds it difficult, in view of political pull, prestige
and other influences brought to bear, to single out a home-
town architect. It is easier to bring one in from afar. To
prevent this, the home-town talent must either urge a costly
and wasteful competition to choose a home-town man, or
else all home-town men must offer their services as a whole.
The latter method has an appeal that is likely to grow
stronger and stronger as citizens begin to grapple with debt
and with plans for having all home-town money spent at
home.

One further effect of the architectural crusade, following
the World's Fair and much accented by the rise of professional land booming and boosting, was what might be called
keeping-up-with-the-Joneses. Not merely in buying architecture, but in buying the same kind the Joneses had bought.
In each part of the United States there are natural traditions of building. Colonists used local materials, and up to
the time of Richardson and McKim, this had pretty generally been the case. New Orleans and other Southern ports
had developed the strange incongruity of Quincy granite
for a number of public buildings, but that was because the
cotton boats took granite as ballast on the return trip from

Boston. Otherwise, people clung fairly well and with great intelligence to what they had.

The new ideas upset all that. New Orleans presently emerged with one of the worst examples of public building to be found in all America. Never was there a greater absurdity than dragging marble to New Orleans to build a bounder of a court house, right on the road to Jackson Square and almost in the heart of the Vieux Carré. It is so outstanding an instance of what happened when skilled architectural salesmanship was in the saddle that it deserves to be proclaimed as the world's worst example. Yet it is, after all, but a sample of what happened everywhere. What! said the neighbors—build a brick court house! The whole town is already full of brick! We must have marble! Or we must have granite! Or we must have terra cotta that looks like marble! In the end they had whatever had been presented by the smartest salesman, although the architect may have cast a deciding vote, or some politician may have thrown in his influence.

The result was that the United States not only changed its style of hat at the bidding of the stylemongers, but changed its building materials at the behest of whatever Tom, Dick or Harry could outsell the other. In time there was no difference in leaving the railroad station at Cosmopolis, Megalopolis or any other 'polis. One came out of the station, one drove through streets like all other streets, entered a hotel like all other hotels, walked into a room like all other rooms, out of which one looked at the same scene and into which came the same sounds and smells of the food one ate in a bastard Beaux Arts dining-room like all other bastard Beaux Arts dining-rooms.

As for schools, one can but repeat the same story. Their

[272]

cost rose to unbelievable heights, but here was Jonesville with a million-dollar high school! There was Smithville with another! While Brownsville had two of them and a Junior High! The bond issue was big, the cost of keeping up the plant would be heavy, but what could Whitesville do? Let the price of land fall in the home town? See people moving away because the children had a better school somewhere else? Never! Jonesville, Smithville and Brownsville were alive and growing. Their citizens got together and pushed and boosted! They were getting somewhere! They had bonded the town and gone ahead, and look at them!

Well—look at them, now the cyclone has passed. One doesn't need to look far amongst the wreckage to discover that the high cost of architecture, based on the present method of landlordism and usury, has drained away the hope and the future of millions. It would have been far better if most of the great array of costly buildings, put up to advertise and promote the interests of land owners and then frantically continued for the purpose of bolstering up the paper values issued against congestion, had never been built. How many towns and cities would now gladly exchange a lot of their buildings for a release from debt? Or for the simpler buildings they might have had if the pressure of land gambling and population hunting had not so betrayed them.

It is a sad and sorry picture, shorn of its emotional esthetic hullabaloo and looked at as a reality. There need have been no such debauch. Architecture, in itself, derives from nothing but the act of building, and is a means to great blessings. Not yet has any people—calling themselves civilized—learned how to use it. Not yet!

There is no date in American history when one can say that any marked change occurred in the manner of building, save only the approximate date of the birth of the steel skeleton. Chicago claims this with more ferocity than seems necessary, or than it may care to exhibit when the whole tale will have been told. But let Chicago pass, and the date 1887 along with it, and let the firm of Holabird & Roche, architects, have the glory that may attach to the Tacoma Building as the first of its kind. The rest of us are now faced with the debt, and while the steel skyscraper isn't wholly responsible, nothing like the billions of debt now hanging over the United States would have been possible, save for a method of capitalizing land values by herding people in steel skeleton buildings that outstripped anything land-lordism had been able to get from the builders with brick or stone.

The steel skeleton merely excited the rate of movement. It did not change the direction. In that there has been no change. The volume of building grew steadily as men grew more and more skillful in looting and destroying one of the grandest natural resource inheritances that ever a people knew. If one had explained to members of the Virginia Company in the London counting-houses that the land system to be set up in the Colonies would finally oblige many millions in America to drink water so infected with sewage as to require chlorination, it would have changed nothing.

In America, forests fell like dry grass in a prairie fire. One can make no serious study of architecture without reading the account of what happened to the store of timber that might have been an endless blessing. "Practically the entire State of New York was originally covered with a magnificent forest of white pine, spruce, hemlock and hard woods. . . .

The forest history of Pennsylvania has been similar to that of New York. . . . The history of lumbering in the Lake States during the greater part of the last century is substantially the history of white pine exploitation. . . . New England has passed through every stage of forest exploitation from the days when only the best white pines and oaks were merchantable to present dependence upon outside lumber and pulp wood. With the exception of a few small areas, New England was, in 1620, a virgin forest, comprising some 39,000,000 acres. In 1920, not more than 5% remains." [1]

Well may the forests have shuddered when the *Mayflower* and the *Susan Constant* cast anchor.

It was the red-shirted high-booted industrial pioneers of Pennsylvania (with all due respect to Chicago) who found the way to do what the builders of the Ames Building could not do. It was the same men, following one another in an impetuous stream as they wrenched coal and iron from the earth, who perfected the rolling-mills that made I-beams, L-beams and H-beams. Like the sharp-eyed business hunters they were, these men who played with steel and who meant to sell it in millions of tons soon found engineers who did nothing but devise more ways of using steel. They found the way to make a building with a steel skeleton, where walls were no longer needed save as screens and wind-breaks. They could then be made no more than one brick thick, be tied to the steel skeleton that carried all loads, and the masons could begin laying them at the bottom or the top or in the middle or wherever time could be saved. Floors could be

[1] *Timber Depletion.* U. S. Dept. of Agriculture. Forest Service, June 1, 1920.

made thinner, partitions thinner, and with high-speed elevators and pipes and wires, the race was on!

The steel skeleton was the signal for such a gambling in land and buildings as must have caused the original shareholders of the Virginia Company to turn in their graves with envy. It left all other betting no more than a piker's amusement. Never was there such a green cloth as the land, with all America rushing to cash in, building like madmen with one hand and piling debt with the other! A building method had been found that turned town and city land gambling into a dazzling glitter. The few poor things who protested were almost lynched as dangerous radicals and progress obstructers. It was believed that the price of land and the rentals to be collected therefrom could rise without end.

The height of skyscrapers was limited after the first feverish flurry. City populations were being shifted so fast that great areas of urban land fell in value. Taxable values in such areas likewise fell and the revenue loss to the city was not made up by higher assessments in the new skyscraping areas, for these demanded vast city expenditures for additional services of all kinds. The game was going so fast that city debt limits, based on property values, could not expand fast enough to permit borrowing the vast sums needed for "public improvements." Some cities, instead of fixing a limit of building height, as a possible means of stabilizing land values and preventing further traffic congestion, applied set-back regulations. These demand that a building shall rise only to a certain height on a street front, and then the walls must be set back just as in a pyramid. There is then no height limit. A building may go a thousand stories, if it starts with a big enough ground area, and it was towards

bigger ground areas that speculators turned. The relation of
paper securities already issued against land inflation and
human congestion left them no alternative (save collapse),
as we shall later see. It is a curious commentary that America's most acclaimed contribution to architecture—the skyscraper—derives from steel mill, engineer, the law and
frenzied finance, in which the architect is no more than a
gambling society's errand boy.

Forcing these greater buildings threw into the rental
market such an area of floor-space as could be filled only
by emptying scores of other buildings, a fact that marked
the beginning of the end. The debt load had reached a point,
not only in land and buildings, but in all forms of public
and private debt, such as no people could longer bear. In
the gamble, public borrowing powers had been signed away
until many cities were literally insolvent. Even in 1929,
when signs of coming foreclosure were written large all
over the United States, skyscrapers were still going up. In
spite of the fact that the last ones built were still standing
empty, new ones were actually going up. Why? Because the
"investment bankers" had sold bonds for the gamble! The
money had to be thrown away in order to pay flotation
percentages.

To attempt to single out any particular building, in all
this general mess, and point out its esthetic merit as a piece
of architecture, or art, seems rather futile. One can scarcely
think of a building that was not more or less a chip in the
gamble. Churches, schools, theaters, hotels, office buildings,
public buildings, all built with borrowed money—all pawns
in the game!

The part played by the church, now stolidly giving its
sanction to and taking its profits from landlordism, is not a

pleasant picture. "Churches which have been tax-exempt for years are now allowed to sell their land at a profit and keep the profit. The potential profits in this field are enormous. The land on which Trinity Church is located increased in value from $3,750,000 in 1885, to $24,800,000 in 1932. The land on which St. Bartholomew's church is located, increased in value from $1,250,000 in 1920 to $3,650,000 in 1932. Some years ago Temple Emanu-El, which was then situated on the corner of 43rd. Street and 5th. Avenue, sold its land at a profit of millions of dollars, although the land had been tax-exempt for many years. Its plot had increased in value from 1900 to 1929 more than 500 percent. The temple was permitted to keep enough money to erect an enormous new plant farther up Fifth Avenue and leave a million dollar surplus. The Madison Avenue Methodist Church made a profit of $650,000 by selling its old site for an apartment house and moving around the corner. Instances of this type could be multiplied many times." [1]

The situation described is by no means confined to New York.

The process by which the great bulk of buildings came into being is perfectly set forth in the Report of the Committee on Site Planning of the American Institute of Architects. The Committee assumes that readers are familiar with the usual activities of landlords, boosters, real estate dealers and speculators, and the network of political dealings and favors that are a part of present American community life, and then traces the sequence of events as follows:

[1] *The Problem of Tax Exemption.* City Affairs Committee Bulletin. New York, December, 1933.

[278]

"(A1) a public improvement; (A2) higher property values; (A3) higher taxes; (A4) more bulky buildings or intensive use of private property; (A5) more people and more vehicles in the streets; (A6) demand for 'relief from congestion'; (A7) specific proposals for new public improvements; (B1) new improvements at public expense; (B2) increased property values; (B3) still higher taxes; (B4) still more intensive use of private property; (B5) still more congestion of people and vehicles in the streets; (B6) demand for more 'relief from congestion'; (B7) new schemes proposed to increase values; (C1) another publicly financed public improvement program—and—so on.

"All through this vicious spiral the public treasury never comes out ahead. Its credit becomes pledged to the limit; some property owners are more or less constantly 'on the make'; other owners have nothing done to develop their own properties, the while they contribute taxes towards the effort to increase the value of the favored owners' property. Is it any wonder that financial processes so inequitable should make congestion profitable to some and to that extent desirable to some—or that the municipality and the neglected parts should be led into bankruptcy?"

This is the history of debt and city land gambling, but it is also the story of American architecture! To refuse to take these facts into account is to fail to understand why our cities were built as they were, and why the procession of palaces and hovels. The gamble has come to an end—for the moment. No doubt it will be resumed as quickly as people can be induced to gamble some more. Owners of unused city land and buildings are champing at the bit. They are eager to shift the present tax and interest load to

[279]

somebody, and no doubt a fresh crop of suckers will appear. But that won't make better cities! That won't pay the debt! As for architecture, the shift will merely raise the percentage of hovels.

XII

ENTER—THE PIPER

IT HAD become clear to smart Americans, soon after the Civil War, that the way to cash in quickly on land, of which vast areas had been acquired and held as investment by Europeans as well as Americans, was to fill the country with people. The old way of waiting for children was too slow. Each shipload of immigrants increased the demand for land. That led to a demand for buildings. Each building increased the price of adjoining land. William Penn had worked the trick when he laid out Philadelphia, as so well told by Mr. John Irwin Bright in his studies of the plan of that city.[1]

Penn marked the city off in squares. He made the streets as narrow as he dared, for to him streets were hardly more than land that could not be sold. He then sold lots, keeping

[1] *Art and Archæology. April, 1926.*

[281]

every other one in his own hands. As lots were bought, the price of neighboring ones rose. Penn and his friends cashed in, although some held on for years. Generally, that is the basis of what is called land-subdivision in the United States. The method is illustrated very simply, by the tale of the man who asked the price of a lot.

"Two hundred dollars," said the realtor.

"I'll take two," said the man.

"That'll be five hundred dollars."

"How's that?" said the buyer.

"Well, you see, the moment you buy one lot, the one next to it goes up fifty percent."

This was the rough basic idea of the men in those old English counting-houses. Had it fallen by the wayside, during the two centuries of settlement? Not at all. The record shows some huge fortunes gathered by those who only sat and waited during all the long years the country had been filling. From the invention of the railroad, it had slowly been carved and plotted, as one line after another opened up great areas and natural resources. As soon as the free land had been sold or given away, the real business of cashing in could begin.

"When the Republicans in their platform of 1860 offered free land to the workingmen of the land, in exchange for a protective tariff, the way was already opened for a tumultuous response. When in the midst of the Civil War the Republicans fulfilled their pledge by beginning to fling the land to the clamoring multitude, the economic revolution was begun." [1]

The gates were opened wide. Millions of all sorts of Europeans were invited in. Invited? They were herded in

[1] *The Rise of American Civilization.* By Charles A. and Mary Beard.

[282]

droves and jammed in the steerage of ten thousand ships. Let us get the true picture at this point, for it is part and parcel of the growth of palace and hovel in American architecture. These millions were wanted, not for their art or culture, but to labor on great railroad and collateral schemes necessary for the land game, and then to buy at an inflated price the land their very labor had made accessible. To study American architecture without looking at these facts and their consequences is like trying to gauge the flow of the Mississippi with a bucket.

Railroads, seen as great tools for opening up land in America, were built by creating a vast semi-public interest-bearing debt. To this was added the infinitely greater and constantly mounting debt known as land values, which, to all present intents and purposes, is undischargeable. It may change hands, but that only changes ownership. Under the present set-up, it remains forever.

All architecture thus begins with a land debt. Not a constant factor, but one that rises steadily with each building operation so that the cost of building must either rise or its quality fall. It only remains to add—as anyone can see by looking realistically at the United States in which he lives— that there is no possible way to get architecture by the land debt process, save in a constantly rising percentage of hovels.

As architects, engineers and builders fell into line with the technique of the steel skeleton and learned to make bigger and bigger buildings, "congestion" began to get in the headlines. In the slums it had annoyed only those who lived there. With the rise of the land-inflation skyscraper game, congestion spread to all quarters. All city streets and sidewalks filled up. The more traffic routes, the more traffic. Rapid transit by rail and concrete highway, offered as a cure, dumped new crowds in the outskirts, but landlords had got there first. Inflated land prices at all rapid-transit outlets forced more congestion. Down went the size of dwellings, down went the size of rooms, up soared both land debt and public debt.

Rapid-transit squeezing and crowding turned congestion into a commodity, dealt with as one deals with any profit-making commodity. The paper values issued against it as "securities" were passed into our monetary and currency systems, and used as the basis for fresh inflations and congestion operations. Few guessed that in order to do away with congestion one would also have to destroy the paper values issued against it as debt! Few were wise enough to see that more than becoming a mere social malady, congestion was a sinister vested interest, holding up the mounting pile of debt.

Suddenly, with a defiance that stunned a proud and conceited people like an icy douche, debt shook itself clear of the maze and took the people of the United States by the throat. Long ago it had taken architecture by the throat, insofar as providing enough decent houses or agreeable communities for people to live in. Now it shook the nation as a terrier shakes a rat!

Looking calmly at the wreckage from the vantage of the present day, it is clear that, from 1900 on, the United States was in a feverish race with debt. Quite a race it was, as billions of paper values poured from the printing presses. The guiding rein and goading spurs for the banking jockeys who rode, in order that millions might bet, or be shoved about as human pawns in the great city gamble in the new steel architecture, was the pressing need to herd and congest people rapidly enough to keep the inflation from collapsing. There had to be higher land prices in order that more paper values might be issued in order that the previously issued paper values be kept afloat. By their very swarming, people gave these higher prices to land and put themselves more and more in debt, to land owners and money-lenders who sold the debt as an "investment." Against the rising billions of debt that rested on nothing but human congestion, skyscrapers rose endlessly, while a million Americans were inveigled into buying houses at prices inflated hopelessly beyond their power ever to pay off the mortgage.

A third of all taxes in New York City is now required to service its debt of two and a third billion dollars. No doubt there has been waste in piling this enormous burden of unpayable debt. The point is that far the greater part has been piled in an effort to serve land and building speculation (exactly as described in the Committee Report of the A. I. A. on page 279) with those amenities that keep land debt afloat—water, police, schools, streets, jails, courts, hospitals, asylums, parks, playgrounds, and transportation underground in which the city is a heavy investor. Well— says somebody—you couldn't have a city without buildings! Quite true, but there could easily be a city without debt— and without taxes!

The two and a third billions is only part of the debt burden on the citizens of New York. All land in the city is also a debt. Whatever its valuation—call it five billions for the moment—it represents debt. It is not usually so figured by professional economists, but what else is it?

Plainly, piling debt by inflating land prices by means of herding people and burdening the land with architecture is the same process that leads the deluded clerk to take money from the till, and then to keep on in the wild hope of somehow putting it back. One cannot stop; one has to go on, using the profits of inflation to make more inflation. When the jig is up, the Federal government must then supply taxpayers' billions in an effort to save the whole inflated debt structure, or hold it together until it can be liquidated by the slow process of foreclosure. After foreclosure, when millions of citizens have lost their all, and the flow of money is resumed, all the old debt will duly appear in new hands.

Architecture by the debt process is the old Roman empire game all over again, although exhaustion now comes not from a shortage of necessities, but from such demands by debt owners that people cannot buy their necessities even though the supply be even more abundant than ever before. Ever since the days of Khufru, it is really very plain that, by one method or another, all builders have been used for ends that were in themselves destroyers of the societies that employed them.

The results of the latest debt collapse will fall, as usual, most heavily on small owners. Skyscrapers, now foreclosed or rigidly deflated, will demand to be written down for taxable purposes, which means higher taxes somewhere else. "The skyscraper has created a new tax problem, and I don't think one of you will live to see another skyscraper go up in this city," said Mayor LaGuardia to one who reminded him that reduction in skyscraper valuations would cause house owners to suffer in proportion.[1]

If only the debt problem was so simple as to be solved by

[1] *New York Times*, February 9, 1934.

[286]

not building more skyscrapers! For the evils now here, money-juggling may palliate for a moment, but it cannot cure. The national game of the American people differs not a whit from the game as played by the Insulls, Kreugers, Hatrys and the Staviskys, whom men exalt, if successful, even as they turn and rend them when their debt pyramids fall.

It is time to attempt two definitions for architectural realists, and they shall be these:

Slums are those human habitations occupying areas where land has not yet risen to a price that will enable the owner to sell for as much as he thinks he can get by waiting for the growth of or changes in the town or city such as will create that demand for his slum land by which alone the price can be raised. In the meantime, slums can be rented to the poor, taxable values kept down, and if things do not get too bad the owner may be able to pay taxes out of rents —there is no upkeep and depreciation—trusting that some favorably located public or private improvement will some day send up the price of his land and give him his profit. It is a sordid tale and so full of tricks and evasions that a fair volume would be needed to describe them. The whole operation, even under the present chaotic order, is a net loss to everyone save the land owner, whose loss is only avoided by taking advantage of the community, if the chance occurs. He then puts the increment value in his pocket and the operation helps to swell the net land debt of the community.

Skyscrapers, on the other hand, are buildings, the first purpose of which is to enable the individual, or group, to cash in on land where, by reason of the swarming of the right kind of people, the price and the assessed tax value have risen so high that the owner must either cash in, if he can, or else build a building big enough to earn a profit on the new higher land price. Failure to do one or the other means that taxes will steadily eat away at the increment that has been added, for no matter what reason. Thousands upon thousands of buildings, including many of the first skyscrapers, were torn down during the great gamble that came to a pause in 1929, not because they were physically worn out, but because the land on which they stood had been inflated to such a price that the standing buildings could no longer earn enough money to pay taxes and overhead, and leave a profit for the owner.

This tale, like that of the slums, is equally full of tricks and evasions, of gambles and swindles (many skyscrapers appear to have been built for no reason save the sale of the bonds!), and the net effect on the community, in terms of money, is more disastrous than the effect of the slums. Skyscrapers demand enormous communal expenses and these turn up in the problems of debt and taxes that are likely to become tiresome, if not ugly, before the present financial debacle is cleared up.

Outstanding in the history of American skyscraping, because of their dramatic bigness, are the Rockefeller Center buildings in New York. They might well be christened the last word in that disorder for which the so-called experts are so skilled in selling to both owner and community. Every ounce of expertness that could be mustered was evidently used to confuse and obscure the social result. It was completely hidden by a series of land-value, architectural and engineering calculations that will have to pass as the consummate example of how realtors, architects and engi-

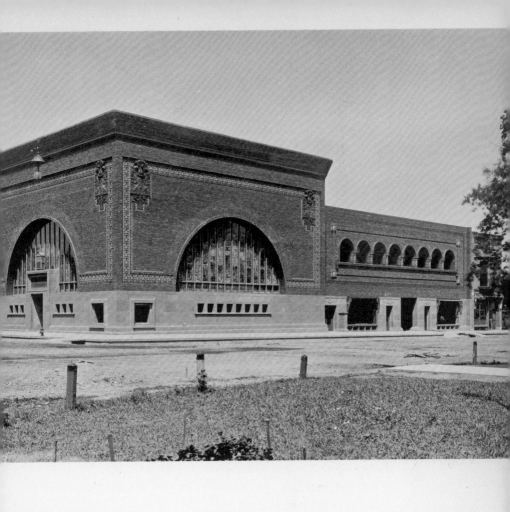

PLATE xx. THE OWATONNA BANK BUILDING (1907)
LOUIS H. SULLIVAN, ARCHITECT

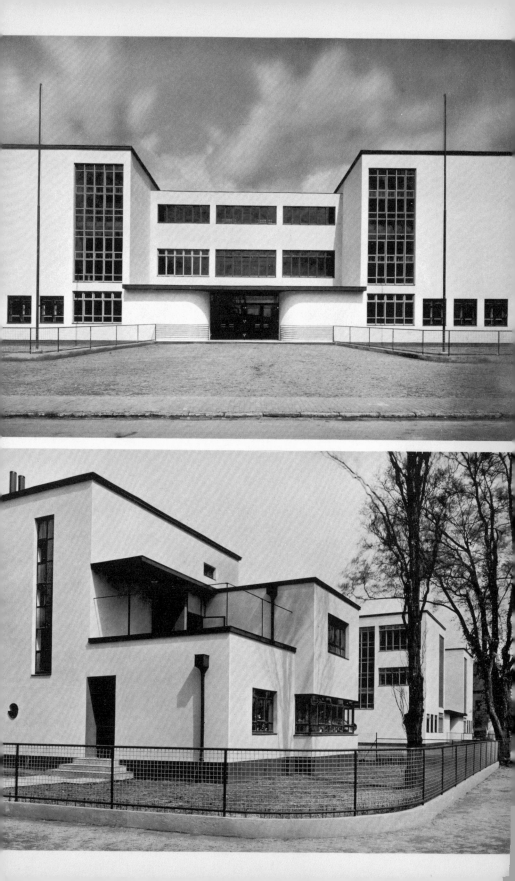

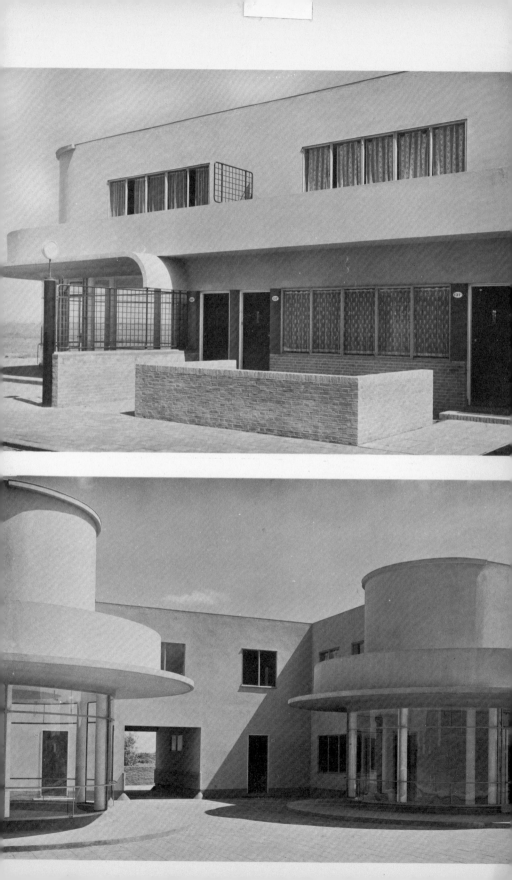

PLATE XXXIII. RESIDENCE OF FREDERICK V. FIELD, ESQ., NEW HARTFORD, CONN. HOWE AND LESCAZE, ARCHITECTS

PLATES XXXVIII AND XXXIX. TWO VIEWS OF AN EARLY
FARMSTEAD NEAR ANDOVER, MASSACHUSETTS

(*Photographs by W. C. Behrend*)

PLATE XL. AN EARLY GRAVEYARD, CONCORD, MASSACHUSETTS

PLATE XLI. A MODERN CEMETERY. (In no other examples of form and arrangement is the decline of craftsmanship and the rise of mass production so plainly apparent as in these homes of the dead.)

(*Photographs by W. C. Behrendt*)

neers proceed to arrive at what they call a "solution." One guesses the tragic result, no matter how it be viewed, as another sad tale of an owner who had in mind a beneficent center of activities in the field of the arts, and who was expertly misled into an operation that bears an ominous resemblance to the Golden House of Nero and the Great Palace of Justinian.

To judge the buildings as pieces of architecture is like dealing with floods and land erosion by completely forgetting the deforestation that set the wild waters in motion. The buildings were based on the expert belief, or the expert hope, that enough children would be born and would swarm on the scene, so that the land rent (reported to be three million dollars a year), plus amortization, overhead, taxes, upkeep, interest and profit, would be payable out of the congestion price to be charged for rentals—at least until the year 2015, when the buildings become the property of the land owner (at present, Columbia University).

The vast debt thus heaped up in a city square must be assumed not only by the living but is intended to be fastened to the backs of generations of children, from the moment they open their eyes on life.

Even Memphis and Thebes were not as cruelly stupid as that.

After five thousand years of a labor that has never ceased and which at times attained both a simplicity and a grandeur before which any sensitive person is rendered very humble— for it is before such works that one comes face to face with the great and noble powers that lie within man—it is plain that the great day for the builders is still ahead of them. Never yet have they wrought more than a fraction of what they might have done and what they alone can do—when the right time comes. Never have they had a chance to put their powers to free use and thus to give a fine form to man's world. For fifty centuries they have been used to build empires that could not endure, cities that could not stand, palaces for kings, temples for priests, and for each palace and temple a thousand hovels arose like a lamentation.

Their day has been long. Their misuse a melancholy betrayal. Some day, one refuses to cease hoping, they will begin to build a civilization. At last their chance will come. Ahead will be neither empires, palaces, temples nor hovels, but buildings befitting a race that has won its dignity of soul, its integrity and its security.

How hopeful does the future look for builders in the United States? The answer depends not upon their skill—never were they so well equipped with tools and materials—but upon the manner in which they are set to work, and that again depends on how resolutely the American people are willing to begin changing the ideas that have so far gone to perpetuate the Roman tradition, until the likeness begins to be almost too ominous. In guessing as to how far the national temper may change, each must make his own speculations. For the wreck left by the gambling frenzy, it is quite unfair to cast much blame. It was a pretty general debauch. Crucifying the bankers—the Insulls, Kreugers, Hatrys, and Staviskys—seems more like the savage act of a society that refuses to look at its own record as now written in its buildings than the act of a people not afraid to see their own image in the mirror. So long as men choose to gamble with land and debt in the hope of being able to live on the profits, who is to blame for whatever happens? The best one can do is to refuse to be misled by the talk and salesmanship of the debt-pilers, and by those who propose to salvage the worth-

[290]

while remnants of American life by schemes which, so long as they do not recognize the basic evils of land ownership and the present debt processes, will only tend, more and more, to make any salvage impossible.

How strange, said Francis Bacon, that men pursue power in order to lose their liberty! How strange also that men pursue debt in order to lose their security!

If one could detach oneself for a moment from the din of ritual and slogan, from the jargon of the economists, crop-destroyers, money-inflaters and price-raisers, and thus get a clear view; if one could see the whole and not merely the pleasant parts and thus get the picture in all its menacing ugliness, one might well feel that all that has happened since men turned back from their emotional consecration to war, in 1919, and began anew the fight for individual gain and security, is what the prophets of old would have called a revelation.

Not the thundering revelation of a stentorian voice crying in the wilderness, but that of a still small voice, saying quietly to a hundred bewildered millions, now swarming at the cross-roads as never before:

Man—look at the world you have made and the palaces and hovels with which you have sought your ends. Look at the picture before you. Look at each other. Look at yourselves.

What have you done to the land?

Where are the pleasant hills, the clean rivers, the quiet valleys, the plains and the forests?

O, the forests, where birds built their nests and where the winter snows were held that water might flow in steady abundance over an earth forever freshened and renewed, in ceaseless fertility and plenty!

[291]

O, the rivers, now so defiled that they stink in your sight!

What, O, Man, have you done to the land that was lent you?

"Lent?" asks the defiant glutton of ownership and usury, "I thought it was given."

But there is no answer. Revelations do not argue. They reveal.

XIII

THE FUTURE

FROM time to time, ever since the days of Louis Sullivan (and even though some of his friends refer to his philosophy as a "lost cause"), there has been talk about "modern" or "functional" architecture.[1] In the North of Europe, generally, after the War, and in Germany and Holland especially, arose many buildings in which architects had thrown away the usual classic and bourgeois forms and studied their task in terms of form and function.

Such architects found clients willing to risk outstanding changes in building looks. In making the change it was wholly natural that those who put up the money should be timid. One has to think about the liveness of an asset in case

[1] There were similar movements in England, as a result of the teachings of William Morris, and in Northern Europe generally under the leadership of Van der Velde, to whose disciples in the German *Jugendstil* and the French *Art Nouveau* movements the name of Sullivan was unknown.

of need, or ease of sale or rental if one is building on chance. Thus one has to reckon on the probable and possible income qualities in these new building ideas. An owner's decision to try a new theory of design is seldom based on any deep and abiding esthetic philosophy, but upon his guess as to what publicity value the building will have.

Just as the old Singer Building in New York gave the sewing machine a boost, so did the 5 and 10 cent business, life insurance, chewing gum, and what not, get similar boosts out of buildings. Over a decade or more, no big-business booster could lay his head on a pillow without dreaming uneasily of how to get his name, or that of his wares, attached to the "highest building in the world." Nor could the embryo landlords, wriggling their way out of the East Side of New York, lie quiet at night, so were they tortured with the dream of a Devonshire Arms or a Walsingham Manor on the Grand Concourse.

Americans had such a passion for going in debt that usurers could scarcely print the paper fast enough. Anything could be sold, if its name could be shouted loudly enough. As it came to be seen that architecture could make a hell of a noise, publicity in buildings grew to be as insulting (to sensitive people) as all other noise-makers, billboards and those forms of American bounderism that have grown out of salesmanship, as forced by the tricks of pyramiding inflations and increments. This is not to belittle form and function as applied to buildings—not by any means—but merely to point out that it is quite unlikely that what is called "modern" or "functional" architecture would have made any headway unless those who put up the money had been able to see the profitable publicity, the search for which now so largely governs American life and behavior.

[294]

As examples in esthetics, those who care about building as an art, were happy to see signs pointing away from the past. The skyscraper, under the new set-back regulations, driven to larger ground areas in order to get a fresh pecuniary vantage, had begun to take form. Hitherto a stylistic medley in two dimensions, it now recaptured a third, and began to emerge as a clean piece of three-dimensional wholeness. The Nebraska State Capitol had given designers a great deal to ponder. Its soaring tower actually served, not merely as a dignified emblem, but as working space for offices. The idea of the costly and useless dome had gone, one hoped, and although the few imitations of Goodhue's great work, so far, are thin and maudlin in comparison with the original, here at least was a definite gain in the use of common sense to plan and design a building.

The competition for the Chicago Tribune Building brought one of the most dramatic answers ever offered in a quest for notoriety, but as topping a building with an apse-like imitation of a Gothic cathedral seemed to possess the most advertising value, that idea was adopted. (No one would assert that the imitation flying buttresses served any other purpose.) Competent judges declared that the design offered by Eliel Saarinen, of Finland, should have had the prize. Some critics go so far as to say that in Saarinen's design lay the ultimate "solution" for the skyscraper. "In Saarinen's extraordinary conception, architecture, long bound with the chains of precedent and bent double with the load of commercial expediency, bursts its bonds and stands up as a free man. It is as though some titanic seed, planted in earth, had suddenly sprung from the mould into the light

[295]

of a shimmering bloom of stone and steel. It is the best design since Amiens!" [1]

Esthetically one can easily agree. Socially, in spite of all deserved praise for the designer who lost his chance, the skyscraper is no more than a gambler's chip in the game of land debt and usury. Until removed from that sphere and given its logical place in a community—if it has one, which is far from having been proved—the search for "solutions" may well be regarded as the emotional mumbling of weak-minded estheticians and petty empire makers. The wreck and ruin of debt and disorder left by the present crop of skyscrapers is enough to make any but a hopelessly stupid people pause and think.

This does not mean that there has been no progress in design. One can mark, all over the United States, many buildings where the competent creative designer has struggled to make the best of all conditions. When free to design a whole building, rather than one façade or a corner, one can note, almost for the first time since Colonial days, the presence of such form in a building as indicates a straightforward pursuit of rightness and a complete willingness to let the form grow naturally out of straightforwardness.

The net result for human beings is the same as at Memphis, Athens, Rome, or any of the seven so-called civilizations that Sir Flinders Petrie has traced in his many years of search.[2] The pyramid had form! So had Karnak! The Parthenon, the Pantheon, St. Sophia, and Amiens! But the social movement of the multitudes behind them had no enduring civilizing form, and it is the slow surge of the multitudes

[1] *The Story of Architecture in America.* By Thomas E. Tallmadge.
[2] *Revolutions of Civilization.* By Sir W. Flinders Petrie.

[296]

that determines the form and the duration of civilizations, not their architecture!

Architecture tells the story. Not yet has that story been used as the lesson!

Whether the lesson has now been learned, or will ever be learned, is anybody's guess. One might suppose that Americans, having suffered enough from the costly uses to which architecture has been put, would now be ready to talk sense about buildings. Emotional fervor over skylines is a pleasant indulgence, but when it comes to paying the cost of the folly, it may be guessed that it would be saner and far cheaper to let the architecture grow out of common sense rather than out of land debt.

From land debt, modern architecture has no escape to offer. Because a building fulfils its function that must of necessity now be based on monetary success, and the hope that it can carry the debt overhead, the social evils and pecuniary burdens thus thrown back on society as a whole are not thereby mitigated. Architecture is not like easel painting, nor is it like any work that expresses ideas in forms that are movable, transferrable and easily destructible. To judge a building as one judges such things, in mere terms of art talk, is to ignore the basic vital factors that make every building either a useful addition or a costly nuisance.

To those who look at the history of building in its relation to the follies and exaltations of men as they are pictured in the empires of kings and priests and in the wayward groping of democracies, with the endless procession of palaces, temples and hovels, it is easy to believe that the spirit of modern architecture is a voice crying in the wilderness. Not the simpering voice of "art," but the vibrant voice of rightness, steadfastly reminding us that it was a great folly to have departed from the simple principles that guided the first men in search of shelter and that comforted the craftsmen for thousands of years. One might easily imagine that the new feeling for straightforwardness in line, form and mass was a heroic effort to throw off the heavy burden of architecture as art, as advertising, as propaganda, and by recognition of basic things let the art emerge from the rightness of the building for the purpose, distorted as are most of our purposes by pecuniary considerations that have no relation to a civilization.

If we are pleased with the ideas that animate the technician who seeks to contrive a machine that will yield the best and most dependable results with the least number of parts and the minimum of energy used in doing its work, why not be equally pleased with the building that results from the use of the same basic idea of rightness? Could anyone tell the difference between the feelings of the painter who has at last put on canvas the idea that haunted his dreams, and the feelings of the technician who at last listens to the gentle rhythmic purring of the aëroplane engine that he too has dreamed and tuned? Do not both feelings spring from the same source? Why all the chatter and delusion over "art" and "artists"?

What makes any work great is simplicity and straightforwardness. Those are the qualities one looks for in a building, and they can be grasped only by looking inside the building as well as at the outside, if one seeks to judge it in terms that have any sense, whether the work be as old as the pyramids or as young as yesterday. The word "modern," as applied to architecture, is neither more nor less than the expression of a conceit. It describes the very ideas that guide the craftsman in the well-doing of anything. What is as old as the instinct of craftsmanship merely comes to life, as though it were boldly suggesting a way out of chaos and into a civilized order of society. We call this instinct modern merely because the word satisfies our ego, as well as our instinct for salesmanship.

If the effort to return to the craft principle of rightness be taken over by the salesmen who seek publicity and more profits, and if to such a purpose there be added the desire to satisfy the vanity of the architect, the result will be as before; another assemblage of insolent buildings and unpayable debts will be added to the American scene of disorder and discomfort. Rightness cannot spring from such a source. It must be born in something much deeper than that, if architecture is to be of any use. What the Greek builders gave to the world was not an enduring form for a building but a lesson in rightness. However intricate were the ways by which the Parthenon became so perfect a form, the methods were none other than the craft feeling for rightness. Other powers and forces put that feeling to rout, and the moment of that civilization was brief. The lesson that remains, nevertheless, is that nothing has ever changed the craft instinct and spirit, and that nothing can take its place as the cornerstone for a civilization.

To change the form of a world that is for the moment lost in the worship of things and in a frantic effort to bring them all into a pecuniary money-price relationship with the life and needs of man, architecture is helpless; but it is inexorable when it comes to writing the record. The moving finger writes, and not all the printing presses, though they run faster and faster to deny the truth and administer their daily opiates, can change a line of it. The American scene, as expressed in its buildings and their surroundings, is exactly as Louis Sullivan described it. The record is plain. One may deny it by refusing to look at it, but the physical form of the land from the Atlantic to the Pacific, as it took shape from the actions and behavior of the American people is as indelible as the heavens. Everything, from the tiniest atom to a nation of a hundred million people struggling desperately for security, takes its form from the purpose pursued.

In architecture, we have been taught to look at the high spots of the record, not only in the past but in our own performance. In the United States, the whole living record is still glaringly before us. It is the one record that cannot be falsified, and it is thus the only one that is worth while examining. Architecture—as expressing the whole building effort of a people—is the one document that can be relied upon to be without self-interest or the will to deceive. From it, wherever one looks, there is to be drawn the fact that nations take their present desperate form from the desperate purpose that now animates them, no matter how gay the palaces or how monumental the temples.

Ignoring the Century of Progress in Chicago in 1933-4, for its buildings belong not in a history of architecture but in one of salesmanship and advertising, there still remains one other thing to be said about modern functional architecture. Straightforwardly done, it often speaks in terms of great frankness, and that is always a gain to any society. One cannot say that this form of frankness has yet exerted any great effect on the moral fibre of the nation, or that the

[300]

idea of using buildings as advertising mediums, and the public weal be damned, has yet been permanently checked, or that some other equally anti-social method of using buildings will not be devised as men continue to pursue debt. So far, the modern movement indicates hardly more than the commercialization of novelty. This will have no effect on the palace and hovel method by which empires proceed to their destination. Talk about gains and savings to be made by the still franker use of steel, glass and all sorts of synthetic products, may mean some interesting flings at the common expense, but such flings will not alter the general result. There will be no social gains in the way of better houses and surroundings and no slowing down of either the land-debt or any other debt process, merely because of new and novel selling methods for architecture.

A great deal of nonsense has been talked by the chief sponsors of the movement called modern, and by those critics who regard a new façade precisely as they regard a variation in easel painting as shown in an exhibition, as though the interior of the building be a secondary or incidental factor in an outward esthetic result. No one will dispute the esthetic point of view upon which is based the plea for a rational honest approach to building. When it comes to saving money by the use of cheaper materials, or methods, or by any of the mass-production processes; or to making architecture a universal servant; or to effecting any useful changes in dwellings and their surroundings, one points out that the whole debt process may be relied on automatically to defeat or offset all gains that architecture can contrive. The present method of dealing with land will effectively prevent any movement towards making whatever may be called modern architecture generally useful in producing a rising state or order and more agreeable living conditions. The accompanying American debt process, following hard on the heels of the land system, cannot permit any permanent reduction in the relative cost of anything. Diminishing costs automatically destroy the foundation of debt, for that can exist only by a constant and continuous cost inflation based on waste and instability. It is likewise plain that the cost of labor saving will more and more be thrown back on the collectivity, by which it must be absorbed through some form of charity, thereby diminishing the net collective spending power. In the light of this vicious circle and these glaring facts, one should swallow any talk about modern architecture with a large grain of salt.

It will be quite useless to hope that any form of architecture will aid in abolishing slums or in restoring blighted areas to pleasurable occupancy, or in repairing tens of thousands of small towns, villages and settlements that comprise the broken-down countryside of the United States, so long as people are reckoned as clickers of turnstiles in the process of pyramiding debt. Looking back at the building done under that method, one can scarcely thrill with delight at the prospect of more of it, no matter how functional it may be or how much we are made to shine with chromium or glass, or settle down in factory-made houses.

The most certain sign on the horizon is debt. It will have to be dealt with, not only as a present intolerable burden, but as a principle. There will have to be a choice. Some day some people, one guesses, may see that debt is no more necessary as a means of setting the builders to work at their proper task of building the physical basis of a civilization than is more salt necessary in the sea. Debt is a noose, choking architecture and completely blocking its use for anything

[302]

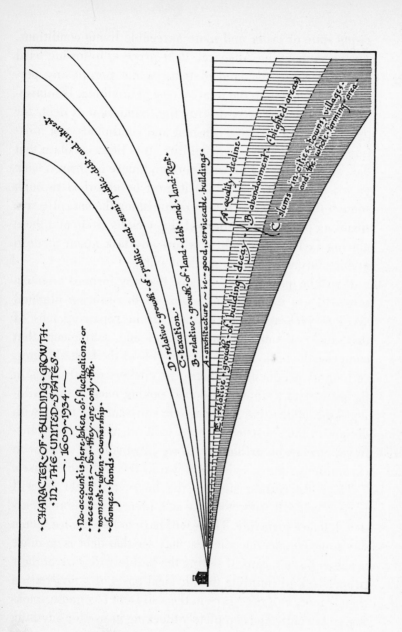

· CHARACTER · OF · BUILDING · GROWTH ·
· IN · THE · UNITED · STATES ·
— · 1609 ~ 1934 · —

· No · account · is · here · taken · of · fluctuations · or
· recessions ~ for · they · are · only · the ·
· moments · when · ownership ·
· changes · hands · — ~

E · relative · growth · of · debt · and · interest ·

D · relative · growth · of · public · and · semi · public ·

C · taxation ·

B · relative · growth · of · land · debt · and · land · Rent ·

A · architecture ~ ie · good, · serviceable · buildings ·

E · relative · growth · of · building · decay ·

A · quality · decline ·

B · abandonment ~ (blighted · areas)

(C · slums ~ in · cities, · towns, · villages ·
and · the · whole · farming · area ·

but palaces and temples. An intelligent society will some day throw it away and learn to issue currency against the creation of realities.

An outstanding example of the debt pyramid is New York, but the situation is relatively no different or more impossible to deal with than that of the great majority of communities, now that the wreck has to be faced. The debt figures for New York, in January, 1934, are these:

Rapid Transit	$683,000,000.
Water Supply	365,000,000.
Schools and Sites	359,000,000.
Streets and Sewers	258,000,000.
Public Buildings	173,000,000.
Docks	172,000,000.
East River Bridges	64,000,000.
Parks and Parkways	50,000,000.
Ferries	42,000,000.
Libraries and Sites	13,000,000.

This money has been expended precisely as set forth in the Report of the Committee on Site Planning of the American Institute of Architects (see p. 279). It was ploughed into the general land and debt gambling scheme, the profits of which were taken by those who were smart enough to get out before the crash, the losses of which are now being taken by those who held the bag when the crash came, while the fresh profits, if any, will be taken by the sly and nimble ghouls who descend upon such wrecks as unerringly as a buzzard marks a dying sheep.

At the moment (March, 1934), land prices in New York have fallen. There has been a steady movement towards a decrease in the population flow that alone sustains land prices. What this means, as an attempt is made to carry the city debt load (now requiring about a third of all taxes raised) and keep up the repairs and improvements of the city's physical functions, may be pondered by anyone with a knowledge of simple arithmetic. It is of course unthinkable to the tax assessors and collectors that land prices shall be allowed to remain lower, yet how to reinflate them in order to collect more taxes without creating fresh debt, the demands of which will be more than can be met by the increased taxation, is one of the conundrums that politicians and office-holders do not like openly to face. The pyramid builders of Memphis kept the great base of the structure on the ground. In the American debt piling process, it is the apex that rests on the earth!

Plainly indeed, any attempt to use architecture under the present debt processes, merely sets up a condition whereunder the more a people builds the greater the number of hovels in proportion to the number of palaces! To put it baldly, yet very truthfully, the art called architecture is at present, as it always has been, an anti-social process!

Before the communities of the United States there are at present two choices and no more. By refusing to incur debt for the purpose of fattening land prices, they may proceed to decay at a rate that will reflect the degree in which they are penalized by the whole outside debt process as it operates to diminish the price they receive for such products as they are able to sell, while it increases the costs of all products they are obliged to buy—a situation already

[305]

exemplified in farm impoverishment and the desperate remedies invoked.

Or, communities may proceed towards insolvency by piling debt in order to produce the increments and inflations that make up the debt pickings for the sly and the nimble, not only up to the period of general insolvency but all during the wreck-clearing process of foreclosure, when the sly and the nimble arrange to transfer the ownership of debt to themselves and by the usual reinflation processes—such as those set in operation by the use of Federal billions—to reappear on the scene with the same amount of debt claiming its legal earnings. In the end, only ownership has been changed.

Up to 1929, it was never doubted that people would swarm in ever-growing numbers and in directions where the turnstiles would remain in charge of congestion-promoters, land-inflaters and debt-pilers. Thus there was maintained the legend known as "Own Your Own Home." It is plain to all but the mentally deficient that a "home" cannot be owned. The word is used by smart advertisers in land-promotion schemes, expressly to set up an emotional illusion under which the sale of land or a house can be made while the buyer is under such a spell as will blind him to the fact that he is agreeing to pay dearly indeed for the land and materials noted in the mortgage, under conditions that render extremely doubtful his ability ever to close the account, save by taking the loss of all payments made when foreclosure arrives. It is also true that the legend has persisted because a large factor in buying land or houses is the hope that the buyer will benefit from a rise in price due to the probable swarming of enough people to add an increment value over and above the price he paid under the illusion that he was being let in on the ground floor.

The legend served its purpose, at what cost and mental anguish some millions of lost-their-own-homers can now attest. The pyramid of unpayable debt hanging over the deluded citizen who was exhorted to buy a home, even by his own government and with all the publicity power it possessed, was cleverly disguised by the use of two simple words—"own" and "home."

Hardly could there be a more infamous betrayal than for any governmental authority to urge the buying of a "home" under present conditions. Whether a civilization can be built only by having every citizen own his dwelling is beside the question. The facts run undeniably to prove that the buyer of a house, on a small payment and a mortgage, has only a minor chance of ever being able to pay off.

"It should be noted that in 1929, 40 percent of the population, and 1933 approximately 60 percent received an income of less than $1,000. Those figures give us a hint as to the nature of our problem. It would be hazardous to venture a guess as to present distribution of family income. But calculations covering the last decade are available and we may say that, during the greater part of that period, the family income of one-third of the population was under $1,200. per year; the range of another third was between $1,200 and $2,000. When account is taken of the cost of promotions, financing, sales, construction of habitations, taxes and the cost of living, it is readily seen that from one-half to two-thirds of the population cannot be housed until a like proportion of habitations has fallen into an advanced stage of decay and obsolescence. It would seem to follow from this relationship that the rate at which habitations are produced by our industrial system can have no direct relation to their occupancy by this group of the population. Seemingly, occupancy by this group is determined by the rate at which houses decay and fall into various stages of obsolescence.

"Faith has led us to adopt fantastic procedures. Generally speaking, we have ignored the facts of physical decay and obsolescence of urban structures; we have allowed our mortgages to run on through time without amortization. It has been assumed that, due to constant growth, the appreciation in the value of the site would run at a faster rate than the rate at which obsolescence and decay took effect upon the structure that occupied it. Thus when we wrecked the structure, time had already transferred its value to the site. Thus urban property ordinarily carries a valuation which represents the sum of the valuations of all the urban structures rendered obsolete by use and time and destroyed. Thus the urbanites not only pay for the structures they occupy and use in the present but they also pay taxes and fixed charges upon a series of structures that have passed into oblivion. We are really paying taxes and fixed charges upon unwarranted hopes and expectations. The facts of the present should serve to demonstrate the absurdity of capitalizing expectations that flatly deny the facts of growth in the physical world." [1]

"The provision of habitations, the same as other things, is preceded under our economy by an advance of credit—that is to say, provision is preceded by the creation of debt. But under this same economy, prices oscillate in time through a very wide range, affecting value in a like degree. These oscillations set in train financial disturbances and disloca-

[1] *Controlling Factors in Slum Clearance and Housing.* By Frederick L. Ackerman. *The Architectural Forum*, February, 1934.

tions which run throughout the whole social and industrial system.

"Out of these two characteristics of our economy have grown the procedures of finance which seek to render absentee ownership immune from the effects of such disturbances. Thus, in the field of home ownership, safeguards have been thrown around the lender, which safeguards serve to increase the risks of the borrower who lives under the belief that his name in the deed makes him an owner in fact. So long as he is a mortgagor with small equity, his ownership is conditional and his position that of a transient paying rent, but carrying the responsibilities of ownership in fact, while assuming the risks of a trader with a small margin. . . .

"Changes of value of habitations do not move with the same velocity in time as is the case with equities upon the exchanges. But in the long run, they move over approximately the same range, and in due course, the effect is very much the same. A wide change in prices will wipe out a small equity the same as a small margin. . . The certainty that the home owner may lose his equity is what provides the factor of safety to absentee ownership in this field." [1]

Until there is a clear program that will insure stability of employment and income, and a freedom from currency juggling in the interests of debt preservation, the exhortation to buy a "home" is a cruel trick to play on a trusting citizen. Whatever any governmental authority may do, in incurring more debt for houses, there should be no attempt to shove the burden onto the workers by giving them a title with a mortgage tied to it. Until stability can be said to have become visible on the horizon—and that is far from being the

[1] *Debt as a Foundation for Houses.* Frederick L. Ackerman. *The Architectural Forum.* April, 1934.

[309]

case as yet—the "Own Your Own Home" movement should be looked upon as on a level with any other of the numberless American rackets.

The vision of what civilization might be, in human terms, with architecture used to build a world of dignity and security, makes vivid the fact that the fight for individual security destroys all security. That fight, now developed into a cold calculation of human beings as debt-payers endlessly passing through turnstiles, has completely dimmed any picture of architecture as a natural road and a sane and healthy process of building a world for man. There have been a few small-scale efforts to build examples of communities in which people might live with decency and comfort: Sunnyside, Long Island City, N. Y.; Radburn, New Jersey; Mariemont, Ohio, and Chatham Village, Pittsburgh, Pennsylvania, but while these efforts contain the germ of a physical idea for building a civilization they can get no further than the germ stage. Around their fringe calls the speculator with the siren allure of his "Own Your Own Home" song, while over the head of the germ example rises the pyramid of debt.

Any talk of city planning, or of improvement in living conditions by the use of the skill and science now possessed by architects, engineers and many social technicians, may be dismissed as mere talk. Until the debt process is abolished, neither science nor skill is to be reckoned on, save as they serve the debt process first and the rest of us afterwards.

"The professional spokesman or exponent of planning seemingly recognizes that growth, expansion or change cannot take place except through the initiative and action of

[310]

those who are actuated by pecuniary motives. So, in attempting to arouse interest and gain support for his plans he rejects visions of a future city filled with amenities; but he emphasizes that beauty pays. He points out the many comforts to be secured by well-planned action; but he states that comforts insure higher valuation and a return per cent. He advocates against congestion and overcrowding; but he would never so restrict as to affect property values and the development of such increments as would follow freedom of action. He takes traffic counts at points where congestion is well-nigh intolerable; but he states that rents, realty values, and, so, tax returns depend largely upon the volume of traffic. So, out of a jumble of contradictory words and phrases, programs of planning are made. . . .

"But towards precisely what social or utilitarian end, if any, are aims, aspirations, and ideals thus directed? Surely the support of programs of action looking towards the creation of greater magnitudes and complexities does not arise out of any promise they contain of bringing satisfaction and comfort to the perplexed. Neither do they hold promise of satisfying individual human needs nor the call of instincts with which we, as a race, have through untold ages become endowed. Nor, furthermore, is support derived from the direct application of the modern matter-of-fact logic of science and engineering. Support does not come directly from any of these sources.

"In order to comprehend and explain the support given to these organized excursions into a condition of greater discomfort and perplexity we must confine analysis to the logic of business. From the business viewpoint it is all plain enough. Greater magnitudes, greater densities, higher velocities, and the compounding of waste and losses, all may be brought to serve readily comprehended ends.

"It may be well to note that when we turn the pages of history, there are to be found but few instances of peoples able to save themselves from the force of their own institutions, when those institutions impose ways of life revolutionary in character with respect to those under which their instinctive traits and physical endowments were stabilized.

"So, it is neither to deny the inferences to be drawn from the past nor to ignore the signs of the times to suggest that, while we may readily produce—through the driving forces of an institutional character—cities even more monstrous than any we have yet been able to conceive in our dramatizations of the urban future, it does not follow that, as the setting for our life grows ever more alien in respect to our genetic background, we will be able to hold and occupy the cities that we build. There is one comfort, however, in the thought that we may not be able to hold and occupy them. They would serve as monuments, commemorative of a people who, worshipping their monstrous institutions, failed to hear the small voices of their own rebelling instincts and who thus became the sacrificial offerings to their own institutional gods." [1]

Whether, in looking at the bewildering record of five thousand years, or in keeping closely to the incredible pattern of building ugliness that has been imposed on the people of the United States by their monstrous institutions of landlordism, usury and the debt processes generally, one speaks of the result in terms of building or of architecture, one

[1] *Cities of the Nth Degree.* By Frederick L. Ackerman, *Journal of the American Institute of Architects.* June, 1926.

simple fact has to be admitted. The great architecture of the world has yet to be built!

Never have the builders had their chance. The great buildings—not needing to be vast—the exalted cities, the fine towns, the harmonious countryside of garden and pasture, of river and forest fulfilling their functions—are still locked in the visions of the dreamers!

If one has sufficient faith to speculate on the time-distance yet to be traversed before the people of the United States will be ready to use architecture as part of a program for building a civilization, one is faced with certain present-day ideas and concepts of food, clothing and shelter that emerge as among the most fantastic phenomena that human life has so far produced. To know that men have chosen to destroy food when millions have not enough to eat is almost to admit the hopelessness of what is called intelligence. Food is destroyed in order to raise the price of what is left or is to be produced. For precisely the same reason a costly attempt has been made to shorten the supply of raw material for clothing in order to raise the price of what is left or is to be produced. Why is it desired to raise prices? In order to validate the very debt that produced the condition under which people could not buy enough food and clothing. It is supposed that by the process of giving value to the pyramided debt now hanging over society and thus making it possible to continue paying interest on that debt and ultimately to repay the principal, people will be able to get enough to eat and wear. But the process by which food is to be put in hungry mouths and clothing on unclad backs does not begin by putting food in hungry mouths and clothing on

[313]

unclad backs, but by a series of pecuniary operations (all of which increase the debt burden), the effect of which it is hoped will eventually get the food to the hungry mouths and the clothing on the unclad backs as an incident in the pecuniary operations.

It then becomes plain that between those who have enough food and clothing and those who have not, there rises a grim series of pecuniary entanglements, none of which have the remotest relation to anything that could be called a program of civilization based on the realities of food and hunger, clothing and nakedness. It is the same in the matter of shelter. The same series of pecuniary entanglements stands between a majority of the population of the United States and a decent house to live in. The percentage of hovels has risen so fast that even the government's own spokesmen now admit the melancholy figures.[1]

When it is then proposed to use architecture, on a vast scale, to build houses, other equally fantastic ideas emerge. For, it is proposed to build houses not primarily as an act of justice or of satisfying the need that follows hunger and nakedness, but as part of a program for validating more debt, restoring the taxing power of communities, and of putting money in circulation, as wages, on the theory that as it is theoretically passed from hand to hand, spending power may be reanimated to a point where people can again assume the debt load and pay taxes and get enough to eat and wear.

Mark the process carefully: A great debt is to be created for building houses, and as part of the effect of spending the money all land owners will look forward to a higher

[1] *The Government Housing Program.* By Robert D. Kohn. *The Architectural Forum.* February, 1934.

[314]

price for their unused land. Every building venture will tend to push up that higher price, as heretofore, and thus defeat any possible continuance of schemes that are predicated on land at a present low price.

The approach to the problem of using architecture to wipe out the slums in which the majority of American citizens live is not by the straightforward method of building houses, but by the devious pecuniary processes in which more debt is to be piled on the present load and in which the houses are to be conditioned not by the needs of people and the will to give all the space, light, sun and the amenities the builders could so easily provide, but by the pecuniary factors that envelop the whole operation in precisely the same way that a shoal of fish is caught in a net. What will emerge from the house-building net will be debt-paying fish, first of all, for the first of all requirements is the payment of debt, and the continuing state of society in which debt is never to cease.

One might, from this condition, conclude a number of things. One might guess that when the word "architecture" got into the language, and was used to imply "art," there was a general acceptance of the idea that buildings were not primarily for the use of man but that palaces and temples were for him to look at. How is it, after all, that the art of building does not apply to all dwellings as the basis of a civilization? Where in the world could such a stupid idea have originated? If the first work of architecture is not to make decent houses for everybody, what is it? What has so misled all nations as to make possible such a procession of palaces and hovels as now dominates the life of man? How is it that in the three hundred years since the first craftsmen began to build those simple houses we now accept as part of our finest heritage, the majority of American citizens cannot pay the rent for adequate houses!

By and large, it looks like a serious indictment—and so it is. It is far more serious than anyone likes to admit. But to suppose that there can now be a right-about-face and that slums can be abolished and decent houses provided for all is only another delusion. The conditions that produced the present disorder will not repeat themselves, so far as the turnstiles are concerned. There need be no doubt on that score. The flow of population can no longer be charted. The urge to escape taxation may become as great as the original urge to migrate from Europe.

All population centres face a taxation problem that its well-nigh insoluble. The flight from taxes is likely to present some strange phenomena, as time goes on. Stability is far in the distance, although abundance lies at man's very doorstep, yet cannot be touched. To say where and how to begin the salvage and repair of the physical United States is no easy task. To say that the beginning must be with the land is to suggest a truth now so strange as to be almost past believing. Yet where does man's destiny lie if not in the land? Though he pile gold into mountainous heaps and though he print money in billions, trillions and quadrillions, his fate lies in the land.

If one can escape from the incessant barrage of pecuniary talk and for a moment be free to consider least common divisors and multiples, the problem before the United States, whatever it may be decided to build, is the relation of man to the land. It can be stated in terms as simple as that, no matter how much the statement may be mauled and clouded by the nimbleness of the experts. There is much talk, or at least some audible whispers, about what is called an economic plan. It will eventually be forced, no doubt, no matter whether men like it or not, but there is still a chance to make the wise and good plan rather than to accept one that will become only the poorer, the more difficult and by far the more unpleasant, the longer the right one is held in abeyance.

Just how, one wonders, would the statisticians chart the speed of progress, using architecture as the undeniably truthful record it is? Suppose they took the simple figures about dwellings? If they started with the arrival of the *Susan Constant* at Jamestown, when there wasn't a house for anybody, and came down to 1934, when the majority of the people of the United States had not a decent one to live in, the decimal would show a remarkable and inspiring progress.

If they started at a slightly later period, say the middle of the seventeenth century, when there were few who had not a comfortable house, according to the amenities of the day and the manner of life, and when slums were unknown even though people had nothing better than a log cabin, the decimal would show a startling and steady movement away from anything that even a statistician could call progress. Or is there some yardstick other than dwellings by which to measure progress, in its physical sense?

In any event, it would seem to be a fair guess, ignoring all statistics and relying on one's eyes and common sense, and taking a good fearless look at the ten thousand tumbledown areas—of which every State has a plentiful share— that the United States had departed pretty far from the ideas and concepts that were noted in those early documents that made a loud noise about liberty and other things.

Or, if one looked intently and realistically at nothing

but the buildings and their surroundings from the moment the train pulled out of the station in New York until one got out on the street in Chicago, or even in Boston or any other city, on any other journey, one would be pretty likely to give less than a tinker's damn for any and all statistics and to say, with some warmish vehemence: "What a terrible mess!" So it is, but it's the record!

How did it all happen? How did it come to be supposed, then taken for granted, then accepted, that anything resembling a civilization, composed of buildings and surroundings, could be built by methods that were producing what was before every eye? What caused the deafness, the blindness, the dumbness? Could we mildly inquire what is to be thought of a system of education that has been growing up in the very midst of these things, this mess that lay between every child and every school, and often in the school-yard and building itself? How is it that education never took the trouble to look at these things—this record that is called architecture—to bring it under observation as a part of all our lives, as it begins with the daily walk of the child to school, and then to challenge and indict it? Indeed, it seems fair to say, on the contrary, that it supposed the record to be an accepted picture of civilization, and that it even helped to fix the current ideas about the record, or lack of them, in the minds of a hundred million people, in the minds of their government officials high and low, in the minds of the teachers and their school, the churches and their preachers, and in the mass of printed matter for which whole forests are daily cut down and which are issued as a standing declaration of faith in the monstrous institutions that are bearing down upon man like an impending avalanche.

A majority of the citizens without adequate houses to live in!

[318]

XIV

THE

CHALLENGE THROWN DOWN

BY THE SPIRIT OF

MODERN ARCHITECTURE

P URSUING the origin of a word is like following the trail of the arch. One knows that there was a first time when a builder found how to span a wall opening without the use of a lintel. A hundred years ago, it might well have been thought that the Etruscan masons were the first to discover the principle of the semi-circular arch. Now we know that its history goes back some thousands of years, but we still do not know that it was first used in Egypt. The trail merely

[319]

disappears at that point, and one then knows that origins are never discoverable. They may be traced, but the end is never to be reached by man.

So one also knows that there was a first time when the word "architecture" was used. One picks up the trail, follows it back, loses it for long periods, until at last it disappears in Roman times. One then comes to know that one can never know when it was first used, what meaning it carried or why it was coined. The best one can do is to make a guess, by gathering up the threads and by noting the changes and ideas that seem roughly to identify themselves with the first traceable use of the word.

By coining words and making buildings, man has left a record. To decipher it, one picks one's way, slowly to discover that both words and buildings have been used quite as much to conceal and obscure as they have to make clear and to reveal. If one chooses to believe that buildings are more accurate than words, as a historical record, because it is more difficult for them to conceal as their bones are laid bare by time, it is no matter to quarrel about. The veil of history falls swiftly and surely and the record of yesterday is already dim with forgetfulness and obscured by those who have a reason for obscuring it. How difficult ever to lift the veil and be sure that one has found some truth!

If, however, one had a suspicion that there was a definite connection between the coining of the word "architecture" and the art of building creatively, the best one can do is to guess from what seems to have happened. To make such a guess, and to put it in words that would be related, in a homely way, to a process and a behavior that appear to be as old as the pyramids, one might then make the following fanciful tale:

[320]

An ardent young Roman advertising agent awoke, one morning, with an idea. He had lately taken the new account of a client, in the column business, who naturally wanted to sell the most columns possible. He had standardized them, using a modification of the Greek models, and it was thought that a good business could be had throughout the empire. There might have to be column works set up at various points, for although the columns were in sections, easily movable, there were items of cost and delay that might tend to cut down the profits of a single work-yard at Rome.

The columns had been approved by the authorities. They were well made and dependable articles and there seemed to remain only the problem of a smashing publicity. Along with columns there were further possibilities of a large business in statues of consuls, senators and generals, and there likewise seemed great chances for many sorts of con-structions—aqueducts and viaducts, theaters and arenas—and as the client of our young advertising agent had a good political connection, the chance seemed to be an unusual one. There was needed a word, a slogan that would not only sell columns but that would proclaim the empire idea in grandiose buildings, and that would also fix the mind of taxpayer and subject with awe and reduce him to that state of submission where he would pay and make no murmur.

Arrived at the office, our young hero grabbed for a stylus and hastily traced the letters of his idea—A R C H I T E C - T U R A. The word was long, but it had a tripping cadence. It was a combination of Greek and Roman. The first part implied mastery, for an *architekton* in Greece was a master worker. The new combination, with a termination by which an old established craft process was labelled in terms of a result, got rid of the idea of the worker. The new word pre-

[321]

sented buildings and their parts in the light of something authoritatively fixed and in which there was nothing to do but conform to the rules and go through with the organized motions. The identity of the worker was a matter of no moment.

There was already a good Roman word for such works, but *Architectura* had a flavor that would make it stand out as far more aristocratic than *Opera*. It was a name to roll on the tongue and that gave the user a sense of having moved up a peg in the social scale, precisely as it pushed the workman down. The very sound of it implied something quite apart from the field of toil, the cutting of stone, the laying of brick, the pouring of concrete.

What would Romans, colonists and subject people say when they were offered not buildings but *Architectura?* Genuine Roman *Architectura,* warranted to impress and endure. The columns would not need to be dated. They would be forever empire-fresh!

The answer was written as time went on. Great imperial avenues, existing for no other purpose than to be lined on either side with hundreds of columns in rows, were built. On their heels followed the rest of the building pageant with which we are familiar. Advertising did its work. If, in the process, it destroyed the idea that building was a creative art in which the delight of finding the right form was a part of the craftsman spirit that had led to the perfections in building from which the Romans borrowed at liberty, what matter?

The destruction was not completed for many centuries. The workmen came back into their own, after the fall of Rome; and up to the moment of the Renaissance, the word *Architectura* was forgotten. It was revived, in the fourteenth

[322]

century or thereabouts, and this time with a disastrous effect indeed. It can truly be said that when the word Architecture came to be coined and used, the days of creative building were over and done with. Henceforth Architecture! The workman be damned. One has but to look at the present battle array, under the banner of Labor, to understand the slow evolution. Once the worker served his training and became a free creative artisan. Today he has no more chance at creating than a robot would have. Once there was a steady flow of creative skill. It was poured into building after building as a means of satisfying new purposes or of enlarging old ones. Workers were learning, advancing, perfecting. Today there is division, sub-division and sub-subdivision. To each an allocated task of following an instruction. Not a breath of creativeness is left. The young Roman advertising agent accomplished far more than he wot.

It is thus wholly natural that there has never been a generally acceptable definition of the word "architecture." It was not invented to define anything but as part of the scheming of empire builders, and that makes a vast difference. But the mystification created by the word is not cleared up by adding the word "modern." Nowhere is there any agreement as to what the two words mean when coupled, but here again arises the same condition that led to *Architectura*. Certain architects believe in the spirit and principle of modern architecture as a fundamental social precept. Others believe that modern architecture is a slogan by which the sale of architectural services is to be increased. Thus there is a stout partisanship, for and against, on all sorts of grounds.

[323]

A safe attempt to get a reasonable meaning might be to say that the basic principle of modern architecture rests on the straightforward approach to a building problem by which those arrangements of space that will insure ease, convenience and economy of use are allowed to determine the form, quite apart from the fact that the resulting form may be strange-looking, or even queer, and may cause a violent protest from those who are accustomed to consider buildings only as they conform to and can be easily catalogued in the inherited "styles" of architecture. Against the lay protest, which is naturally swollen by those architects who are used to dealing in stock "styles" and who have no creative ability—of which there is a vast number in the profession—there might be set off a gain, providing those who never thought of a building, save as it satisfied their animal necessities, were to find that modern architecture challenged them into thinking, even against their will.

Into the idea of modern architecture there also enters the prime element of cost, for no money is to be wasted in the uselessness that has cost so many billions already, as blind worship of "style" was worked so successfully in the name of art. One can hardly dispute this premise of cost any longer. It is now beginning to be seen that all buildings are paid for out of the total common production, no matter to whom they belong. The palace and hovel theory of architecture conforms to the methods of distributing wages and profits and to nothing else. The record is squarely before us. The crop of skyscrapers and debt is set off by a volume of slums and dilapidations that ought to make any American hang his head in shame.

The item of cost, in modern architecture, is still far from being intelligently fixed. Under our present pecuniary proc-

[324]

esses, even a most perfect example of modern architecture might not serve more than a brief period. In fact, the duration of income-producing value in skyscrapers has often been no more than ten years while others were insolvent from the moment that digging began. In an intelligent society, moving definitely in the direction of civilization, where stability is to be sought as the result of the wise use of land and its resources, a first principle of building—which is stability—would play its natural part. Buildings would then be made, not as a result of gambling in or the manipulation of land values, or the flotation of investment bonds, but just as they were made for centuries—to serve and last, long and well.

There is a further word to be said about the cost of modern architecture. Because of the straightforwardness of the approach to the problem and the will to achieve the utmost in simplicity, it does not follow that cheapness will result. Many examples of real modern architecture, so far as plan and design are concerned, are costly, if well done, while many others are examples of the poor building resulting from trying to save money. Modern architecture demands not only the highest skill in workmanship but also a far better knowledge of how to use the new materials that are sought as part of the logical approach than now exists. The workmen are not to be found who know how to use and combine the new materials now so freely advertised and used.

Modern materials, whether chosen for looks or for use, are the product not of practice but of theory. They did not originate naturally as workmen sought a better way, but have been worked out in laboratories. There is all the difference in the world between the craft and the laboratory, for the priceless knowledge gained by the workman, as he advanced step by step, is no part of the present picture. The process of getting the needed knowledge will be that of training a new band of builders. The step-by-step process departed when the architect came in. The traditions and the running interest of the building craftsmen could not continue in the face of the steady shower of drawings and blueprints that descended upon them. The laboratory then took up the question of finding new materials and substitutes for old ones, as part of the business game that was to overtake everybody and everything. The result is the critical technical situation that now confronts the disciples of modern architecture. The workmen to build it properly are few and far between. The evolution cannot be a natural process resulting from carrying knowledge over from father to son unceasingly and with no breaks. That process came to an end many years ago.

Somewhere within the outline of these facts and ideas lies the principle of modern architecture, as we understand its challenge to honest building. Its forms will of course be in sharp contrast to those that result from designs where the "style" of the outside is chosen and the inside fitted to it.

It cannot be maintained, by the advocates of modern architecture, that the idea is brand new. Although it is called modern, it has been the governing principle in all creative architecture. Up to the time of the Renaissance, every variation in building was no doubt looked upon as a modern adventure. It had, no doubt, its opponents and its acclaimers. For long, after the Renaissance, the idea was buried in the new faith that the self-conscious "artists" were doing their best to popularize. Buildings, they said, began with a style for the outside, and thus one should hire a stylist.

Like the arch and the word "architecture," one traces the new idea to points where the trail disappears and where the scent is lost. In many minor buildings that have survived, and notably in the older part of the United States, it is plain that the craftsmen escaped, for a moment, from the handicap of style. They created, and let the form grow out of the purpose, even though they clung to their craft traditions when it came to framing a window or putting on a dormer. In America, one picks up the trail of the idea with the writings of Louis Sullivan and the work of Despradelle, but that is merely the re-finding of the scent.

In 1826, Karl Friedrich Schinkel, then a young but well-known German architect, went on a journey to England. Arriving in Manchester he was amazed to see the building forms that were growing out of the industrial centralization that steam had made possible. The grimy smoke-filled air of Manchester filled him with a nausea and it was then, though quite without any understanding of the force that had been let loose for good or for evil, and which was later to engulf men in bewilderment, that he exclaimed, in his notes of the journey: "Every great age had had its style of building. Why shouldn't we have ours?" Then, apparently after a little reflection, he wrote: "Emphasize construction by its articulation; use materials frankly; no useless parts; all clear and natural." [1]

For centuries there had been no need to say anything as plain as that. The Romans, in their grandiose schemes, learned to conceal with marble facings, but the Romanesque

[1] *Betonen der Konstruktion durch die Gliederung, offenes Zurschaustellen des Materials, kein Bauteil ohne Zweckbestimmung, alles klar und echt.*

and Gothic builders went back to their honest crafts. They lost them again, and then Schinkel, confronted with the horrors of the first English factories, and yet startled with the barren forms, cried aloud an old truth. No one can say that he was the first to cry out since the Renaissance. The trail merely disappears and is picked up again, just as it emerges with Sullivan, whose words were so akin to Schinkel's that they only the more emphasize the eternal truth, if one is to build for the sake of Man, and not for the purpose of debt and usury.

It is also true that if one searched with diligence, one would find that even among the architects, ever since they arrived on the scene, there were those who wanted to break away from the limitations imposed by the styles. As time went on there were those who grew bolder and bolder and who went as far as they dared or as their client would permit in breaking with the outworn traditions of the past. No one can say when there first took place the actual sharp break that might fixedly mark the beginning of what we now call modern architecture. One may easily be convinced that the challenge of our day was issued by the engineers. They had to deal with stresses, strains and loads, in terms of pure technique. They were not bothered by forms, and although they were prime agents in the mad race with debt, there came a demand for such technical daring and adventure that certain forms began to stare superbly at the architectural hash of the historic styles. New clean sharp outlines and masses awoke the old feeling, nearly smothered to death by the sheer weight of sham, for forms that were genuine, real, frank, honest. There were grain elevators and a bridge or two, and then there came some factories, warehouses and even the great freight terminal in Chicago, designed by

McLanahan and Price, and growing naturally out of the theories of Louis H. Sullivan.

Tracing the spirit of modern architecture is merely the process of approaching sources that are undiscoverable. It might well be said by an American that the Brooklyn Bridge was the first great modern structural form to challenge the dead language of the styles, even as it remains one of the most superb works, in its whole concept, ever achieved by the builders. But a Frenchman would remark that the Eiffel Tower wasn't so bad (1889), and the Englishman would inquire whether there were not some pretty modern ideas in the Crystal Palace (1854). The German would here interrupt to point out that although Schinkel never got to build anything, there was the design for the department store in Berlin (*circa* 1840), and so by easy stages, one is back in the presence of a group of building craftsmen where the thing that we call modern architecture was no more than the common sense with which men set about all their tasks.

All mechanical activity was then alive and humming with the search for form, although no one guessed it. It was an age of terrific waste, yet one of ceaseless searching for the simpler and the better. If we call it the age of efficiency, it is well to remember that our yardstick was money and the result a riotous squandering. Efficiency, at the present moment, is something about which man knows nothing at all. It cannot be calculated in terms of money and can only be known to man when he rids himself, as he will some day, of his present clumsy and wasteful pecuniary measuring devices.

But even the efficiency of waste began to produce forms that compelled admiration, and the discovery was called "modernism" because, as already pointed out, it pleases

[329]

us to think that we are originators. "Modernism" penetrated all the arts and slowly the idea of applying it to buildings began to take root. There developed a cult and some schools and their followers. Business men also began to take an interest. They saw the chance of using these new and bizarre forms to get advertising. The buildings that resulted were often no more than a trick imitation, for concern was not with the principle upon which the art of building rests, but with advertising.

Undoubtedly there is an attraction value in a striking form, but the principle of modern architecture has nothing to do with a striking form as the object in view, just as it also allows no thought as to how violent the break with past forms may be. There can be only the thought of working out the problem to its complete logical end. One can think about the form, choose the materials that conform, and make all possible adjustments as between plan and design, but what must come is a form that grows naturally out of the logical arrangement of the enclosed space.

Here again, the resulting building may be as great a social waste or menace as the crop of palaces and hovels heedlessly imposed on the American people and by them accepted as architecture. Before there can be any sane use of modern architecture, or any profound movement in the direction it points, there has to be manifest a logical civilizing purpose in the acts and behavior of the American people. Ahead of the builders must be some clearly seen purpose as related to life and not to debt, a purpose leading towards civilization, a purpose that is in tune with science as Nature's law of efficiency and that is in tune with the deepest spiritual and ethical implications of that law. Technical science has its place only as a part of that law. Unless it

[330]

be tempered by the clear concept of Man as the one object of all effort at betterment, science becomes no more than an agent for business. At the present moment this is so true that it is well-nigh impossible for science to deliver its findings freely to men, in building or in anything else. First, it must be passed through the pecuniary turnstiles of debt and profit, and then filtered out to men at the highest price the traffic will bear.

Thus it is not difficult to understand that modern architecture, even as an approach to civilization, is a long way from having gained its freedom to move in defiance of the land and debt processes that have so long governed the production of palaces and hovels, and that are still accepted as the processes of providing shelter for anything or anybody. But it is equally easy to understand, if one looks at modern architecture as something more than a new tool for salesmanship, why the spirit behind it is not only the voice that urges a return to that rightness that once animated the craftsmen, but the voice in which there may be read a kindly note of warning. No race of people, no matter how rich their natural resources, can move farther than chaos if they persist in using architecture as a device for piling debt and living by usury.

It is time to look at the record, the spirit of modern architecture is saying. Time to look at our own record, written by us, in the buildings that make up the United States. It is the one record that cannot be falsified. Those who make our buildings cannot escape fixing the image of those who inspire them. Architecture—to add still one more attempt at a definition—is only the pen that traces and records the human basis on which people are moving at a given period in what is called Time. The spirit of modern architecture begins,

[331]

not with buildings, but with the ways and purposes that animate the people that happen to be flowing by. Only out of a new purpose can a new record be written.

Consider, as one of the unhappiest examples of the failure to use even a penny's worth of logic, even as the spirit of modern architecture was forbidden the premises, the recent public building development in the city of Washington. Although life in this, our world, now obliges anyone with a sense of humor to spend most of his time laughing, the seven- or eight-ring architectural circus now permanently installed in Washington ought not to be missed by the busiest chuckler. A walk—it would take some days to explore all the corridors—through this amazing display of architectural bookishness would lead one back to a full understanding of that little jingle of Edward Lear's: "They went to a sea in a sieve, they did."

It is true that governmental departments in Washington were for years scattered all over the place, as though swept out of the Capitol and dumped on the first vacant lot. Their quarters were inadequate and without dignity, but the pickings of private landlords were so sweet that it took fifty years to have the government do its work in its own buildings.

With the mounting tide of prosperity, some years ago, enough pressure could be mustered to put through the Congress a plan for bringing the great part of the vast army of governmental employees in Washington into that series of buildings now occupying the Triangle, as it is known, which runs from the foot of the Capitol grounds to Fifteenth Street, diagonally across from the Treasury, and is bounded on its long sides by Pennsylvania Avenue and the Mall. One risks small challenge in guessing that the general idea of arrangement and looks was part of the time-honored plan for making Washington a faithful Roman replica. The origin of this idea and the steady determination to perpetuate it are linked, in the minds of most seasoned observers, with the Commission of Fine Arts, for that body has a powerful say as to what the public buildings of Washington shall look like. The result of the choice is more and more evident. To those who believe it a pity to use the national capital as a costly undertaking in "style" embalming, the result is lamentable.

Suppose that before any ground had been broken, there had been set up a "Commission of Ordinary Intelligence to Consider What Is Best to Be Done about Buildings for the Federal Government in Washington." Every building has to begin by a study, no matter how casual or how serious. In this instance, the study should have been extremely serious, and should have been made by a group of well-rounded minds. It is clear, if one takes a good look at the world, that what are called experts are far too often the agents of confusion. Their vision of life is obscured by some kind of a measuring device.

Suppose there could have been set up a Commission of such as signed that memorable document in the cabin of the *Mayflower*, people who had not lost their sense of that comradely togetherness by which they knew they were to stand or fall. They could see a problem in terms of human effort, of that effort that has to go into the making of anything, and of that effort that has to go into the paying. They would have a horror of debt and could not be browbeaten by bankers nor bullied by newspapers.

Before them was a problem in architecture, although they would have called it one of building. Before there could be

[333]

any wise answer as to what to build and where to build it—
the basis from which every building has to spring, for good,
if rightly decided, and otherwise for ill—there needed to be
an unemotional turning over of a few facts. It needed to be
done by people without fear and with a sense of trust.

"The Commission," would run the report, "deems it a
duty to point out and give warning, as prime factors affecting government buildings in Washington, that the costs of all
government are increasing ever faster. As the members of
the Commission believe that progress towards civilization
would show a steadily decreasing cost and volume of government, they are forced to conclude that the United States
is not only headed in the wrong direction but is increasing
the rate of movement.

"This fact in itself gives rise to a grave question as to the
wisdom of doing any building until direction rather than
speed becomes the guide, but the Commission further notes,
as part of this prime fact, a tendency towards that paternal-
ism that not only undermines the ethical and physical alert-
ness of a people but that encourages them more and more to
regard the public funds as a source of special favors, and to
seek those favors by methods that are completely subversive
of any hope of building a civilization. Again, and as another
aspect of the major fact, there is growing up a bureaucracy
that steadily entrenches itself and which will, if it continues,
present another insurmountable barrier to a people that
hopes to create a civilization.

"In the light of these facts, the Commission deems it
highly unwise to push governmental functions into any
further concentration and believes that further to encourage
these ominous tendencies in our national life, by the erection
of an assemblage of costly buildings, would be a betrayal

[334]

of public trust. The Commission further points out that as the cost of any buildings will involve the public debt, no plan should be undertaken that does not propose to salvage the cost of the land from the increments that will result from the spending of public money. Unless this is done, no public building program should ever be undertaken anywhere, for otherwise the national treasury becomes a pocket that tempts too many citizens to pick it with impunity and, far worse, by connivance.

"In studying the amount of space required by the various departments, the Commission is forced to note some melancholy facts.

"(a) The more space used by the Department of Agriculture, the worse becomes the condition of the farmer, while it is also noted that although millions of dollars have been spent in teaching farmers to grow larger crops, it is now proposed to pay them handsomely for not using the information. It would seem clear that under such a state of things the larger part of the functions of that department are sheer waste.

"(b) It is also noted that the greater the activity of the Department of Labor, the greater the relative unemployment, and less and less are people willing to work for a living if they can get it by using their wits or their skill in pocket-picking.

"(c) In the matter of Commerce, the Commission records its belief that the active pursuit of trade by the government is hardly more than a war-making activity, and that it is time the exchange of products between nations be put on a basis that will remove every form of exploitation and the present unceasing battle of all nations to export all possible unemployment to any or all other nations.

"(d) As for our Interior, the Commission suggests it would be well to transfer all attention, for some time, to the Edges, with a view to preserving the small remnant of Manners that now remains, and with a further view to the ultimate merging of all governmental functions in a Department of Manners. The Commission records, with all possible emphasis, its faith that the only basis on which a civilization can be built is an ever-growing diffusion of justice and a complete economic security for every human being.

"(e) In the matter of Justice, which is likely to be attained through manners but never by law, the Commission notes the rising tendency to lawlessness, the mounting cost of crime, and a slow sinking of individual honor. It suggests that these ominous facts are due to the theory under which individuals have the power to tax any and all citizens and to take tribute from them as though under letters of marque. The Commission is forced to the conclusion that the basis for Justice is completely missing."

And so on, by a body of men and women whose common sense and comradeship have not been blunted by publicity-hunting and who could still look a fact in the face. Fearlessly they would think and speak, and thus the Commission would conclude "that there could be no greater waste of public money than to build more government buildings until the course of the nation had been re-charted by navigators who knew something about sailing the seas that lead to civilization."

Thus should a public building program begin. Not in the schemes of politicians hunting votes or popularity, nor on the draughting boards of architects and engineers, but in the chart-room of civilization. Such are the questions that

[336]

needed an answer when the Triangle circus was heading for Washington and the Roman hoops were being made ready for architects to jump through, even though the principles of modern architecture were not to be allowed on the premises.

Of course, they were not to be allowed. The eminent trio who had the most say were Mr. Mellon, Mr. Smoot and Mr. Hoover. One guesses they would not object if one classed them as leading disciples of the Roman idea for Washington, but who also believed that architecture is something imposed from above rather than a living thing that, in order to come to more than a sickly hot-house bloom, must have its roots in a soil far richer than that of a dead imperial past. Some of the architects chosen to design the buildings had ideas, and there were others who bewailed the whole program and protested at the waste. If, however, there had been a commemorative postage stamp issued when the plans were decided, the legend would have read: NO IDEAS WERE PERMITTED.

One may remark that business does not so approach an undertaking. No one would have so acted in the face of such an expenditure as part of a business move, without seeing that the world was ransacked by some competent person in search of ideas that would save all possible money and who would secure all knowledge that would lead to the most profitable result. If an architect presented himself and showed a type of building in which every worker could have abundant natural light, those responsible would at least have examined his project.

If another had proposed to give equal space and more light at half the cost of the Roman plan, they would at least have been interested. Even though they were not so intelligent as to apply the same logic to a building that they would apply to the making of aluminum, beet-sugar or to mining, they would have felt it a duty to see that money was not thrown away in gobs on a doubtful scheme. As a possible mitigation for what happened, let us admit that it might have been thought that no one would object, no matter how much money was wasted, so long as Washington was made the outstanding word in lavish magnificence, and that it was even the duty of those responsible to seek the imperial splendors of Rome rather than a democratic simplicity.

At that point one is thrown violently back on the tradition and confusion that have grown around the word "architecture," just as the poison ivy embraces and throttles the tree that is nearest. The spirit of modern architecture might be likened to a valiant attempt to kill the poison ivy of confusion, of mystification and of snobbishness, to make clear that a building demands the same logic that men in their senses apply to the making of anything, from a needle to a battleship. The form of what they make is determined by the purpose for which it is to be used. Not always do they make pleasant forms, for they often get lost in tradition and moss and salesmanship, as do those who pretend to know better.

If with all the aforesaid facts and ideas before them, a Commission of Ordinary Intelligence had been overruled and it had been decided that politics or party welfare demanded a series of buildings in which heaps of papers might be passed back and forth, then might have come a straight business question. Many factors would have to be faced. First, the effect of herding great numbers, obliged to use

[338]

the same streets at the same time. If no way could be found of avoiding that—for reasons that would not be tolerated in an intelligent society—then would come the question of an extended series of low buildings or a condensed series of higher ones.

In the matter of cost, ease of working and operating, and effective use of space, here might be a logical place for the skyscraper, as the disciples of modern architecture would have pointed out. Instead of the present miles of corridors with their blank invitation to spontaneous aimlessness, one would have a compact building designed to take advantage of all possible floor area and natural light, and at far less cost than that of the Roman Triangle. The open space would permit such a building, for it would cut off no light from others. There would be a great gain in space for traffic and parking by the saving in ground-floor area.

There would be the esthetic problem of so building as not to spoil the present scale relations of Capitol and Monument, but that might easily be solved by choosing another site. By an extended process of land condemnation the government could recover the land that never ought to have been let out of its control, and thus recoup itself for the huge cost of land in whatever move it makes. Each move grows costlier, while the parallel growth of the city could hardly be more expressive of the sacrifice of comfort, convenience and economy to land exploitation.

In Washington, the whole building record tells the true and melancholy story, in spite of the finer things, of the usual political and pecuniary pulling and hauling, with land owners holding the key position and taking their profits at the expense of the public treasury. The waste, in support of the ideal of a Roman necropolis under landlordism,

[339]

produces one of the most unhappy results. Citizens, from afar, who come to look at the focal point in their national life, go away with the idea that the country's best brains have here had their say.

Why should they not think so?

Where else should the spirit of modern architecture be more insistently seeking the logical approach?

Why force Washington into a rigid pattern in order to satisfy the liking for a style that is as dead as the design for the first locomotive?

Why make Washington the outstanding example of the architectural blare of Roman imperialism?

Why not make it the pre-eminent exhibit of that rightness in building that leaves the builders as free to find fitting forms as the bird is free to choose a branch?

Why not set about finding the worthy forms for it to express, in a definite and concerted movement towards civilization?

That is the challenge of the spirit of modern architecture!

XV

SOME SPECULATIONS

ON THE POSSIBILITY

THAT MAN MAY SOME DAY

USE ARCHITECTURE TO BUILD

A CIVILIZATION

I F civilization can be defined beyond the vague assertion
or assumption that it is a social advance over the equally
vague social state known as barbarism, it might be said to
be (or that it ought to be) the manner of living graciously and
agreeably under such a method of using land and its resources that no member of the collectivity could be deprived

of the food for his hunger, the clothes for his back, shelter and the chance to develop his creative (not acquisitive) powers.

Architecture might then be defined as the work of arranging agreeable and convenient buildings in pleasant surroundings, that progress civilizationwards might be steady and with a generally rising well-being. In a society so headed, architecture, instead of being known as an "art," or as that damnable and completely undefinable bit of snobbishness, a "fine art," would be esteemed as a healthy normal process of doing healthy normal things related to the general perfecting of buildings and their surroundings for everybody.

Under such a program, what a world might be made by the builders! Such towns—such cities—such a land! Their order, convenience and serenity pass the comprehension of all but the dreamers. They would be the physical setting for a civilization that had become possible to a race that had learned how to use land and money so that goods and services might be fairly and plentifully exchanged with no resort to debt.

If in the midst of the present wreck and confusion, it were desired to make a plan in which architecture should fully play its useful part, we are faced with a grim and dismaying fact: No one knows where to build the houses in which the people from the slums and broken-down communities are to be put. The drift of population can neither be foretold nor plotted, as during the period of the great gamble. Never have the people of America had a purpose or a plan based on stability. The act of turning natural resources into money, and of then putting that money into the form of wealth known as debt, depends, for the maximum quick and safe return, upon instability and waste, upon inflation and pyramiding. There is nothing in American life that emerges clearly as a conscious social purpose based upon stability. The best one can do is to guess that while there are latent forces of intense idealism, waiting to be tapped, the general vague purpose of the majority is best described as the hope to own and live without working.

Let us assume, if but for a moment, that the people of the United States were agreed that the purpose before them was to give dignity, security and abundance to all citizens, and steadily to move forward in the direction of civilization. There would then be some planning to be done. To undertake such a plan—and nothing else would suffice if civilization be the goal—there would have to be a complete new method of dealing with land and using money. Under such a method we would begin to throw away, little by little, thousands of our present communities, replacing them with new ones, founded not on the will to save present debt, but upon the idea of using land and its resources, with no debt, sensibly to restore human life to decency and dignity, and to create an economic security that could be taken away from no one. All this is possible. It would be architecture set free —at last—and for the first time in the history of civilizations. It would be a program for a hundred years and would offer an adventure as thrilling and exciting as ever befell a race. There would be useful employment for everybody and presently, out of the wreck and chaos of anarchic individualism, there would begin to emerge the foundations for a civilization.

To those who say that such a plan and program are impossible (or who fall back on the hallowed phrase of the coward, "this is not the time"), the answer is this:

They said that he who said he would send messages over a wire by pressing a button and getting a click at the other end was a visionary dreamer.

They said that the man who said he would carry the human voice over a wire so that men could talk with each other over any distance was a visionary dreamer.

They said the same thing of the man who said he would not only send messages, or carry the human voice, but would transmit every known sound from the sigh of a child to the triumphant peal of an orchestra from one end of the earth to the other and with no wires at all!

What folly to say that anything is impossible!

Only that is impossible which cannot be imagined!

But a civilization has to be imagined before it can be built!

The day will come—boldly optimistic as the belief may seem—when men will give up trying to master the degrading and unmasterable wiles of debt and usury, of trying endlessly to pass golden camels through the eye of a needle under the delusion that it is the road that leads to either happiness or civilization, and will set about the building of a world and the flooding of it with such architecture as men have never known.

The skill is here—at this moment! The materials are here—at this moment! The workers are here—at this moment! Everything is ready to begin a task in which a simple and beneficent architecture shall flow naturally out of the search for rightness, just as it once flowed into the great buildings and gave them all the beauty we now admire and cherish.

Everything is ready? Well, everything but the courage, intelligence and good will that shall begin to destroy the ideas that have to go!

Let there be no illusions on that score. The task of setting the builders to work to repair and rebuild the physical United States is far more than the issuing of manifestoes and the creation of more debt. That way lies only more chaos. First, there has to be prepared a foundation of human purpose, resting serenely in the heart of man. The present task of architecture, if one may for a moment think of it as a benign spirit that waits patiently for man to grow in honor, dignity and integrity, and to develop that complete sense of rightness that the craftsman knows, is not to make plans, designs and schemes for which there is no foundation ready, but to await a race of people with the intelligence and good will to wish to build a civilization, to find a people that seeks not to drown the sound of its inhumanities with the blare that Rome used to hide its crimes, but to make the humanities the only basis for building.

Over and over have the builders been ready for the task. Over and over have they seemed to be laying a foundation. Many have been the visions. Many are the fragments that have endured to make us remember them and to keep alive the faith. Only within the last half century has it begun to be dimly realized that while a nation may call a part of its building architecture, it is the whole record that has to be read if one takes any interest in the truth or the future. Hiding behind palaces in order not to see the hovels is merely the refuge sought by cowards.

Thus, to those who still believe that the instinct for craft

[345]

rightness is a sign that man has the power to escape from the fear that led to the invention of the monstrous pecuniary institutions of usury and profit, there is the solid hope that some people, somewhere and some day, though it be no more than a handful of survivors, will have grown to such stature as to be able to see art and architecture in their entirety.

"For years we have been handed the mutilated image; for years men have tried to divide art into two branches, calling one 'fine' and the other 'industrial', each incapable of surviving in such isolation. The wish, no doubt, was to make us believe that the 'industrial' arts were so soiled by the degradation of labor that they could not enter the regions of pure beauty, as though beauty did not draw from materials its only outward form." [1] Such a people, to whose eventual appearance the undaunted look forward, will have re-caught the immortal undertones of the great cosmic pageant and so, being without fear, they will hear, above all other sounds, the still small voices of themselves, saying:

"Come then, ye by whom the common things of life are clothed with beauty. Come in one harmonious throng. Come, engravers and lithographers, moulders of metal, clay and plaster, founders of type, printers on cloth and paper, jewelers, goldsmiths, potters, ironworkers, masons, carpenters, embroiderers, tapestry-weavers, bookbinders—artists, artisans, comforters, who give us the joys of form and color! Benefactors of men, lead us on our way to the community of the future. It holds out the hope of more justice and more joy. You will work in it and for it. From a society more

[1] *Vers les temps meilleurs.* By Anatole France.

[346]

equal and more happy, there will spring a more lovely and more agreeable art." [1]

Why doubt that such a day will come, and that people will then say to their builders:

Build us a fine and pleasant world. Out of it there will emerge a natural beauty that may be called art, or a natural art that may be called beauty. It will not matter by what word we shall choose to call it, and it may well be that no word will be needed. Debt has gone. Usury has ended. The hopeless order of price and profit has been swept away. Land is for use and no man can rent it to another.

Make a plan—and let the beginning of your plan be this —a fine and spacious room for every man, woman and child. To every soul its sanctuary. After that, such other buildings as may become needed and that we can contrive and afford.

As a beginning—for the builders who shall at last set to work for a society that is resolved to build a civilization— what could be a better mark to aim at than for everyone a fine and spacious room, sun-lighted or sun-shaded, as one might choose!

[1] *Idem.*

SUGGESTIONS FOR

COLLATERAL READING

Architecture, Industry and Wealth
   William Morris

News from Nowhere
   William Morris

Chartres and Mont St. Michel
   Henry Adams

The Autobiography of an Idea
   Louis H. Sullivan

A Guildsman's Interpretation of History
   Arthur J. Penty

Sticks and Stones
   Lewis Mumford

The Nature of Gothic
   John Ruskin

The Esthetic Basis of Greek Art
   Rhys Carpenter

Form and Colour
    L. March Phillips

Beyond Architecture
    A. Kingsley Porter

A Short History of the Building Crafts
    Martin S. Briggs

A History of Architecture in the American Colonies
    Fiske Kimball

Erewhon
    Samuel Butler

INDEX

INDEX

[353]

[354]

[356]

[357]

The most important
book ever written.
THE ETHICS OF SEXUAL ACTS
By Rene Guyon

6354